LIFE LIST

LIFE LIST

A Woman's Quest for the World's
Most Amazing Birds

Olivia Gentile

BLOOMSBURY
New York Berlin London

Published by Bloomsbury USA, New York

All papers used by Bloomsbury USA are natural, recyclable products made from
wood grown in well-managed forests. The manufacturing processes
conform to the environmental regulations of the country of origin.

LIBRARY OF CONGRESS CATALOGING-IN-PUBLICATION DATA

Gentile, Olivia.
Life list : a woman's quest for the world's most amazing birds/Olivia
Gentile.—1st U.S. ed.
p.   cm.
ISBN-13: 978-1-59691-169-7 (hardcover)
ISBN-10: 1-59691-169-7 (hardcover)
1. Snetsinger, Phoebe, 1931–1999.   2. Bird watchers—United States—
Biography.   3. Bird watching.   I. Title.

QL31.S557G46 2008
598.072'34—dc22
[B]   2008027036

First U.S. Edition 2009

3   5   7   9   10   8   6   4

Typeset by Westchester Book Group
Printed in the United States of America by Quebecor World Fairfield

For my grandmother, Dorothy Fischer

INTRODUCTION

WHEN I WAS twenty-three, I fell in love with a bird-watcher. I'd just finished college and was living in rural Vermont, not because I loved mountains and open space but because I'd gotten a job as a reporter at a small-town newspaper. I was skeptical, in fact, about mountains and open space. Most of my friends had moved to New York City when we graduated, and I would have, too, if a newspaper there had only hired me. Instead of writing about the election between Bill Clinton and Bob Dole and the emergence of capitalist China, the sort of work I'd fantasized about when I decided to be a journalist, I was writing about the new ice cream cart that had set up shop in the town of Springfield and the county prosecutor who'd been arrested for drunk driving.

I met Tait through a friend at the paper. He had big blue eyes, lots of curly blond hair, and a gentle, almost angelic way about him. He was a few years older than I was, and when I asked him what he'd been doing since college, he said he'd mostly been studying birds, as a field assistant for various research projects. One summer, he'd lived in a tent on top of a mountain in Vermont, in a spruce forest, and observed the behavior of the rare and reclusive Bicknell's

Thrush; not long after that, he was sent to Panama, where he tried to figure out whether the Slate-throated Redstart could nest in the sparse trees on shaded coffee plantations.

When he wasn't working, he watched birds for fun, in the ponds, swamps, and woods near his house. By "watched birds," I don't mean that he sat around, like you do when you watch TV. Bird-watching, the way most people do it, is a lot like hunting, which is why some practitioners prefer the more active-sounding term "bird-ing": you have to know where and when to look for birds, you have to chase them down, and, when you find them, you have to figure out what species they are—often in just a second or two, before they fly away. Tait, like most birders, kept a "life list" of all the species he'd seen and identified, and he was always looking to add new ones, or "life birds."

He told me he'd gotten interested in birds when he was about ten and his mother set up a birdfeeder outside their kitchen window. At the time, she was home-schooling him, and she asked him to take an inventory of all the birds and other animals in their town. One of the first natural history books ever published was *The Natural History and Antiquities of Selborne*, an account of the flora and fauna in an English township by the local pastor, Gilbert White; the book later came to be known simply as "White's Selborne." As an homage, lit-tle Tait called his inventory, which was written in pencil on lined paper, "Tait's Bartonsville." A few years later, he got a scholarship to attend a boarding school in upstate New York, where he was shy with his peers but was encouraged by his teachers to walk in the woods and fields and look for birds.

I'd never given birds a moment of my attention. But when I looked through Tait's binoculars, I saw their subtle loveliness: the lemon yellow of a warbler's breast; the slow wing-beat of a hawk in flight; the curl of a heron's long, slender neck. Through Tait, I also learned to hear birds—their hoots, chuckles, trills, and caws—and it dawned on me that they were everywhere, even in winter, when the world looked barren. I learned, too, that birds had evolved from a small two-legged dinosaur called a theropod, which grew feathers, probably to keep warm, and which eventually used those feathers to take to the air. There's no need for fantasies like *Jurassic Park*: every time you see a bird, even a crummy little sparrow, you're looking at what's left of the dinosaurs.

I was so taken with Tait and his passion for the natural world that it took me a while to recognize his depression. It slowed him down almost every day, and when it was bad, it paralyzed him. He'd forget things, pace, sleep too much, and cry. He'd been on and off medication for a while, he told me, but it never seemed to do much good.

All the same, every morning just before dawn, even when he was at his worst, he woke up to listen to the birdsong. He'd lie on his back in the purple-gray dark, eyes open and alert, and sift through the chorus to identify each species. If I was awake, he whispered the names of the birds so I, too, could appreciate the music. His connection to nature was so powerful, I realized, that it penetrated his depression better than medicine could, better than I could. I wondered if he would be alive without it.

We eventually broke up, which was crushing to both of us. He was still on my mind several years later, when I was studying writing in New York City. Most people barely notice birds, even in bucolic Vermont. Why had they come into focus for Tait? Had he already been depressed when they did? Why, exactly, did they soothe him so? The other birdwatchers I'd met through Tait seemed to approach the pursuit with similar ardor. Did they need salvation too?

I decided to write some sort of essay on birdwatching, and I called a few bird clubs near my home in Manhattan to see what they had going on. One man misunderstood and thought I was interested in joining his club. He tried to encourage me. "Who knows?"

he said. "Maybe you'll be the next Phoebe Snetsinger." The man
had never met Phoebe, but he knew all about her—as most birdwatchers do, it turned out—and he told me a little. That was back
in 2001, two years after her death, and I've been piecing together
her life ever since.

Phoebe wasn't meant to be a housewife. Her father was Leo Burnett,
founder of one of the biggest advertising agencies in the country
(the Leo Burnett Company, in Chicago), and she inherited his intensity and drive. As a little girl in the 1930s, she was a tomboy who zealously memorized baseball statistics; when she was a teenager, in the
1940s, she wanted to be a psychologist, then changed her mind and
decided to be a chemist. By the time she graduated from college,
though, it was the era of Ozzie and Harriet. Earlier in the century,
women had broken down all kinds of barriers, but in the postwar
years there was a backlash: women were once again supposed to
marry young, have as many kids as possible, and devote themselves
entirely to their families. A few women tried to flout the norm and
take up careers instead, but most of them didn't make it very far.

Shy and unaccustomed to making waves, Phoebe married a few
days after she graduated, became a housewife in the Minneapolis
suburbs, and had four children in quick succession with her husband, David, a scientist who taught at the University of Minnesota. She was a thoughtful, loving mother, but she couldn't
muster much gusto for cooking and cleaning, and by her early
thirties, she was "starving for some kind of outlet that didn't re-
volve around raising a family," as she wrote later. (She had company. She was thirty-two in 1963, when Betty Friedan published
The Feminine Mystique.) She tried being a Sunday school teacher
and a Girl Scout leader, but didn't take to either. Then, one sunny
spring morning when she was thirty-four, when only one of her
kids had started school and the youngest two were still in diapers,

a neighbor took her out birdwatching. As she beheld the blazing orange throat of a Blackburnian Warbler that was perched in the top of a tree, she had an epiphany akin to a religious awakening. "I had never seen anything like it," she wrote, "and at the same time, I realized that the bird had probably been in the trees in my own back yard every spring I'd been alive. It was as if a window opened up." She began birding with her neighbor once or twice a week, mostly in the woods around their houses, and keeping a life list, which grew slowly at first, since it takes a while to learn how to "spot" birds in trees and shrubs, not to mention how to tell one kind of bird from another. A couple of years later, when the family moved to a suburb of St. Louis, she found a bird club to join, made more friends than she'd ever had before, and started to sharpen her skills.

Once she'd mastered most of the birds near home, though, she wanted to travel around the country and the world to see more; most of all, she wanted to spend time in the tropics, where the vast majority of the ten thousand bird species live. It was, people were saying, the Golden Age of birding: it was easier than it had ever been to get around in the tropics, and while a great deal of rain forest and other habitat had recently been destroyed, there hadn't yet been many extinctions. Throughout her forties, when her kids were in their teens, Phoebe wrote poems about feeling trapped, out of place, and depressed in the suburbs, and about wanting to flee to the jungle, where she belonged.

In 1981, when she was just a few months shy of her fiftieth birthday, she was, to her shock and devastation, diagnosed with advanced melanoma and told she had less than a year to live. Since there were no good treatments, she decided to spend her final months chasing birds wherever she could, a plan her family supported. She went with "bird tours"—a new phenomenon at the time—to Alaska, Australia, Suriname, and India, always thinking each trip would be her last. As it happened, however, her doctors had been wrong, and a year after her diagnosis, her body was robust, her spirit was exuberant, and she was starting to wonder how many species she could find before she was forced to stop. "I know the balloon will burst some day in the next few years," she wrote to a friend, "but meanwhile life is *so good*."

In the years that followed, Phoebe crisscrossed the globe with ever-deepening abandon, staking out rare and spectacular birds in the wildest places on earth. She still took tours, but she chose increasingly fringe ones, and as time went on she took more trips on her own, hiring local guides to show her around. She slept in yurts, at truck stops, and by the side of the road; she traveled in tiny planes, in canoes, and on horseback. Once, she was chased by tribesmen with ten-foot-long spears; another time, she was boatwrecked in the middle of the ocean. On the island of New Guinea, she was carjacked, kidnapped, and brutally assaulted by five thugs. Ten years after being diagnosed with terminal cancer, Phoebe had become obsessed with the notion of seeing eight thousand species, more than any other birder in history. She had also lost the capacity to take into account her family, her health, and her safety.

Phoebe liked to write things down, and I've been able to reconstruct her life through her papers: the poetry she wrote in her forties, letters she sent to friends and family, notebooks she kept on trips, and articles she contributed to the newsletter of her bird club and various magazines. When she was sixty-five, she started working on a memoir, and it was almost complete when she died.

I interviewed Phoebe's two brothers, Dave, her widower, who still lives outside St. Louis, and her four children, now in their forties and fifties, all of whom have careers in the natural sciences. The Snetsingers are private, dignified people, but they shared with me what they were comfortable with, and they allowed me to read and excerpt Phoebe's papers. I interviewed dozens of her friends, most of them birders, and found that a lot of them had stories worth telling, too. I tried out birdwatching myself, and I eventually took bird tours of Kenya and Peru, two countries in the tropics with particularly large numbers of species.

This book is about Phoebe, and about birding, a way of life I wanted to better understand. But it's also about the larger questions Phoebe's life raises. What happens when society pushes you into a role that you aren't meant to play? If you're told that you only have a short time to live, how should you spend it? Where is the line between dedication and obsession, and when does obsession cross the line into pathology?

What does it mean, ultimately, to live, and die, well?

Chapter 1

IT HAD BEEN a long, nasty winter, even by Minnesota standards. At first, it was numbingly cold. "Keep Your Overcoat
Buttoned Up," the *Minneapolis Morning Tribune* warned, with midwestern understatement, in mid-January, when the temperature
was five below zero. Over the next few weeks, it often got down
to twenty-five below. "Another battery-destroying, toe-freezing,
window-frosting day of cold, cold weather is predicted for the
Twin Cities today," the paper said in early February. In March,
there were three blizzards, each ten days after the last, each with
winds so fierce that you couldn't see. At one point, the wind was
so strong that it kicked up the soil, which mixed with the snow
and turned it black. Roads, schools, and stores were closed; telephone and power lines went dead; kids jumped from their roofs
into thirty-foot-high snowdrifts. "Winter May Be City's Worst in
43 Years," the *Tribune* declared.

It was 1965. Phoebe was thirty-four, and she lived with Dave
and their four little kids outside Minneapolis, in New Brighton, an
industrial town that was turning into a suburb. Penny was six; Tom
was four; Carol was three; Sue was one. Dave, who had grown up
on a farm, was a professor of agriculture on the St. Paul campus of

the University of Minnesota. His specialty was the relatively new field of poultry nutrition: he tried to figure out what to feed laying hens and chicks so the chicks would grow quickly and make for healthful, tasty meat. He taught, performed experiments, wrote papers, and sat on committees. Phoebe stayed home with the kids, which meant, of course, that she got to see their first steps and hear their first words, but also that she spent much of her time running after them, changing their diapers, and cleaning the house. When she could get out, she did some volunteering for the League of Women Voters (she was a Democrat with misgivings about the Vietnam War) and the Girl Scouts (for a while, she was a troop leader). She and Dave taught Sunday school at the local Unitarian church, not because they were particularly religious but to give their kids a sense of community.

Although Phoebe's parents gave them a little money each year, they lived primarily off Dave's salary as an associate professor, and so they'd bought a small, one-story house with a single bathroom, the sort of house where you don't get much privacy no matter which room you're in. There were only three bedrooms, Sue's nursery was a refurbished bathroom, and the living room was barely big enough to fit all six of them. The house was in a big field, though, near a lake and some woods, and they spent a lot of their time outdoors. Together, Phoebe and Dave planted pear trees and raspberry bushes and grew cucumbers and sweet corn. The kids had a tire swing and a sandbox, played in the woods, and wrapped themselves in cucumber vines to pretend they were ancient Romans. In the summer, the whole family swam in the lake together; in the winter, they used it as a skating rink. After a big snow, Dave would load the kids in a sled and drag them, pink-faced and smiling, around the property with his tractor.

In the winter of 1965, however, Dave was away on sabbatical. He'd gotten a fellowship to visit Oak Ridge National Laboratory in Tennessee, one of the places where the nuclear bomb had been developed, to learn to incorporate radiation into his research. He was mixing radioactive markers into chicken feed so they'd bind to the calcium, iron, and other nutrients in the feed. When he x-rayed a bird that had been given this feed, the markers showed where the nutrients were, which helped him figure out if they were getting absorbed.

Phoebe stayed behind with the kids, only one of whom— Penny—had started school and two of whom—Carol and Sue— were still in diapers. I don't know a lot of details about how she managed, but it couldn't have been easy. With Dave gone, she didn't get to take many breaks. Since the weather was so bad, she couldn't even go outside on some days, which meant that she saw no other adults. The little house would have been loud with children's cries. By springtime, she wrote in her memoir many years later, she was "starving" to do something that didn't involve kids. She "badly needed some mental and physical diversion," she wrote elsewhere. Once, when a reporter asked her about this time in her life, she said that her kids had been making her "kind of crazy."

She had probably started feeling frustrated well before that winter, even if it took the winter to bring things into focus. In high school, she'd gotten all A's and planned to be a psychologist. She'd gone to one of the best colleges in the country, Swarthmore, in Pennsylvania, where she got almost all A's and was chosen for Phi Beta Kappa, the national honor society. Early in college, she decided to be a chemist and loaded her schedule with advanced math and science classes. But, like many women who went to college in the 1950s, she got engaged when she was a senior—she had her "ring by spring," as the saying went—and put aside her plans for a career. She taught for a while before she and Dave had kids, but since 1958, when Penny was born, she'd been a housewife.

Phoebe was shy and didn't make friends easily, but she had one good friend in New Brighton, another shy, brainy housewife named Elisabeth Selden, who lived nearby with her husband and four children. The Selden kids were older than the Snetsinger kids, so Elisabeth had more freedom. She devoted a lot of her time to the civil rights movement, the Senate campaigns of Hubert Humphrey, and other liberal causes, and she opened her house to foreign exchange students at the University of Minnesota. In the spring and summer, when it was nice out, she watched birds.

One sunny morning in May 1965, after the snow had finally melted, Elisabeth had Phoebe over to her yard. According to Phoebe's memoir, Elisabeth gave her some binoculars, pointed to a branch in an oak tree, and told her to look. What she saw "nearly knocked me over with astonishment": a black-and-white bird, no bigger than a child's hand, with a yellow head, shiny black eyes, and a throat the color of a ripe mango. "I thought, 'My god, that is absolutely beautiful.'" The bird, Elisabeth said, was a Blackburnian Warbler, and it had come north from South America to breed. She must have told Phoebe that dozens of species of warbler—all little and bright, with voices like flutes—came north every spring. "Here was something that had been happening all my life, and I'd never paid any attention to it."

It was as if she'd seen a "blinding white light." When she got home, she couldn't wait to put the kids down for a nap so she could see if there were birds in her own yard. She bought binoculars and a field guide, and she hired one of Elisabeth's daughters, Anne, to baby-sit once a week so she and Elisabeth could go exploring together. One day, they saw dozens of Great Blue Herons tending to nests in some dead trees near a marsh. The nests looked flimsy to Phoebe—they were just bunches of sticks—and it looked to her like they might fall out of the trees. But then it occurred to her that Great Blue Herons had been raising their young the same way for millions of years, since long before the evolution of humans. "Once again, I was totally staggered."

Later in the spring, she and Elisabeth saw another kind of heron, an American Bittern, skulking in some grass near a swamp. It was mating season for this bird, too, and, as they watched, it froze, pointed its bill in the air, and began "the most amazing" courtship display: again and again, it bowed forward, shook its head violently from side to side, let out a deep, booming call, and returned to its starting position.

With Elisabeth's help, Phoebe started learning to identify some birds. It's tough: you have to know which "field marks" set a species apart from similar ones, and you have to find them fast, because birds don't stick around. You have to know, say, that the Magnolia Warbler has a band of white on its tail, that the Prairie Warbler has a bright yellow breast, that the Blackpoll Warbler has long, pointed wings, and that the Connecticut Warbler has a big bill. If you work hard at learning all these field marks, however, you get to a point where you don't have to think about them so much. You start to recognize birds viscerally, like you recognize your friends.

The effort pays off, because once you've identified a bird, you can appreciate it on a deeper level. If you know you're looking at a Blackburnian Warbler, for instance, you also know that it spends most of the year somewhere between Peru and Panama, usually at about two thousand meters above sea level; that it subsists, for the most part, on caterpillars and beetles; that every April, it flies north across the Gulf of Mexico and settles for the summer somewhere between Georgia and Saskatchewan, where it looks for a mate and builds a nest, often in a high branch in a hemlock tree; and that the female lays three to five white eggs with little reddish blotches that hatch around early June.

Phoebe also started keeping a life list, as Elisabeth surely did.

There were "surprises and new sights in every bush and tree," so the list got a bit bigger almost every day. "It was a season of euphoria," she wrote later. And: "It was a season of true magic, perhaps all the more powerful because of its belated entry into my life."

A picture of Phoebe was taken not long after she started birding, probably by Dave. She's sitting in the woods, on a stump or a rock, with binoculars hanging from a strap around her neck. Her black hair is cut in a smart, practical crop, and she's wearing a button-down blouse that she likely chose for its simplicity. She's not looking at the camera, but off in the distance, no doubt to see if there are birds. Her legs are a little spread—she's ready to spring up—and her hands grip her big black binoculars. She looks peaceful but intent. The sun shines on her from behind.

Dave and Phoebe had met as teenagers, in the farming town in Illinois where they both grew up. Dave's family had one of the town's most successful dairy farms; Phoebe's father commuted to Chicago to run his advertising agency. Dave and Phoebe started dating, shyly and from afar, when they were both in college, and they got married the week after Phoebe graduated, when she was twenty-two and he was twenty-three. They didn't talk much about their innermost thoughts and feelings, maybe because they both came from families where no one did, but it appears that during the early years of their marriage, when their kids were young, they were happy together. According to Elisabeth's daughter Anne, their baby-sitter, when they were all in the lake together, Dave would swim up behind Phoebe and put his arms around her; when Dave was about to come home from a trip, Phoebe would put on nice clothes and lipstick. "They'd look at each other and be so happy to see each other."

They were good parents, too. "I never saw either of them lose their tempers at the kids," Anne says. "Each kid was allowed to be an individual." The kids all consider themselves lucky: they weren't coddled or doted on, but they knew they were loved, and they have good memories of their time in Minnesota. With their mother, they baked cookies and brownies, read *Charlotte's Web*, listened to Pete Seeger and other sixties folksingers, and, beginning in 1965, looked for birds. One day, in the woods, Phoebe found the nest of a Great Horned Owl, so named because it has two pointy tufts of feathers on the top of its head that look like horns. She took the kids to the nest again and again to see chicks hatch, fuzzy

Great Horned Owl

and white, from their eggs; grow into fierce, silent hunters; and, finally, fly off to fend for themselves.

In the summer of 1965, just a couple of months after she'd introduced Phoebe to birding, Elisabeth's husband got a job in Washington, D.C., and, to Phoebe's great sadness, the Seldens left
Minnesota. Afterward, Phoebe continued birdwatching at her and
Elisabeth's regular spots, but it must have been a little lonely—and
difficult too, since she was still a novice. Dave, meanwhile, was getting frustrated at work. After he'd returned from his sabbatical, the
poultry science department had been combined with two other
departments at the School of Agriculture, animal science and dairy
science, and his new boss knew little about poultry. Over a school
vacation, Dave took some undergraduates to St. Louis for a tour of
the Ralston Purina Company, which makes animal feed. The man
who took them around had been in Dave's graduate program, and
he offered him a job developing poultry feed, on the spot, a job
that paid much better than his professorship did and would allow
him to do more interesting research. So, in the summer of 1967,
Dave and Phoebe decided to move the family to a suburb of St.
Louis named Webster Groves.

It was a lot fancier than New Brighton. The houses were ram-
bling and grand; there was a country club and a gourmet grocer's.
Most of the men were doctors or executives who commuted to St.
Louis. Almost all the women were housewives, and a lot of them
were active in social clubs: the Engineers' Wives Club, the Kappa
Kappa Gamma Alumnae Club, the Greater St. Louis Home Econo-
mists. Some of them took classes at the Webster Groves YMCA on
"Entertaining with Elegance and Ease." ("Learn to set talked-about
tables, serve memorable meals, plan parties with a theme, [and] make
your own table linens and clever centerpieces," the Y advertised.)
With help from both sets of parents, Phoebe and Dave bought a

house three times the size of the one they'd had in Minnesota. It was old, white, and elegant, with a portico, gleaming arched windows, high ceilings, and big airy rooms. There were five bedrooms, six bathrooms, a formal dining room, and two studies.

In Minnesota, they'd had a lot of land; in Missouri, they had a lot of neighbors. There were about ten families on the block, many of them Catholic, each with four or five or six kids. Right away, the Snetsinger kids—ages three, five, six, and eight—made a lot of friends. They'd play outside all afternoon with them, until Phoebe called them to dinner at six. A lot of the mothers on the block were also friends, meeting during the day for lunch or bridge, but Phoebe didn't fit in with them, and she was more interested in getting to know other birdwatchers. She called the St. Louis chapter of the Audubon Society and was directed to a club right in her town, the Webster Groves Nature Study Society, with hundreds of members from around the city. They studied all kinds of things, but most people in the club focused on birds, and there were field trips twice a week to look for them. Later, Phoebe described the group as "the answer to my prayers."

"WGNSS," as it's called (pronounced WIG-ness), had been founded in 1920 by a quirky Quaker couple, Alfred and Elizabeth Satterthwait. Alfred was an entomologist for the federal government; Elizabeth was a housewife who, it was said, descended the stairs in their house by sliding down the banister. They didn't have any children, which might explain their wholehearted devotion to the club: they held meetings at their house, organized and led field trips, gave talks at local schools to recruit members, and helped send some of their protégés to college. So a whole generation of Webster Groves kids learned about birds and other aspects of nature from the Satterthwaits, and this generation, in turn, taught the next. By the late 1960s, when Phoebe joined WGNSS, there were bird clubs all over the country, but she was lucky to fall into such a vibrant, learned one. "As a novice, I couldn't have been in better hands," she wrote later.

At this point, the club was mostly adults. A lot of the men were of retirement age and had been birding since they were kids; some of them must have learned from the Satterthwaits themselves. There were a few women among the old-timers, too, but, for the most part, the women were like Phoebe—housewives in their thirties or forties who'd taken up birding when their kids were young, as a reprieve. Most had finished college, and some had gone to graduate school. One woman, Martha Gaddy, had graduated from law school and passed the bar exam, but no one—including her father, who had his own law practice—had been willing to hire her. Instead, he hired Martha's husband, whom she'd met in law school, while Martha stayed home to raise their kids.

The weekly birding trips were on Thursday and Saturday mornings. Phoebe couldn't usually make the Saturday one, since her three older kids were out of school then, but she almost always got a sitter for Sue on Thursdays, and the outings, she later said, became the highlight of her week. She once told one of her friends in WGNSS, "On Thursdays, I'm not someone's daughter, mother, or wife. I'm me." She would meet the other "Thursday birders," mostly women, at eight o'clock in the parking lot of the local shopping plaza, beneath, appropriately, a light pole that was adorned with a huge plastic dove. An old-timer would be on hand to lead the trip, usually Kyrle Boldt, a retired insurance salesman from Texas who called the women "Sugar" and carried a thermos full of Bloody Marys in the field. They'd pack into a few cars—Kyrle would lead the way in his Chevy—and go to whatever park, pond, or patch of woods seemed to hold the most promise that day. Kyrle would help the group spot the birds ("It's right there, Sugar, can't you see it?") and figure out what they were, as the Satterthwaits had done in their day.

Common species—the cardinals and crows we all see everywhere—were pretty much ignored on these trips. The point was to find rare or elusive birds: owls that didn't budge until nightfall, woodpeckers that blended in with the branches, warblers that were passing through on their way north or south. As it happens, St. Louis is a great place to behold bird migration, since a lot of species migrate up and down the Mississippi River, probably to avoid getting lost. When the Thursday birders saw something good, one of them would race home to activate the "Rare Bird Alert" telephone tree so the rest of the club would have a chance to see it, too.

Kyrle and the other old-timers taught Phoebe to talk like a birder. When you're trying to tell someone else where a bird is, you use clock terminology: "noon" means it's right in front of you, "nine o'clock" means it's to your left, "three o'clock" means it's to your right, and so on. A bird that's "teed up" in a bush is relatively easy to see, while a bird that just does a "fly-by" is harder. "I'm on it!" you'll say, triumphantly, when you spot a bird you've been hearing in the brush. If you see a bird well enough to identify it definitively, you can "tick" it off on your list, but you might still wish you'd gotten a better look at it, in which case you'll mark it as "BVD," for Better View Desired. A species you keep missing is a "jinx bird" or a "nemesis bird" or a "grip-off." A species you really want, or "need," is a "target" bird, and you might feel a real "dip" if you miss it.

Most people in WGNSS kept a whole bunch of lists, including a life list, an "area list" of the birds they'd seen within a fifty-mile radius of St. Louis, and a "year list" of the birds they'd seen in the fifty-mile radius that year. While 350 bird species were known to exist in and around St. Louis, a lot of them were hardly ever seen, and barely anyone saw more than 225 in any given year. If you had a "year list" of two hundred or more, you were inducted into that year's "200 Club" and feted in the WGNSS newsletter, *Nature Notes*. Cheating on lists was rare. If you got caught pretending you'd seen something that you hadn't, the whole club would shun you.

In January 1968, Phoebe started keeping a year list. She systematically kept track of it, and of all her sightings, in a spiral notebook that she began that month, too. She wrote down the names of all the birds she saw each day, sometimes adding a few notes on their field marks. If a bird was new for her year list, she wrote its name in ink; if it was also a life bird, she added a red underline. She wrote the names of all other birds in pencil. When there were birds that had stumped her, she wrote down what she thought they were but didn't count them. She marked any rare birds with an asterisk.

She made a lot of friends during her first months with WGNSS. At Purina parties and gatherings in the neighborhood, Phoebe felt uncomfortable and said little, but when she was with her new birding friends, she was talkative and vivacious, according to Dave. Birds seem to have given her a medium of connection that enabled her to overcome her shyness, which was probably a big part of their appeal.

She got excited about other aspects of nature, too. Whenever possible, she attended the club's botany, entomology, and geology field trips. She'd studied some astronomy in college, and she started taking an interest in stars again, often setting up a telescope on her roof at sunset. Soon, she was thought of as a resident expert, and in the winter of 1968, the editor of *Nature Notes* asked her to write a series of articles on the sky. The first installment, "Apologia for Stargazing," was published in February. "The night sky now offers some of the most splendid viewing opportunities of the year, and darkness still comes early enough for even young children to be exposed to the beauty and majesty of all that is going on beyond our minuscule world." In that article and in two that followed, Phoebe explained how to locate various constellations, how they got their names, and some basic scientific facts about them. (Binary stars like Eta Persei, she explained, are "two very close stars, one bright, one dimmer and somewhat larger, revolving around a common center of gravity.")

But then May came—her first in Missouri—and, as she explained to her readers, she lost interest in the project: "The night skies can wait. After all, one can always see the 'spring' evening sky even in February simply by rising at 3 A.M. But May days come only in May, and since I was unable to spend the night with the telescope if I wanted to get up with the warblers, something had to give. There have been some moments when it seemed that I made the wrong choice—such as one very wet and vain search through dripping underbrush for an elusive Connecticut Warbler . . . But nevertheless the warbler fever struck me full force this spring, and I rather hope it's incurable."

Birding, in some ways, is like a religion. Some people get hooked on birds gradually, but many others have an experience like Phoebe's, an awakening triggered by a "spark bird." Many religious people seek to transcend the everyday by praying or meditating; birders seek transcendence by spending time in nature. Bird clubs give them a sort of church, a community of like-minded people who offer companionship and support. So although Phoebe found her religion on that fateful morning in May 1965, her conversion wasn't complete until more than two years later, when, serendipitously, she found a thriving congregation.

Phoebe put a lot of effort into teaching the kids about nature. One Saturday, she took them into the woods to look for mushrooms. She had them carefully examine each fungus, then look in her field guide to try to identify it. "The children quickly learned to scrutinize the undersurface of the caps of the stemmed mushrooms in order to distinguish the pore fungi from the gill fungi—a basic step in classification," she wrote in *Nature Notes*. At night, through her telescope, she'd show them the rings of Saturn and the reddish tint of Mars. Once, she woke them in the middle of the night to see a lunar eclipse, when the earth's shadow falls upon the moon, turning it a spooky orange.

She taught them about birds, too. Tom, a shy, studious little boy, was the most interested, and some of his happiest memories from childhood are of standing on the roof with his mother on spring mornings to look for warblers. (When I was interviewing Dave, I stepped out onto the roof, and I was struck by the sense of remove I got, which Phoebe and Tom must have gotten, too. Though I could see plenty of other roofs, I was practically engulfed by verdant treetops.) One day, she let him skip school so he could go with her and the nature society to see the raucous mating dance of the Greater Prairie-Chicken: while the female chickens watch, the males fan their tails, stomp their feet, hoot, cluck, and jump up and down. Each male has two sacs of yellow skin on its neck, which inflate like balloons as the bird dances.

She was creative about entertaining the children inside, too. An uncle of hers was a professional puppeteer in Hollywood, and she had him teach her to make puppets as he did, with papier-mâché heads, stick bodies, wire arms, and cloth dresses. She taught the kids to make the puppets, built them a theater out of an empty refrigerator box, and helped them think up and put on shows, which they did, with zeal, for many years. "She was a pretty typical mom," Sue says, "but our house always seemed to be more fun."

On the other hand, Phoebe was bored by a lot of the other things that she was supposed to do—and enjoy—as a housewife. She cooked dinner every night, but she stuck to simple meals like macaroni and cheese and hamburgers, and the kids were in high

school before they realized that vegetables could be bought un-
frozen. As the children got older, she assigned each of them the
task of making one meal a week and taught them to do their own
laundry; a housekeeper came once a week to help her with the
cleaning. She took the kids shopping for clothes, but not with
much enthusiasm, they say, and she bought her own clothes in
bulk, at dime stores. She had Dave buy their furniture and whatever else they needed for the house, and "she wasn't much for dec-
orating things around here," he says. He handled the gardening
and landscaping, too, though she got upset when he clipped the lilac
and forsythia bushes, which she thought should be allowed to grow
wild.

Dave had two main responsibilities at Purina. The first was devis-
ing experiments to be carried out on chickens and other birds at
the company's research farm, which was a couple of hours west of
St. Louis, out in the country. He went to the farm regularly to
check on the research, and, depending on how it turned out, he
might suggest changes in the feeds being sold. His other responsibility was customer service. He took calls from farmers and meat
companies with questions about Purina's chicken feeds, and he
visited some of the bigger customers in person. In the fall of 1968,
about a year after they'd moved to St. Louis, he and Phoebe hired
a sitter so she could go with him on a short trip to meet with some
customers in Texas—one of the best places in the country for
birding, largely because it's a way station for migrants heading to
and from the tropics. Of the roughly nine hundred bird species
that have been recorded in the continental United States, more than
six hundred have shown up in Texas at some point.

Their first stop was El Paso, the desert town on the Mexican
border, where Phoebe had "part of a day and a rental car at my
disposal," she wrote in *Nature Notes* when she got home. "Knowing

nothing whatever about the area, I simply headed for the largest green spot on the city map," which turned out to be a dry, scrubby canyon on the edge of town. It was, she wrote, so different from the terrain she was used to that it "might as well have been on some other planet." "The plants—mostly cactus-like—I couldn't even begin to cope with; besides, there were too many intriguing flutterings in the scrub growth to investigate." She used a field guide to help her identify the birds, almost all of which were unfamiliar. "A literally breathtaking sight that I will never forget was my first view of a Black-throated Sparrow. This stunning fellow hopped up on a bush about two feet away from me, and we stared at each other for an ecstatic sixty seconds or so before he decided he'd seen enough of me and went his way." When I looked up a picture of this bird, I expected to see something dramatic, but it's just a little gray thing with a black and white head. Phoebe was likely made ecstatic by its novelty, and by her exotic surroundings. She and Dave also stopped near Lubbock, where she found a "lovely roadside cemetery" full of birds. "How very pleasant it is to be naïve enough to be excited by things which the natives of an area take for granted."

At the end of 1968, her first full year in St. Louis, Phoebe had 166 birds on her year list; her life list was probably at around 250 then. She surely enjoyed the spring of 1969 in St. Louis, but it couldn't have been as exciting as the previous spring—she was going to the same places to see pretty much the same birds—and the trip to Texas had whetted her appetite for more travel. In the summer, at her suggestion, the whole family took a road trip out West for a couple of weeks. They split their time about evenly between Colorado and Arizona, with stops in the Rocky Mountains, with its fir forests, meadows, and glaciers; the Native American ruins of Mesa Verde; the Grand Canyon; and Petrified Forest National Park, a dramatic landscape of red, blue, and yellow buttes. They spent most days hiking; most nights, they cooked outside and camped.

The trip didn't work out as Phoebe had hoped, however. She wanted to walk slowly and linger among the birds, while her "goal-oriented family" wanted to cover a lot of ground, according to a *Nature Notes* piece she wrote afterward. At the end of one hike, to an alpine lake in northern Colorado, "I felt ecstatically happy with all the new birds and flowers to investigate, but also full of agony knowing I could not stay long enough even to begin to absorb it." Later, they drove past the jagged San Juan Mountains of southwestern Colorado, "some of the loveliest scenery I have ever been in," she wrote. "Even along the road the flowers were incredible, and my imagination ran wild at the thought of the beauty hidden in the more remote areas of this range. But Mesa Verde was our goal for the day, and we could not linger in the San Juans." Then, when they got to the Mesa, "time permitted only the merest skimming of the surface."

Much of the time, Phoebe walked by herself, way behind Dave and the kids.

Phoebe happened to get into birding when it was in the middle of a revolution.

It used to be that if you liked birds, you shot them. In any case, that's what gentlemen in England did after the country started to industrialize, in the early nineteenth century. Cities were getting big and polluted, and people were longing to reconnect with nature. The rich, who had lots of free time, began going to the woods to collect plants, bugs, and rocks. If you were a man, you might also collect birds—bloodily, with your shotgun. Once you'd shot a bird, you'd figure out what it was, then skin, stuff, mount, and display it. The idea was to amass as big and varied a collection of bird skins as possible. A few decades later, when the United States started industrializing, bird collecting took hold among the upper class here. "Begin by shooting every bird you can," a manual urged young American gentlemen in 1874. By then, a few British and American men were making a living as ornithologists at museums, but most of what they did was shoot and skin birds, too.

Milliners were also preying upon birds. In the late 1800s, a hat with feathers was a status symbol for women in London and in the big American cities. Some hats had just a few feathers; some had dozens; and some had a whole bird, "mounted on wires and springs that permit the head and wings to be moved about in the most natural manner," according to an article on ladies' fashions in *Harper's Bazaar*. As many as five million American birds were being killed each year to make hats, which was causing the populations of many species to plummet.

In 1896, Harriet Hemenway of Boston, an heiress and nature lover, decided to try to put a stop to the bloodshed. At a series of tea parties, she told her friends about the mass slaughter they were contributing to and tried to get them to renounce feathered hats. Eventually, she and hundreds of other ladies founded a club "to discourage the buying and wearing, for ornamental purposes[,] of the feathers of any wild birds . . . and to otherwise further the protection of native birds." They called their group the Massachusetts Audubon Society, after the bird artist John James Audubon— who, for the record, shot a lot of birds himself, but who introduced many Americans to avian beauty. Audubon groups were soon founded by women in a dozen other states, and the groups ultimately united to form the National Audubon Society. Audubon members boycotted hats with feathers, lobbied for laws to protect birds, taught kids to make birdfeeders, and took walks to see birds in the country. The first real binoculars were invented around this time, which made it possible to see birds well without shooting them first.

Many of the "gentlemen naturalists" who collected birds for

fun and study also joined the Audubon Society, and they, too, campaigned against hat-makers. But they didn't see a problem with continuing to shoot birds themselves. They killed them in relatively small numbers, they argued, and they thought it was impossible to properly identify and study birds if they weren't right in front of them, on trays.

A notable dissenter was Lynds Jones, one of the country's first professors of ornithology, at Oberlin College in Ohio. Killing birds wasn't just inhumane, Jones thought; it was also counterproductive. "The old grind that a 'bird in the hand is worth two in the bush' may still apply to other things, but it certainly does not apply to the birds," he wrote in 1897 in an ornithological journal he edited, the *Wilson Bulletin*. "We want to know *them*, not simply their skins." To that end, Jones and one of his students, William Leon Dawson, suggested to *Bulletin* readers that instead of collecting birds, they keep lists of them. First, they were to keep "daily horizons" of the birds they saw each day. Over time, these lists would establish which species occurred in their towns, how common they were, and whether they were migrants or permanent residents. The process of taking systematic notes would also "stimulate the powers of observation," according to Dawson. "It will be a surprise to some to find how many species of birds may be seen on a little early-morning-before-breakfast ramble." Second, at the end of each year, readers were to compile a list of all the birds they'd seen since January 1—this was an "annual horizon"—and note any changes from the year before. These lists would help chronicle long-term patterns in bird distribution.

A third kind of list, "the life horizon," had no scientific value but could provide the bird student with "delight." "This is, in short, a list of all the birds he knows in the field," Dawson explained. It was to include "only those species which he has actually met and so can identify afield." If such a list were kept "merely for the sake of numerical comparison with some rival observer," it would be "as vulgar as a collection of tobacco tags," in Dawson's view; but if, on the other hand, the list was "rightly conceived," it could be "a source of legitimate satisfaction." "To be able to add year by year to your list of bird friends is no mean ambition. It will incite the student to a careful scrutiny of his own surroundings and give zest as well to the vacation trip or change of residence." He concluded, "A day is happily spent that shows me any bird that I never saw alive before."

When collectors still insisted that the only way to identify a bird with certainty was to shoot it, a young man from New York City, Ludlow Griscom, set out to prove them wrong. As a boy, Griscom had watched birds in Central Park, probably to get away from his parents, who were followers of the self-professed psychic Madame Blavatsky. In 1911, when he was twenty-one, he became the first American to attend graduate school in ornithology, at Cornell, where he wrote a master's thesis on how to identify ducks and geese with binoculars. It wasn't a question of determining what distinguished each species—the collectors had already done that—but of figuring out which of these distinctions could be gleaned in the field. After earning his degree, Griscom was hired as an ornithologist at the American Museum of Natural History in Manhattan, whereupon he tried to work out the field marks for birds around the country. In his spare time, he tried to shake up the Linnaean Society, the main bird club in New York, whose older members were still using shotguns.

He was just as much of a sportsman as the old-timers were, though. "Charge!" he'd cry to his protégés, most of them young men, as they set out to look for birds in the woods. Later: "Gang, let's have a council of war." "Someone find a bird with some zip in it." And finally, when one turned up: "Unprecedented!" Griscom and the men who admired him kept lists of the birds they saw each day, each year, and over the course of their lives, and they didn't think trying to outdo one another was "vulgar." (As in the Webster Groves Nature Study Society, people wanted other club members to respect them, so they didn't dare lie about what they'd seen.)

One of the youngsters in the Linnaean Society who followed Griscom around was a passionate art student named Roger Tory Peterson, who, like Griscom, came from a troubled home and had likely taken up birdwatching to escape it. In the early 1930s, Peterson started working on a book that would illustrate Griscom's teachings, with simple drawings of each species in eastern North America and arrows pointing to the most important field marks. Each bird also got a short writeup that emphasized the ways it was different from similar species: the Cape May Warbler, for instance, was "the only Warbler with chestnut cheeks"; the Scarlet Tanager was "the only bright red bird with black wings and tail." The book, published in 1934, was called *A Field Guide to the Birds: A Bird Book on a New Plan.* It was pocket-sized, so it could be carried around, and it advised readers to "keep a life list."

Field Guide became a huge bestseller, made thousands of American men and women start watching and "listing" birds, and put to rest the idea that birds had to be shot to be identified. Audubon chapters and other birdwatching clubs were founded around the country, and clubs that already existed, like WGNSS, grew dramatically. Soon, Peterson published a guide to the birds of the West, and shortly after that he helped write one for the birds of Britain, where collecting had also fallen out of vogue and watching birds had taken hold in its place.

The next revolution in the way people enjoyed birds—the one that was under way when Phoebe got started—began just after World War II. Americans were more mobile after the war: they had more money and leisure time, roads were better, gas was cheaper, and it was possible to take airplanes around the country and the world. In the early 1950s, Olin Pettingill, an ornithology professor at Carleton College in Minnesota, published two books, *A Guide to Bird-Finding East of the Mississippi* and *A Guide to Bird-Finding West of the Mississippi*, that helped people birdwatch in unfamiliar places, directing them not just to the part of the country where a particular bird could be found but to the exact bog or forest or cliff or meadow that was the best place to stake it out. Around the same time, Peterson, along with a friend from Britain, took a hundred-day road trip around the national parks of the United States and Canada and published a spirited book about it, *Wild America*. Like his field guides, it was hugely popular, and it inspired a generation of young birdwatchers to set out in their cars.

By the late 1950s, a few birders were even going abroad, mainly to the tropics. The closer you get to the equator, the birdier it gets: the tiny country of Panama, which is just north of the equator, has almost a thousand bird species, more than have been recorded in all of North America; Peru, which is just south of the equator, has a whopping eighteen hundred. One birder from Kansas, Dean Fisher, saw the birds of the Pacific Ocean from the deck of a Navy cruiser in the mid-1950s. Upon his discharge in 1958, he and one of his shipmates set out to see the birds of the world in a camper. They took the newly built Pan-American Highway to South America; sailed from Brazil to South Africa; drove on a track in the sand across the Sahara; sailed from Morocco to Spain; and drove east across Europe, the Soviet Union, and India. At the border between India and Burma, the Burmese police wouldn't let the camper pass, so Fisher and his friend shipped it to Australia and got around the rest of Asia by bus and by thumb. Eventually, they flew from Saigon to Perth and drove around northern Australia (where, incidentally, Fisher met his future wife). They left the camper in Australia and flew home. In all, the trip took three years.

There weren't any field guides or bird-finding books for these countries. In every new city, Fisher would look for a natural history museum and ask to see the bird skin collection, which he'd take some notes on. Then he'd drive to whatever parks, forests, or beaches were on his map. When he saw a bird he couldn't identify, which happened all the time, he wrote a description of it in hopes that when a field guide was published, he'd know what he'd seen. Though he missed countless birds while his head was down to write, he ended up adding about three thousand species to his life list, bringing his total to about four thousand (of the 8,600 species that were recognized at the time). Fisher was, by far, the leading "lister" of his day.

During the 1960s, more and more people watched birds far from home—though not many women, since they were usually busy raising kids. Like Fisher, Ben King was from Kansas, and he also got assigned to a Navy cruiser in the Pacific. When he was discharged in 1962, he hitchhiked around Asia and Australia to see birds, ran out of money, got a job teaching ballroom dancing in Korea, and hitchhiked some more. Joel Abramson, a doctor from Miami, got to know the birds of Asia while serving in Vietnam in the mid-1960s. He'd take sick call at his Army base first thing in the morning, then look for birds around the base and in the jungle. "I didn't want to be captured [by the Viet Cong], so I'd find a place off the trail to sit, my back to a tree," he says. "I knew I'd see people before they saw me." Other birders went to graduate school in ornithology as a way of funding foreign travel. You had to come up with a respectable dissertation topic, but you could spend a lot of your time poking around.

As the environmental movement began and gave rise to eco-tourism, it occurred to a few guys to try to design bird tours. Peter Alden graduated from college in 1967, inherited a little money in 1968, and decided to "piss it off on round-the-world bird-watching," as he told me. When his money ran out, he talked the

Massachusetts Audubon Society into letting him lead birding trips for its members to Mexico, Kenya, and other exotic places. So Alden got to keep birding abroad, and the people who took his tours got to start. Over the next few years, several other bird clubs started running similar tours.

Most birders didn't have the time or money to go abroad, but many went on far-flung road trips with their bird clubs, often with a copy of *Wild America* in the car. Once, in the late 1960s, a high school student in Pennsylvania named Ted Parker talked a couple of men in his bird club into driving to Florida for a weekend to see a rare bird that had recently been spotted there. They left on Friday night, drove for twenty-four hours straight, saw the bird Sunday morning, and headed right back, returning home just in time for work and school. Ted and his friends started calling themselves the IDIOTS, short for "Incredible Distances In Ornithological Travel Society," and they adopted the motto, "It's a good thing there's no bridge to Cuba." A few years later, when he was in college at the University of Arizona, Ted became a birding celebrity when he saw more species in North America in a single year—626—than anyone had seen before, though he ended up dropping every course at school but golf. The previous "Big Year" recordholder had been Peterson, who saw 572 species in 1953, when he was traveling the country for *Wild America*.

In 1968, the year Phoebe and Dave went to Texas together, a few birders who'd done some traveling founded a national bird club, the American Birding Association. It wasn't aimed at protecting birds, as the National Audubon Society was, or at studying them in depth, as some academic societies did. Instead, the new club catered to "the vast majority of birders who are interested in birding for its value as a hobby and sport," according to the first issue of the club's journal, *Birding*. To that end, club members would help each other find birds in different parts of the country and around the world, exchange information about helpful books and equipment, and compete against each other for the highest lists. "Competition adds zest to life," an early issue of *Birding* declared. At the end of each year, *Birding* would publish its members' life list totals and the totals of any other lists they kept, such as year lists, North America lists, and state lists. In 1969, the first year this was done, the member with the highest life list was Stuart Keith of California, with about three thousand species. (Fisher, Alden, King, and Abramson hadn't joined the club yet.) The man in second place had about fifteen hundred species, and the man in third had just under eight hundred.

Though there were no women in the top ten, at least one would have qualified. Her name was Bertha Massie, and she was a plucky accountant's wife in her sixties who'd gotten her start in the Webster Groves Nature Study Society. After her kids were grown, Bertha had started taking Audubon and other nature tours to see new species, and by 1969, when the American Birding Association was founded, she'd been around the world. She'd occasionally go out with WGNSS's Thursday birding group and tell the young housewives about some of her adventures. She used to say, "When they pass the cake, take a piece, 'cause you don't know if it's gonna come around again."

"I hung on her every word," Phoebe wrote many years later, in her memoir. "What a simply *wonderful* way to live!"

A few months after the Snetsingers took their trip out West, in January 1970, Purina sent Dave to Mexico to meet with some customers, and Phoebe decided to go with him to see birds. They hired a sitter for the kids, all of whom had started school by this point.

In Mazatlán, on the Pacific coast, "it was depressing to see the blight of resort civilization," Phoebe wrote in a *Nature Notes* piece. "But the birds were lovely, perhaps more poignantly so because it was obvious such fragile creatures could not long hold their own." At one point, a flock of Roseate Spoonbills flew over her, with wings "stunningly pink against the blue sky." (They're called spoonbills because, oddly enough, their beaks look like long wooden cooking spoons.) On a boat-trip to a few nearby islands, she saw Magnificent Frigatebirds, which have bright red pouches under their necks that inflate like giant balloons, as well as thousands of Brown Boobies, which nest in massive colonies to ward off predators. "The sky and the rocks were filled with the comings and goings of the boobies, a truly unforgettable sight."

Later, Phoebe accompanied Dave to a ranch where he had a meeting. "It was glorious," she reported. "Tropical hummingbirds were everywhere and Vermilion Flycatchers so common that I almost stopped catching my breath when I saw one." Their bodies were a resplendent shade of red, which was set off dramatically by jet-black wings. "Most glorious of all" was a Painted Bunting, which had green wings, a red body, and a blue head, and which stayed put for a while, "showing me just how beautiful he was from all angles."

Dave's final meetings were in Mexico City, a virtual birding wasteland, so one morning, Phoebe rented a car and drove to a forest outside the city that she'd heard about from Bertha. Initially, to her "utter panic," she got on the highway in the wrong direction—the signs were only in Spanish—but she made it to the forest by nine, in time to see the morning mist in the tops of the trees. It was, she wrote in her notebook, "a *most* beautiful & impressive forest," with "towering" firs and pines with "enormous" cones. Once the mist burned off, she saw birds everywhere. She wrote down the names of the ones she recognized ("gorgeous!" she wrote in the margin next to one) and took a lot of notes on the ones she didn't, in hopes of figuring out what they were later.

Then she realized that a man was following her. Heart pounding, she walked quickly toward the car, and he soon disappeared. But at the car, there was another man, and this one, alarmingly, had a gun. When she asked him what he wanted, he replied in Spanish, and she got the impression he was saying he'd been guarding the car. She got in quickly, which seemed to upset him. Later, she realized he'd been demanding a tip. She'd been "naïve, and very lucky," she reflected in her memoir many years later. At the time, however, all she felt was a surge of adrenaline, and she drove back to the city with "confidence and daring." The whole day had cast an "intoxicating spell."

She wrote in *Nature Notes*, "My husband tells me he can now detect by the gleam in my eye—or lack of it—whether or not a prospective site for a business trip holds enticing birding possibilities—and he's beginning to suspect that I don't go along entirely for the purpose of keeping him company."

A few days after Phoebe returned to the St. Louis winter, the "spell" wore off, and she crashed.

This was when she started writing poetry. She treated it as a diary, and though Dave had a vague idea that she was writing it, she hardly ever mentioned it and didn't show him any poems; she might have been ashamed of her dark feelings, and she clearly didn't feel comfortable communicating them. Dave first read the poems decades later, upon her death. They were typed up and carefully centered on white paper, with the date in the bottom right corner of each page.

On February 7, 1970, less than a week after her return from Mexico, Phoebe wrote a poem called "Sickroom." She was surrounded by cold, sterile walls that made her feel like she was in a tomb, she wrote. Though the tomb had windows, the glass was one-way: she could look out and see that other people were happy, but no one could look in and see her. "I have been there, too, from time to time / In that outer life where beauty swells one's soul. / But now can be forever, and emptiness eternal / In the cold and sterile whiteness of my tomb." A few days later, she likened herself to a skeleton with hollow bones; all the marrow, once throbbing and red, had been "crushed." She could still move and talk and act like everyone else, but, in truth, she felt dead.

She wrote dozens of poems that winter and spring. Her heart hung slack; she was lonely and bitter; her days were full of secret, searing pain. She felt she wasn't living honestly. She admired the son of a friend who was going to jail for refusing to fight in the Vietnam War, she wrote he was serving his conscience, as well as hers. She, on the other hand, lived "a sensible life of compromise and conventional achievement," which made her more of a prisoner than he.

She sometimes criticized Dave brutally. In one poem, which he only told me about, she accused him of not being able to appreciate beauty, and even of having "no soul."

With spring, she wrote a few happier poems. She could smell the sassafras on the trees and hear the song of the cardinal, she wrote, and she, too, felt resurrected. She sometimes thought of spring in sexual terms—as an orgasm, intense but finite, or as a lover, tenderly seducing the virgin green earth.

One poem was an ode to Joseph Wood Krutch, a nature writer who had just died. Krutch began his career as an academic in New York, but, after writing a biography of Thoreau, he quit his job and moved to the Arizona desert, where he ended up spending his happiest years. In her poem, Phoebe said it was cruel that Krutch had died in the spring, when the desert was most alive. On the other hand, she wrote, there was no good time for those who loved the earth to depart it.

Some days, she believed that she, too, could be bold and change her life. "Today is clay, gray and unshapen / I'll take it in my hands to warm, / To soften and to mold." She could either infuse the clay with energy, and "be a god," or "leave both time and self unrealized / Formless and cold." She also wrote that late at night, when she was alone, she was able to break free from the confines of her stark reality, to dream and even to be insane. These were her "most fulfilling" hours: "I love the potential of the night / The primordial formlessness." The night was a womb, warm and moist, out of which could be born her true self.

Still, she knew that change was hard, and sometimes violent, like the amputation of a limb.

Chapter 2

I N 1935, WHEN Phoebe was four, her father started an advertising agency in Chicago. It was the middle of the Depression,
and people thought he was nuts.

Leo Burnett was born in 1892 to parents of Scottish descent
and grew up in a small town in Michigan, St. Johns, where his father, Noble, owned a general store. According to a family history
written many years later, Noble was mild-mannered and kind, but
Leo's mother, Rosa, had a violent temper. A couple of times, in
anger, she ripped off the clothes she was wearing and tore them to
shreds. Once, she threw a carving knife at Leo.

Noble had trouble making the store turn a profit, largely because he was too generous in extending lines of credit to customers.
As his debts mounted, he suggested to Rosa that they mortgage
their house, but she wouldn't hear of it. Desperate, he boarded a
train to Detroit to try to negotiate a different loan. But the train
crashed, and he was badly hurt. Rosa had to run the store for months
while he recovered. From then on, she turned away whenever he
tried to kiss her, according to the family history. The store soon
went under, and Noble filed for bankruptcy.

Leo, the eldest of Noble and Rosa's four kids, got a part-time job at the local newspaper when he was twelve and the store's debts were piling up; he probably wanted to help out the family and escape the house at the same time. He was short and awkward, and, as he later said, "a pimply-faced kid who wasn't much noticed, except for the pimples." He worked hard, however, and in 1910 he went on to the University of Michigan, where he studied journalism.

Around the time he graduated, his father's store closed, and he decided to go into advertising instead of journalism, since it paid better. In his twenties and thirties, Leo worked in the ad departments of two car companies, one in Detroit and one in Indianapolis, and at a small ad agency in Indianapolis. During this time, he met his wife, Naomi, and they had two sons, Peter and Joe. In 1931, the year Phoebe was born and two years into the Great Depression, Leo was put in charge of the Chicago office of a big New York agency, Erwin, Wasey & Company.

As the Depression worsened over the next couple of years, Erwin Wasey went downhill, and three of its clients—Green Giant, Hoover, and Real Silk Hosiery—told Leo that if he went out on his own, they'd follow him. He was forty-three. He borrowed against his life insurance to help pay the rent and his eight employees.

As Leo saw it, most ads were either boring, unbelievable, or both; he vowed that the Leo Burnett Company would make interesting, credible ones. To that end, he told his staff to identify a product's most compelling feature—the deliciousness of peas picked at the peak of their flavor, for instance—and capture it with an image and a plainspoken headline. "Keep it simple," he told his staff. "Let's do the obvious thing—the common thing—but let's do it uncommonly well."

He decided that the company's symbol would be a hand reaching for a cluster of stars. To welcome visitors, the receptionist set out a bowl of apples.

Years later, Leo said, "I always figured that I was less smart than some people, but that if I worked hard enough maybe I would average out alright." He must also have been worried about ending up like his father, penniless and rejected by his wife. So he worked every day but Christmas, often past midnight, and with such abandon that he looked a wreck: his hands were always covered with ink, his vest was never buttoned right, and he tended to neglect his fly. In elevators, he stood just inside the doors so he could be the first one out when they opened. Once, he was so eager to get to work that he hopped in a cab and barked, "Fifteenth floor!"

In the company's first year, it billed just under $1 million. By 1940, when the economy was a little better, it had a few more clients and was billing $3 million a year. It picked up some big accounts after the war, and in the 1950s it grew explosively, both because the economy was soaring and because Leo and his staff thought up a lot of successful campaigns. They tended to orient their ads around a fictional character, or "critter": two of their biggest blockbusters were Tony the Tiger, for Kellogg, and the Marlboro Man, for Philip Morris. By 1960, the Leo Burnett Company had nine hundred employees and was billing more than $100 million annually, which made it the sixth biggest ad agency in the country. Its symbol was still a hand reaching for some stars, and it still gave apples to anyone who came by.

Leo, age sixty-nine, was still CEO, chairman of the board of directors, and chairman of the Creative Review Committee, which gave final approval to all ads. The *New York Times* described him as a "sparkplug with a feverish pace." *Time* put him on its cover and called him the "Midwestern Marvel."

He worked as hard throughout the 1950s as he had early on, and he was a gruff and exacting boss. When someone showed him a draft of an ad, his standard response was, "Not good enough." Or he'd say, "You don't really like that, do you?" Other times, he didn't have to say a thing. When he didn't like something, his lower lip would protrude. The more upset he was, the more his lip stuck out, and employees gauged his reactions according to—in their words—the Lip Protrusion Index.

But he could be ebullient. "Goddamn good!" he'd exclaim when he liked an ad. One of his clients observed, "When the pressure is hardest and things look blackest, Leo will leap up in the middle of a meeting, look around, grin, and comment, 'Isn't this fun?' " Once, for a speech at an advertisers' convention, he wrote a bubbly poem:

> When the day's last meeting is over,
> And the VPs have left for the train,
> When account men are at bars with the client,
> And the space men have switched off the brain,
> We shall work, and, by God we shall have to—
> Get out the pencils and pads,
> For finally, after the meetings—someone must get out the ads!

He once said, "I have always felt that advertising could be something to get excited about. To take pleasure in. To regard as worthwhile, meaningful, respectable. Something to do thoughtfully and well."

In the 1950s, as the company grew, Leo started sending around a lot of memos. Many of them gave instructions on how to make "Burnett-quality" ads. "Be thorough," he wrote, "even if you have to stay after hours to button up the job and do things that you might consider menial in relation to your title—down to licking the envelope and taking it to the post office if necessary." A bunch of memos warned against greed. "If you ever find yourself putting major emphasis on counting the money, pretty soon there won't be much money to count."

He set an example by keeping his salary modest, giving away stock to the executives who sat on the board with him, and setting up a profit-sharing program that benefited lower-paid workers. Meanwhile, the company kept growing. In the early and middle 1960s, Leo and his staff thought up the Pillsbury Doughboy, the Man from Glad, the Maytag Repairman, and the "Friendly Skies" of United. Between 1960 and 1965, billings rose from $100 million to $200 million per year, and the number of employees rose from nine hundred to twelve hundred.

By this time, Leo was seventy-four, and the younger men on the board were restless. They wanted more say over ads; they wanted to open offices overseas; and they wanted to change the profit-sharing system, which still benefited lower-paid workers. Some of them thought the company should go public, which would enable them to sell their shares and get rich. Leo, on the other hand, liked things the way they were. He particularly opposed the idea of taking the company public, which, he thought, would dilute its standards.

A power struggle between Leo and the rest of the board ensued, which Leo eventually lost, largely because he'd given away so much of his stock. The official line is that he chose to resign the CEO post, which may or may not be true. As of June 23, 1967, his new title was "founding chairman," and he still had seats on the board and the Creative Review Committee. Later that summer, however, the new CEO and some of the other top executives asked him to stop attending Creative Review Committee meetings, claiming that he was still dominating them. According to the new CEO, this was a "terrible moment" for Leo, but he didn't put up a fight.

At Christmastime, Leo made one final power play, in the form of a major speech at the annual company breakfast. He wasn't trying to regain control, but to make a case for his old-fashioned values. "This agency means everything in the world to me, especially its philosophy and its character, and so does its future," he began. "Not just next year, and the year after that, but ten, twenty, even fifty years from now, especially if my name is still connected with it." In a tone at once wry and grave, he warned that if the company changed too much, he might demand that his name be taken off the door. "That will be the day when you spend more time trying to make money and less time making advertising—our kind of advertising . . . When you lose that restless feeling that nothing you do is ever quite good enough . . . When you begin to compromise your integrity—which has always been the heart's blood, the very guts of this agency . . . When you lose your humility and become big-shot weisenheimers."

He most feared the day "when you lose your respect for the lonely man—the man at his typewriter or his drawing board or behind his camera or just scribbling notes . . . When you forget that the lonely man—and thank God for him—has made the agency we now have possible." In that case, he said, "I shall *insist* that you take my name off the door . . . Even if I have to materialize long enough some night to rub it out myself, on every one of your floors. And before I de-materialize again, I will paint out that star-reaching symbol, too. And burn all the stationery. Perhaps tear up a few ads in passing. And throw every goddamned apple down the elevator shafts."

In the video of this speech, the audience roars with laughter at the end. Leo looks out at them, triumphant. "Keep right on with what you're doing," he says earnestly, "but more of it. More of it."

Phoebe's mother, Naomi Geddes, was born in Mansfield, Ohio, not far from Cleveland. Naomi's mother, Anna, was an immigrant from Alsace-Lorraine; her father, George, was the son of a congressman who represented northern Ohio. George's parents didn't approve of his marriage to Anna, probably because she came from a poor, undistinguished family. George worked for a newspaper and as a real estate salesman but never made a good living. In 1901, when he was forty-two, he died suddenly. Anna was left to raise and support Naomi, who was eight, and her younger sister. They moved to Detroit, where Anna opened a diner.

Naomi liked books and wanted to be a librarian. After finishing high school, she studied library science at the Detroit Public Library and worked as a cashier in her mother's diner. In 1917, when she was twenty-four, she was reading a book at the register when a customer introduced himself and asked her how she was liking the book. His name was Leo, and he wrote ads for Cadillac. "He wasn't tall, handsome, or that type . . . but there was something about his personality and bearing that intrigued me," Naomi said years later, in a biography that the Leo Burnett Company wrote after his death. "He was a charmer. The *darlingest* sense of humor." Over the next few months, Leo courted Naomi, often by bringing her books. They got married in 1918, when he was twenty-six and she was twenty-five.

Peter was born two years later, in 1920, by which time they were living in Indianapolis and Leo was working for LaFayette Motors. Joe was born in 1923. Phoebe was born more than seven years later, on June 9, 1931. (When they named her, they weren't thinking of the little gray birds called phoebes. They just thought Phoebe was a pretty name.) Around this time, Leo began running the Chicago office of Erwin Wasey, and the family moved to Glencoe, Illinois, a fancy suburb on the North Shore of Lake Michigan. Most of the men were executives in Chicago; there were country clubs and debutante teas and fashion shows.

Leo was almost always at work, especially after he started his company, and Naomi pretty much raised the kids by herself. The second verse of the poem Leo wrote about hardworking ad men goes like this:

There are those who romp with the children,
Or spend some time with the wife,
There are those who catch trains right on schedule,
And lead the suburban life,
There are admen who live just like people,
And are known to their daughters and lads,
Though we envy the life they are leading,
Still—someone must get out the ads.

During the Depression, Naomi was grateful to Leo for being such a good provider. "My God!" she told his biographer. "Everyone we knew had suffered financially and many men had no jobs at all. I thought he was a miracle worker." Later, however, she often got frustrated and angry with him. "Leo was always so busy we hardly had time to discuss family matters." Instead, she wrote him notes and left them, along with bills and various reminders, on his desk at home. "One day, I was fed up with this arrangement—of him just reading my notes instead of talking with me. I went to pieces. 'This isn't a life, it's a business. This isn't a home, it's an office.' By this time, I was hysterical and screamed, 'I'm not a wife, I'm a secretary.' Leo never looked up during this dramatic scene but kept reading my notes and said, 'And a damned good one, too.'"

While the Leo Burnett Company had many women employees, most of them were secretaries, not copywriters, and Naomi often helped Leo when he was working on ads aimed at housewives. Once, she wrote him a memo on "Why I haven't an automatic washer" and what it would take to sell her one. "[Y]ou would have to guarantee that the machine wouldn't need servicing for at least two or three years and not just one year. You would have to convince me that my present hot water heater could supply enough hot water for 5 consecutive loads." In a speech to the company, Leo once said that Naomi had "contributed so much more to this business than meets the eye . . . I am sure you know that many of the ideas I take credit for are actually hers."

Phoebe's brothers, Peter and Joe, remember some fights between their parents, but they think of them as having been very close. They also say that for the most part, no one in the house talked about or showed their feelings for one another. "We weren't demonstrative," Joe says. "We're Scotch."

The three Burnett children liked their father, but they didn't see him much, and when he did something with them, it was usually at their mother's suggestion. Leo was often involved in the production of radio shows, and he sometimes took the kids to the studio for broadcasts. Though the kids got to meet some famous people this way, such as the popular radio hosts Art Linkletter and Arthur Godfrey, the outings didn't bring them much closer to their father.

Naomi had a thoughtful, progressive approach to parenting. In Indianapolis, she sent Peter and Joe to a private school where children were encouraged to figure out what interested them, think creatively, and play outside. When Peter developed a stuttering problem, she took him to a clinic at Vassar College in New York, and it cured him. She abhorred the practice of corporal punishment. Once, when she found out that Joe had been spanked by the father of one of his friends, she confronted the man and told him to pick on someone his own size.

She was attentive, sometimes greeting the kids after school with fresh-baked cookies, but she gave them an unusual amount of freedom. "There was always something crazy going on in the house," says Phoebe's best friend from grade school in Glencoe, Peggy

Beman. At one point after they'd moved to Illinois, Joe persuaded his parents to let him order a monkey from a company that sold animals to zoos. He kept "George" in the house, in a cage made of chicken wire. But the monkey sometimes got out, ran around the neighborhood, and stole people's mail. When it got nervous, it would scream. Naomi eventually made Joe donate his pet to a zoo.

As soon as she could walk, Phoebe followed Joe around; she had the sense, early on, "that boys did more interesting and enjoyable things than girls," she later wrote in her memoir. In Glencoe, they lived near some lagoons that were good for collecting clay, which they'd bring home to shape into works of art. They also collected frogs, snakes, and turtles to keep as pets. They took apart motors. They threw water balloons at each other and had rambunctious fights with the garden hose. They listened to Chicago Cubs games on the radio and memorized the team's statistics religiously. When she was about ten, Phoebe wrote to the *Chicago Daily Tribune* to correct a mistake in an article about infielder Stan Hack, and her letter ran on the editorial page.

She wasn't interested in girly things. Peggy, whose family lived on the same block as the Burnetts, remembers that Leo once gave Phoebe a dollhouse that had been custom-made by one of his clients: it sat on a big platform and had electric lights and ornate furniture. Peggy thought it was amazing, but Phoebe was unimpressed. Sometimes, Peggy says, she would play with the dollhouse while Phoebe listened to a Cubs game on the radio.

Peggy didn't know any other families in Glencoe like the Burnetts, and she felt privileged to be in their lives. There were a lot of successful businessmen in town, but Leo seemed more creative and interesting, and there weren't many mothers as laid back as Naomi. Of all the children in town, the Burnett kids always seemed to be having the most fun, in Peggy's view.

Phoebe didn't have many other friends at school; she was shy, and, besides, the kids at school probably seemed less interesting than Joe, whom she later described as "my idol and role model." When she wasn't playing with Joe or Peggy, Phoebe was often reading. "She was kind of an introvert, a homebody," says Peter.

Her teachers noted her shyness, her smarts, and her determination. "Phoebe continues to go on her way quietly, yet observing everything which happens," her third-grade teacher wrote in a report card. Her academic skills were "outstanding," and she set high goals for herself and met them. "No task seems too big for her. Sometimes I am quite appalled by the enormity of a certain plan she has laid out for herself. But she always comes out all right. For such a tiny child she has surprising energy and perseverance." According to the teacher, when Phoebe set out to accomplish something, such as learning to do a cartwheel, she proceeded in an "orderly way" until she was successful. "She may take a few knocks on the way but she 'grits her teeth' and begins again."

In pictures from this era, Phoebe looks like a happy kid. In one that was taken when she was about five, she's standing in the yard with a watering pail, smiling. She's got a lot of brown, curly hair that could use a brushing. She's wearing overalls, and one of the straps is falling off of her shoulder. It looks like she wants to get back to playing. In a picture taken when she was about seven, she looks just as happy, but this time she's lying on her stomach reading a book. Someone has tied her hair back on one side with a big white ribbon. She's got one hand on the book, and she's using the other to prop up her chin. She's engrossed.

Though Naomi and Leo were wealthy enough to fit in on the North Shore, they didn't take to its stodginess, and in 1942, when Phoebe was eleven, the family moved from Glencoe to Lake Zurich, a farming town farther from the city. By this time, Peter was twenty-two and was studying engineering at the Colorado School of Mines; Joe had just finished high school and was about to join him there. The next year, they both went off to war.

In the early 1940s, most people in Lake Zurich still lived and worked on farms, and a whistle sounded at noon to tell them to go in for lunch. There were still blacksmiths and creameries and other businesses that catered to farmers. The whole town got together for a picnic every September and for boys' basketball games on Saturday nights. On Lake Zurich itself, there were summer resorts that attracted people from the city, which was about an hour away by train.

The Burnetts bought a farm with a white clapboard house, some barns and silos, and seventy acres of land that Leo saw as a massive blank canvas. He hired a farmer to plant thousands of trees and wildflowers and admonished him to get rid of every last weed. Sometimes, on the weekends, Leo would strap a tank of herbicide to his back and go at the weeds himself. Naomi, more practically, grew roses and vegetables and raised chickens. She joined the Lake Zurich Women's Club, which ran the town library, met for book discussions, and held blood drives. She had a housekeeper but did a lot of housework herself. Some weekends, Leo and his staff had meetings at the farm, and Naomi served them sandwiches and tea.

Phoebe later said that country life "very much suited me." At first, she went to a one-room schoolhouse where she had only three classmates, but she didn't mind, since she'd "never been a particularly social creature." She got all A's, without much effort. In the afternoons, while her schoolmates were milking their families' cows, she took walks and rode an old workhorse around the farm. She had a pet goose, some cats, and a beagle. She also read a lot, as she always had. Joe remembers Naomi being worried that Phoebe spent too much time alone in her room, reading or doing her homework.

She met more kids once she was at the town's high school, where there were about thirty-five students in her class. She worked on the yearbook and the newspaper and joined the drama club. She also joined the 4-H club, in which she learned some farming skills and raised ducks. The club was run by two local farmers, Clarence and Helen Snetsinger, and their sons, one of whom, Dave, was a year ahead of Phoebe in school. For a while, Dave was president of the 4-H club and Phoebe was secretary; later, he was the editor of the high school yearbook and she was the assistant editor. Once, he invited her to a school dance, but only because his first choice had rejected him. Otherwise, Phoebe didn't go on many dates.

In her high school compositions, she was often nostalgic for her adventures with Joe. One essay began, "This may sound rather fantastic, but we actually did have a monkey." She also wrote that Joe had once talked her into giving him some of her savings so he could send away for French-language records, which he ended up playing endlessly. "I have heard that French is a beautiful language, but it was certainly pitiful to hear my brother try to pronounce it, especially since he thought he was doing remarkably well."

She wrote about her parents, too, and, it seems, she got a kick out of them. She made fun of her mother for keeping her up until midnight to rearrange the furniture in the living room and for taking her to donate blood but refusing to give her own. She made fun of her father for trying to fix a broken furnace by kicking it and for attempting, one weekend, to learn to play the mandolin. In one essay, "Father's Lake?," she explained with both amusement and distress that her father was constructing a lake on their farm. "The creation of such natural wonders as forests, mountains, lakes, and the like, it seems to be generally conceded, can be left only to the loving care of God and time. Far be it from my father, however, to yield to such an orthodox conception." She thought the lake was a "disgustingly obvious" display of wealth, and she could tell that the neighbors thought so too.

As an adult, Phoebe would talk about her mother with fondness but would say that she resented how little time her father had spent at home, and that his company had always come first.

A lot had changed for women in a short time. In the early 1900s, women fought for the vote, and they got it in 1919, the year after Phoebe's parents married. When the Depression started, women went to work in record numbers to help support their families, though usually in menial, low-paid jobs. During World War II, however, when many men were away, women got good jobs in the factories that were making weapons and office jobs that they wouldn't normally have been considered for; they were also admitted to law, medical, and graduate schools in higher numbers than ever before. The government set up child-care centers to help working women, and Norman Rockwell celebrated them in his *Saturday Evening Post* cover "Rosie the Riveter."

Later, Phoebe said that when she was young, she never gave much thought to marriage and children; instead, she dreamed of her career. In 1946, when she was fifteen and in tenth grade, she wrote a composition called "Psychology—My Vocational Choice." "Being still in high school, I am as yet undecided as to my career, but psychology interests me immensely, and I believe my future lies in that field." She liked the idea of studying the mind and helping people. "[A] specialist in this branch of science is as necessary and important in the treatment and study of the human mind, as the family doctor is when it comes to a case of scarlet fever." To prepare for her career, she intended to go to a college with a good science program, such as Northwestern, the University of Wisconsin, the University of Illinois, or the University of Michigan. After that, she would go to graduate school.

By this time, Joe was a graduate student in architecture at the Illinois Institute of Technology in Chicago, and he spent a lot of time at home in Lake Zurich. At one point, he ordered a make-your-own sailboat kit, and Phoebe helped him put the boat together. They tried to learn to sail it but didn't get far, according to one of Phoebe's compositions, "I Never Did Like Boats." Through his girlfriend, who was from Lake Zurich and went to Bryn Mawr, the women's college in Pennsylvania, Joe learned about Swarthmore and suggested to Phoebe that she apply. It was co-ed (she didn't want to go to an all-girls school); its campus was a lot like the Burnett farm, with lots of trees and flowers; and there was an honors program that fed into the top graduate schools.

During her senior year of high school, Phoebe was class secretary and editor of the yearbook. In the spring, she was honored for her "good citizenship" by the Daughters of the American Revolution of Illinois. She graduated from high school as valedictorian in June. In the fall of 1949, she began at Swarthmore.

In the late 1940s and early 1950s, when Phoebe was in college, the gains women had made during the war years were lost, and then some. Women were fired from their wartime jobs to make way for the returning men. The day care centers closed. The Servicemen's Readjustment Act of 1944, or GI Bill, paid men who'd been in the military to go to college and graduate school and gave them loans to buy houses and start businesses. A young woman's best bet was to find a good man—and to make him happy by attending to their home. "He's head man again," the women's magazine *House Beautiful* told its readers when the war ended. "Your part . . . is to fit his home for him, understanding why he wants it this way, forgetting your own preferences."

It was fine for a woman to work right after she was married, especially to put her husband through college or graduate school. If she and her husband could get by without her paycheck, however, she was supposed to quit working once they started having kids.

Otherwise, she was "rejecting" her role as wife and mother, as one *Life* article asserted. "She may find many satisfactions in her job, but the chances are that she, her husband and her children will suffer psychological damage, and that she will be basically an unhappy woman." In *The Common Sense Book of Baby and Child Care*, which was published just after the war and was a bestseller for years, Dr. Benjamin Spock declared that working mothers risked raising "maladjusted" kids. Knowing this, he said, "may make it easier for her to decide that the extra money she might earn, or the satisfaction she might receive from an outside job, is not so important after all." Besides, a woman who stayed home with her kids was serving her country—and, Spock implied, helping to fight communism. "You can think of it this way: useful, well-adjusted citizens are the most valuable possessions a country has, and good mother care during early childhood is the surest way to produce them."

Women were told to think of homemaking as a career. A housewife is a cook, nurse, dressmaker, decorator, teacher, and business manager, an article in *Ladies' Home Journal* said. By raising her children well, she's doing her part to preserve "culture, civilization, and virtue." So, when the census-taker asks, "let her write her occupation proudly: 'housewife.'" Though magazines sometimes ran articles about female writers and actors, these women were portrayed as housewives first and foremost. A piece in *Ladies' Home Journal* about the homemaking skills of the poet Edna St. Vincent Millay concluded, "Now I expect to hear no more about housework's being beneath anyone, for if one of the greatest poets of our day, and any day, can find beauty in simple household tasks, this is the end of the old controversy."

In the early 1950s, television took off and spread the idea that women should stay home. The housewives on *Father Knows Best* and *The Adventures of Ozzie and Harriet* are beautiful and glowing. Lucy of *I Love Lucy* wants to be a singer like her husband, but she has no talent and is portrayed as a fool. During all these shows, there were commercials that showed happy housewives made even happier by floor wax and flour. (A lot of them were produced by Phoebe's father and his staff. Leo didn't necessarily think women should be housewives; he was just doing his best to make the products look good.)

The average age of a bride soon dropped to twenty, younger than it had been since the 1800s. The younger the woman, the more marriageable she was thought to be: "A girl who hasn't a man in sight by the time she is 20 is not altogether wrong in fearing that she may never get married," a psychiatrist wrote, with some hyperbole, in 1953. Most women were having kids by their mid-twenties. The average size of a family went up from two children to three and a half, and many women had had four kids by their early thirties.

On college campuses, women got mixed messages. On the one hand, they could study to be scientists and professors. On the other hand, they were told that they'd end up housewives no matter what. In 1955, Adlai Stevenson, the Democratic politician, told the all-female graduating class at Smith that there was a lot they could do to fight communism "in the humble role of housewife—which, statistically, is what most of you are going to be whether you like the idea or not just now—and you'll like it!" According to Stevenson, the "typical Western man" did such specialized work that he risked losing his "wholeness of mind." "You may be hitched to one of these creatures we call 'Western man,' and I think part of your job is to keep him Western, to keep him truly purposeful, to keep him whole."

College deans—most of them men—thought women should get training to be wives. "The considerable, and apparently increasing, majority of college women will, and should, devote the first two or three decades after graduation to building and maintaining homes and families," wrote Lynn White, the president of Mills College, a women's school in California, in 1950. So, White said, "Why not study the theory and preparation of Basque paella, of a well-marinated shish kebab, lamb kidneys sautéed in sherry, and authoritative curry . . . A girl majoring in history or chemistry could well find time for one such course which, we may be sure, would do much to enliven her own life and that of her family and friends in later years. It is rumored that the divorce rate of home economics majors is greatly below that of college women as a whole." Mills College and many other schools started offering "feminine" courses, including some on how to have a good marriage.

Women students took the hint. Only about one in three women who went to college in the 1950s ended up graduating; many of the rest dropped out to get married. A lot of the women who stayed in school didn't study much. One woman at Smith told a writer that "a girl who got serious about anything she studied—like wanting to go on and do research—would be peculiar, unfeminine. I guess everybody wants to graduate with a diamond ring on her finger. That's the important thing." Many women got engaged in their senior year and were married the week after graduation.

A few women put off marriage and kids to try to have careers, but, for the most part, they didn't succeed. One survey taken in the early 1950s found that more than half of women who graduated from college and tried to enter male-dominated fields either didn't get jobs or ended up as secretaries. Many graduate schools took a few women, but it was hard for them to get jobs when they were finished. In a memoir about her years as a graduate student at Harvard in the early 1960s, Jill Ker Conway, a historian, said that as soon as she and her friends had defended their dissertations, the men were hired as Harvard professors and the women—no matter how well they'd done—were sent on their way. "[T]he intellectual world that gave us such joy," she wrote, "was not open to women in any but the most fleeting sense."

At Swarthmore, which was known for its intellectual rigor, you couldn't take a course on making paella, but, beginning around the time Phoebe got there, you could attend lectures at night on "Premarital Relations," "Postmarital Adjustment," and "Responsibilities in Marriage." Many women took their classes seriously, but they were criticized for it. "I grant that intelligence is the Swarthmore woman's crowning virtue, but intelligence without social grace is nothing," a male student wrote in the *Swarthmore Phoenix* while Phoebe was there. "I believe that most of the girls here realize that it is a pretty girl's world . . . and realizing this, they try to combat it by going to the other extreme and showing how really smart they are instead of striking a happy medium by attempting to cultivate their femininity along with their intelligence."

Another man published a piece that same day that was supposedly a defense of Swarthmore women; he praised their "character, personality, and intelligence" and said these were traits that most Swarthmore men valued. He still thought the women at the school should take more care with their looks, however. "While the Swarthmore man may not base his opinion of a woman on whether or not she is a glamour girl, nevertheless this does not preclude the possibility that he might desire that she would keep her personal appearance in an attractive enough state so that she wouldn't be mistaken for an Italian woman waiting in line to be de-loused after the Allied victory."

When she first got to college, Phoebe thought she wanted to be a chemist; she pictured a career in which she was always studying and growing, she later said. During her freshman year, she took two semesters of chemistry and two semesters of math. She also took German, which was recommended for chemistry majors, and introductory classes in philosophy, government, and psychology. By the end of her second semester, she'd taken ten courses and gotten ten A's. In her dorm, she became good friends with another ambitious freshman, Peggy Ann Woford, who had been the valedictorian of her high school in Kentucky and wanted to be a doctor. Peggy was on the field hockey, basketball, and tennis teams and had a boyfriend, Bob Groves, whom she'd been dating since high school and who was a sophomore at Lafayette College, a short drive from Swarthmore.

During her sophomore year, Phoebe took twelve classes, two more than most other students. She took more chemistry and more math, a class on the philosophy of science, and introductions to physics and astronomy. The astronomy class was taught by Peter van de Kamp, who was known around the world for his research on the positions and movements of stars. As part of the class, Phoebe studied stars through the telescope at the campus observatory. "Excellent student in my astronomy course," van de Kamp wrote in a note for her file with the registrar. "Did superior work on practical assignment, which I am now using in an article to be published in an astronomical magazine." She also spent a lot of time in chemistry and physics labs that year. She got mostly A's. She was roommates with Peggy, who was still with Bob. She didn't go on many dates herself.

At the end of her sophomore year, in the spring of 1951, Phoebe applied for and was accepted into the honors program in chemistry, which put her on track to attend a top graduate program and become a professor or research scientist. As an honors student, she'd take mostly seminars with only a few other students and do a lot of lab research and other independent work. Instead of getting grades as she went along, she'd take a series of oral and written exams during her senior year that would be administered by professors from other schools. Though a fair number of women in Phoebe's class chose the honors programs in English and government, she was one of the only women who decided to try for honors in science. Her professors would all be men, too.

She spent the summer at home in Lake Zurich. She had two summer jobs while she was in college, according to her file at Swarthmore, one in advertising research (presumably at the Leo Burnett Company) and one as a part-time secretary at the town high school; she probably held one or both of these jobs in the summer of 1951. While she was home that summer, she was also asked out by her old friend Dave Snetsinger.

No one had a better reputation in Lake Zurich than the Snetsingers. Dave's father, Clarence, was on the school board, the village board, and the county farm bureau. His mother, Helen, was on the Parent-Teacher Association and taught Sunday school. They made a good living on their farm, which had been in Clarence's family since the late 1800s and had dairy cows, chickens, and pigs. When they had first gotten married, Helen had assumed she'd stick around the house, but she found that lonely and decided to work with her husband in the barns and fields. In the summer, the whole family sold picnic food and gave pony rides to visitors from the city who'd come to enjoy the lake.

As the leaders of the 4-H club, Clarence and Helen taught children to raise animals and grow vegetables and took the kids to fairs to show off what they'd done. In 1946, when Dave was in high school, the National 4-H Council invited club leaders from around the country to write an essay that could be the basis of a short movie about American farming. Clarence and Helen wrote about how their eldest son Bob once raised a calf that got sick and died, whereupon he sold the carcass and spent the proceeds to start a strawberry garden. Of the eight hundred essays that were submitted, the Snetsingers' was judged to be the best, which is particularly impressive considering that neither of them had finished high school.

"Farmer Writes Son's Life, Wins 4-H Club Prize," the *Tribune* reported. The Snetsingers weren't actually in the movie—it was shot with actors in Indiana—but they got all dressed up to see the premiere in Chicago and won a twenty-foot-long freezer from Sears.

Dave is an Abe Lincoln type: tall and lanky, with a quiet and self-possessed but somewhat stiff way about him. Like the Burnetts, the Snetsingers kept their emotions to themselves, but unlike the Burnetts, they all spent a lot of time together. Dave worked hard on his parents' farm, helped them run the 4-H club, and helped with the picnic stand on the lake. He worked hard at school, too, and in high school he was second in his class. In addition to editing the yearbook, he was captain of the basketball team, which made him something of a town celebrity. According to his class's senior poem, he was "friendly to all."

In 1948, he graduated from high school and went to the University of Illinois, in Urbana, on a Reserve Officers' Training Corps scholarship. He studied agriculture, a new academic field then, and got mostly B's. He dated a woman from Lake Zurich, and their relationship grew serious enough that she transferred from another school to be with him.

They'd broken up by the summer of 1951, when he and Phoebe went on their first dates. He doesn't remember much about their early relationship, he says, but it seems to have been more friendly than ardent. (If he did remember their early dates, I'm not sure he'd tell me about them. Each time I met with him, he was polite but guarded, particularly about his marriage.) They talked to each other easily, he says. Since they were two of the only kids from their school who'd gone to college, it must have appeared that they had a lot in common, though Dave says he was intimidated by Leo and Naomi. Phoebe surely admired Dave's status in town and liked how family-oriented and approachable he was compared to her father, whom she'd never really gotten to know.

When they were back at college in the fall, they exchanged some shy letters. Dave says that at first, he was afraid to sign his letters "Love, Dave" and wrote it backwards—"Evol, Evad"—instead until Phoebe finally signed one of hers "Love, Phoebe."

Meanwhile, Phoebe had a full schedule of honors classes. In the middle of the semester, however, in a decision that shaped the entire arc of her life, she dropped out of the honors program, saying she didn't want to be a chemist after all. She figured out that since she'd already taken some German classes, she could switch her major to German and still graduate on time. She enrolled, late, in a German class and three other humanities classes. She ended up getting mostly B's in them.

She told Dave she was sick of labs and wanted to take classes outside the sciences; she said something similar to one of her cousins many years later. That can't be the whole story, though. She was twenty, she was starting to focus on men, and, in all likelihood, she was scared. Maybe she was worried that her lab work made her seem "peculiar" and "unfeminine," to Dave or to men in general. Maybe she got the sense that because she was a woman, she wouldn't make it as a scientist anyway. At some point along the way, Peggy Woford decided not to be a doctor, either.

Phoebe might also have been influenced by her brothers and the women in their lives. Peter had gotten married six years earlier, when he was twenty-five and his wife, Georgia, was nineteen. He was working as an engineer for oil companies, figuring out how to store petroleum in natural cavities deep beneath the ground; Georgia was staying home with their four-year-old daughter and was about to have another baby. Joe was twenty-eight, working as an architect, and getting ready to marry his fiancée of many years from Lake Zurich, Diane, who had graduated from Bryn Mawr but intended to be a housewife.

Over Christmas vacation, Phoebe saw Dave in Lake Zurich,

and they wrote to each other some more in the spring of 1952. Phoebe took more German literature and a class on Shakespeare that semester and went back to getting A's. At the end of the school year, she went to Dave's graduation, and they dated over the summer, in Lake Zurich. In the fall, Dave reported to Fort Eustis, in Virginia, to begin fulfilling his commitment to the Army. He was assigned to the Transportation Corps, which meant that he'd be learning to direct the transportation of soldiers and supplies in a war zone. It looked like he'd soon be sent to Korea.

Phoebe returned to Swarthmore for her senior year. By this time, she'd impressed the professors in her new department, most of whom were women. "She is an outstanding student," one professor wrote in a note for her file, "a person of unusually attractive qualities of mind and character, and has a quiet but strong personality. My opinion of her academic work is recorded in the grade of A . . . but my respect for her goes far beyond the academic level." Another professor wrote, "Miss Burnett is one of the finest and most reliable girls whom I have come to know within the last fifteen years . . . Her industry and perseverance are remarkable, her gift for learning a foreign language quite impressive, her manners and character a pure joy. She is not a ball of fire in conversation but she never talks any nonsense, and she is less shy now than she used to be." Though her thinking wasn't "highly original," it was "broad and solid and open to suggestions."

Peggy Woford and Bob Groves were engaged by the time Peggy and Phoebe started their senior year, at which point Bob was entering medical school at Yale. They'd get married as soon as Peggy graduated, and she'd work in Connecticut for a few years to help put him through school. Peggy had become a star at Swarthmore: she was the number one player on the women's tennis team and had been chosen for Mortar Board, a women's social club. Later in the year, she won a campus-wide poetry contest. She was described in the yearbook for 1952–53 as "[f]riendliness personified" with a "warm smile for everyone." She was "brilliant but won't admit it" and could do "a semester's work in one night when pressed." She was also "modest, sincere, and easy-going."

By contrast, there's a catty edge to the description that was written of Phoebe. She was described as having "curly hair and curly eyebrows" (her eyebrows were full, not curly) and it was noted that she had a "healthy appetite" (in some pictures from this era, she looks a little plump). It was also said that she "steps on children" (I don't know what that was a reference to) and "studies at night" (I guess that was uncool). On the other hand, she was described as being "unselfish as they come" and as having a "shy smile," a "warm friendliness," and a "keen scientific mind."

Phoebe and Dave were in close touch during the fall of Phoebe's senior year, and he drove up from Virginia a few times to visit her. They'd go to Philadelphia, take walks on campus, and watch lacrosse games. She had to be back in her dorm by eleven P.M., and he slept alone, in a hotel. On one of these visits, they decided to get engaged. They didn't discuss the matter at length, Dave says; by the standards of the day, "it was just time to get married." Back then, instead of fretting over the question of marriage, "you just went and did it." He couldn't make it home to Lake Zurich that Christmas, but he gave Phoebe a ring to show to their families.

When Phoebe told Naomi she was engaged, Naomi asked her if she was certain she was in love, as Joe recalls. "Mother," Phoebe said, "if I'm willing to change my name to Snetsinger, which I don't even know how to spell, of course I'm in love." Naomi sent a notice to the *Tribune*: "Mr. and Mrs. Leo Burnett, of Old McHenry Road near Lake Zurich, announce the engagement of their daughter Phoebe to Lt. David C. Snetsinger, son of Mr. and Mrs. Clarence Snetsinger."

In the spring, Phoebe took more German literature classes, got more A's, and was one of twenty-eight students in her class of about two hundred to be chosen for the honor society Phi Beta Kappa. She graduated on June 8, 1953. (Naomi submitted another announcement to the *Tribune*: "Phoebe Burnett is Phi Beta Kappa Swarthmore Graduate.") The next day, Phoebe, Dave, Peggy, and Bob drove to Lake Zurich together for Phoebe and Dave's wedding.

It was held at the Burnett farm on June 13, four days after Phoebe's twenty-second birthday. Joe and Diane, who were newlyweds, were there, as were Peter and Georgia, their daughter, and their baby boy. Dave's family, the principal of Phoebe and Dave's high school, and some of Leo's colleagues came, too. The minister of a church in town performed the ceremony. Peggy Woford was the maid of honor; Dave's brother Bob was best man. "Phoebe Burnett Becomes Bride of Lt. Snetsinger," the *Tribune* reported the next day. The paper must have sent a reporter to the wedding, as there was a detailed account of it. "The setting for the ceremony was a semicircle of shrubbery with accents of white geraniums," according to the *Tribune*. "The bride wore a 3/4 length white pique dress, a short tulle veil, and aqua colored shoes. She carried a bouquet of white gladiolas and lilies of the valley."

In one picture, probably from just after the ceremony, Phoebe and Dave are standing on the lawn together. There are other people around them, but they're looking at each other and beaming. In a picture taken later, though, Phoebe's gotten sick of all the pomp. She and Dave have just cut the cake, and Dave is trying to feed her a bite of it on a fork. He's smiling and holding the fork near her mouth, but she's not opening wide enough, and her arms are crossed stubbornly.

Dave remembers that at the end of the night, Naomi looked at Phoebe and said wryly, "I hate to see that brain go down the kitchen sink."

One of the last pictures shows Phoebe and Dave walking out of the farmhouse, toward their car. Dave is still wearing his wedding suit; Phoebe has changed into a blouse and skirt. Naomi stands in the doorway behind them, her eyes bright. People have lined up on either side of the doorway to throw rice at the couple, who are smiling and ducking their heads. The next shot is of them in the car.

About six weeks after the wedding, in July 1953, an armistice was signed by Korea, China, and the United States, but Dave still had to go to Asia as part of the peacekeeping effort. He started out on a base in Japan, where he took a course on what to do in case of a gas or atomic attack. At the end of October, he was sent to South Korea to help coordinate transportation. He worked seven long days a week, slept in a tent that was usually freezing, and counted the days until he could go home.

Phoebe had it better. She'd gotten a job teaching science at a girls' school outside Philadelphia, Baldwin, whose stated purpose was to prepare girls for Bryn Mawr. At Baldwin, students were expected to study hard and to learn to do things that most girls didn't, like work with wood and play basketball. Later, Phoebe would say that she'd loved her time there and that it had made her consider a career as a teacher.

Meanwhile, Dave applied for an early release, which was granted in March 1954. In April, he finally got to move in with Phoebe, who had signed on for another year at Baldwin. During the summer, he worked as a camp counselor, and he got a job for the next academic year as a third-grade teacher at a boys' school not far from Baldwin. In the fall, both Dave and Phoebe applied to graduate school at the University of Illinois at Urbana—he to the Ph.D. program in agriculture, she to the master's program in German. Under the GI Bill, Dave would get a free ride and a living stipend to cover both of them. He was under the impression that Phoebe was just as excited about going back to school as he was, but she later said that she just "went along" with him.

She might have wanted to stay at Baldwin but didn't feel comfortable communicating that, or didn't feel entitled to. As Dave says, "It was assumed, then, that the husband's career would take priority."

Until Dave got back from Korea, his and Phoebe's relationship had almost always been long-distance. In Pennsylvania and when they were at the University of Illinois, they grew closer and had a lot of fun. She wasn't into cooking or housework, but he didn't expect her to be, and they each pitched in. At her suggestion, they got a puppy, which they named Sherry, after her favorite drink. She also decided that they should build a sailboat together, like the one she'd built with Joe as a teenager. Dave talked Phoebe into giving camping a try, though she was horrified when, on their first night in the woods, their tent filled with bloodthirsty mosquitoes. They started going camping and taking road trips with Peggy and Bob, who'd also gotten married; Peggy was working in a lab to support them while Bob finished medical school at Yale. By this time, Phoebe's father was rich and famous, but she and Dave lived simply, and mainly off their own income. Phoebe rarely told anyone that she was Leo Burnett's daughter.

Dave made a lot of home movies during this period, which he lovingly edited and titled; a road trip they took to Florida, for example, was "Christmas 1957: A Snetsinger Production." Most of the footage, of course, is of Phoebe, and as she plays in the waves or feeds the dog or runs through a field, she looks vigorous and happy, even radiant. According to Dave, the two of them didn't talk much about their feelings or what they wanted for the future, but they both assumed that they'd have kids, and that she would stay home to take care of them and keep house.

In graduate school, Phoebe took classes in German language, literature, and history and got all A's without much effort. She also taught German to undergraduates. She got her degree in August

1958, when she was twenty-seven. At that point, she was five months pregnant.

About a year earlier, the *Chicago Tribune* had taken a comprehensive survey of hundreds of young suburban housewives in Illinois. According to one article, only a third of the women said they were leading the lives they'd pictured as teenagers, and many were feeling cooped up and bored. "[W]hether she has the talent and training of an artist, a writer, or an anthropologist, she spends most of her time doing housework, which is rapidly undone by her children." One woman told the paper, "Education leads us one way, reality forces us to stay home."

Overall, though, the series was upbeat. The concluding article, "We Never Had It So Nice," reported that the average suburban housewife was "amazingly content with her lot." She liked watching her children grow, making her husband happy, and making their home "clean and pleasant." "Today's young suburban housewife is as blessed as she is busy—and she knows it . . . She wouldn't exchange the diapers, dishes, and dandelions for a career, a lost youth, or a castle in Spain."

By the time Phoebe got pregnant, Peggy Groves had quit her job to raise children, and Joe's wife was also at home with their kids. Phoebe probably didn't consider the possibility of working after she had her baby; even if Dave had supported such a plan, which he well might have, most people would have thought her irresponsible and weird. In any event, she was tired of teaching German, Dave says, and excited to be a mother instead.

Dave was still working on his dissertation, an analysis of which amino acids chicks needed to be fed to grow the fastest. When he was a kid, chicks had hatched in April and weren't big enough to be killed for meat until August, but research was showing that with the right diet the turnaround could be considerably faster. Graduate school was stressful for him, he says. He had to work hard to do well, he was unsure of himself, and he had to devote much of his time to teaching undergraduates.

Penny was born on December 18, 1958. Naomi sent her housekeeper to Urbana to help Phoebe and Dave out for a couple of weeks, and they got advice from *The Common Sense Book of Baby and Child Care* by Dr. Spock. Dave finished his dissertation around this time, went on the job market, and got hired as a professor at the University of Minnesota. At the end of the school year, the family moved to New Brighton. The following spring, Phoebe got pregnant with Tom, and a few months after he was born she got pregnant with Carol. Dave thought three kids were all they could handle, but Phoebe thought they should try for a fourth, maybe because she loved being a mother to infants, or maybe because raising kids had become a substitute for the career she'd given up. Sue was born in 1964, when Phoebe was thirty-two.

Each time a new baby was born, Naomi sent her housekeeper to help out for a while. Phoebe made it clear to Dave that she didn't want him to be the sort of father that Leo had been, and that wasn't what he wanted either: he helped a lot with the kids when he was home, even getting up in the night to give them bottles, and they all say that he was a great, engaged dad. But much of the time, of course, Phoebe was on her own with them. She spent most of each day changing their diapers, cooking for them, feeding them, putting them down for naps, and cleaning up after them. At one point, Tom, Carol, and Sue were all in diapers.

During these years, there were many more articles in newspapers and magazines about young, educated housewives, and a consensus began to form that a lot of them were unhappy. In 1960, the *New York Times* wrote that for women who'd been to college, "[t]he road from Freud to Frigidaire, from Sophocles to Spock, has turned out to be a bumpy one." According to the article, "Many young women—certainly not all—whose education plunged them into a world of ideas, feel stifled in their homes. They find their routine lives out of joint with their training. Like shut-ins, they feel left out." That same year, *Newsweek* reported that housewives were suffering from a "deep, pervasive" discontent; there was an NBC special on "The Trapped Housewife"; and *Redbook* ran a story called "Why Young Mothers Feel Trapped."

Women would feel a lot better, these pieces claimed, if they carved out an hour here and there for themselves. The *New York Times* article quoted one woman who forced her kids to take a nap after lunch so she could read; another woman said she hired a sitter once a week and sat in the lobby of the Waldorf-Astoria. "Next to renting another apartment, the Waldorf lobby was the only place I could think of where I could go and not talk," she told the *Times*. The *Redbook* article invited women to write in with their own ideas for feeling less trapped, but the ones that were published, including "The Day We Threw the Blanket Out" and "I've Found a Schedule that Really Works," focused on how to be a better, happier housewife.

A mother and writer from the suburbs of New York, Betty Friedan, had a different idea, and it resonated with women around the country. In 1963, when Phoebe was pregnant with Sue, Friedan published *The Feminine Mystique*, which called on women to figure out what their interests were, find some child care, and begin careers. As long as women were housewives, they would be living through their husbands and their children, Friedan argued. "The only way for a woman, as for a man, to find herself, to know herself as a person, is by creative work of her own," she wrote. "If women do not put forth, finally, that effort to become all that they have it in them to become, they will forfeit their own humanity."

Friedan asked, "Who knows what women can be when they are finally free to become themselves?"

Chapter 3

IN 1970, AROUND the time Phoebe turned thirty-nine and a few months after she wrote, in her poetry, that she felt like she was inside a tomb, she and Dave took the kids on another camping trip out West. Like the last trip, this one was a couple of weeks long, but this time they only made two big stops, in Yellowstone and in the Grand Tetons. Penny, who was eleven, had come to dread spending time in the outdoors with her family; she'd decided that she liked cities, not wildernesses, and she would have preferred to stay at home, hanging out with her friends and making money baby-sitting. The other kids were all enthusiastic about the trip, though. Tom, who was nine, still liked birds, and Carol, who was eight, was developing such a passion for being in the mountains that her family and friends had started calling her Marmot, after the furry rodents that live at high altitudes. (A few years ago, Carol officially changed her first name to Marmot, and, at her request, that's what I'll be calling her for the rest of the book.)

This trip seems to have gone better for Phoebe than the first one did, perhaps because it was less harried. Though she didn't write a *Nature Notes* piece this time, she took some effusive field notes: she saw an elk with "gorgeous antlers," a "magnificent" bull moose, and a lot of "intensely red" wildflowers. She'd also figured out, by this point, that if she gave the kids a quarter for every life bird they found for her, they'd walk a little slower. Dave says he "tolerated" Phoebe's slow pace, but he wasn't thrilled about it.

At home, she was writing a lot more poetry. She was preoccupied, as she had been earlier in the year, with figuring out the direction of her life, though at this point she was more thoughtful than despairing. She wanted to sit in darkness and silence, ignoring all importunities, she wrote; only then could she figure out who she was and live fully. She thought she'd changed significantly since her school days, when she was involved in "the youthful game of dissecting the universe / to make ourselves believe we understand." Instead of analyzing things, she wanted to experience them. One day she wrote a note to herself rather than a poem: "When I was young I spent so much time looking for absolutes only to discover, half a lifetime later, that there aren't any. Ultimately everyone is left with himself as a reference point."

She wrote many poems about wanting to try harder to connect with people. She was awed by birds, stars, and flowers, she wrote, but they didn't care about her; her love only had an impact when she gave it to humans, which she very much wanted to do. "My living can become significant to some / And I can build eternity with love." In another poem, she declared, "I refuse to be consumed / Without a cry of pain, / I will not melt into the night / Embittered and alone." Rather, she would share her days and her feelings with others: "I wish to live, I've love to give, / And hope to pass along."

Though she wrote some poems that were harshly critical of Dave, she also wrote some about loving him and the family they'd made together. In one poem, "Thoughts on a Photograph of the Orion Nebula," she said that even though other worlds were possible, she wouldn't want to live in them because she wouldn't be with him and her other "earth-loves." In "Family," she imagined herself, Dave, and the kids as spiders in a web. She and Dave were at the center; the kids surrounded them, spinning their own designs and making their way toward the edge. Sometimes the kids tugged hard at the web, but it was strong, and would endure.

Later, she'd tell Dave that she resented him during this time: he was free to grow in his career, while her own growth was stunted because she had to take care of things at home. He did like his work at Purina, and he'd already gotten a couple of promotions, which meant he was spending less time doing research and more time supervising other scientists. But, he says, he didn't know then that Phoebe was jealous of his career or that she was doing a lot of painful soul-searching. "I didn't realize it was as bad as it was. I was doing my thing." When he asked to see the poems she was writing, she told him they were private and refused.

By 1970, millions of women had read *The Feminine Mystique*, and the modern feminist movement was taking off. Many women were starting careers, as Friedan had urged them to. Maybe if Phoebe hadn't been so passionate about birds or if her family had needed money, she would have gone back to teaching, but as it happened she started approaching birdwatching as a career. A lot of her friends in the Webster Groves Nature Study Society didn't take birding too seriously, and they noticed, beginning in the early 1970s, that she did. She went out by herself more than they did, took more notes in the field, and was more bent on seeing every possible bird. At home, she read *Birding* and studied her Peterson and other bird books. At the end of 1970, she made the 200 Club for the first time. In her notebook, she marked the bird that put her over the top with an exclamation point.

By this time, when she was after a bird, she lost track of all else, just as her father did when he was at work. One friend says Phoebe drove "like a trucker" when she was birding and took U-turns in the middle of the road. (This same friend says she was intimidated by Phoebe because she knew all about the stars and planets and could sing "Ode To Joy" in German.) Her friend Claudia Spener says she once got a call from the telephone tree when she was in the middle of entertaining a friend. When she and her friend got to the place where the rare bird had been seen, Phoebe was already there, and Claudia approached her to say hello and introduce her friend. But Phoebe was so absorbed with finding the bird that, to Claudia's surprise, she pretty much ignored them.

One March morning in the early 1970s, Kyrle Boldt, the retired insurance salesman, offered to drive Phoebe, Claudia, and their friend Marjorie Richardson to a swamp to see if any swallows had migrated north yet. As they turned off the highway onto the dirt path that led to the swamp, however, they saw that the path was covered with ice. Kyrle wanted to turn around: if it got any warmer, he said, the ice would melt, the road would turn to mud, and they'd get stuck. Claudia and Marjorie were fine with aborting the mission, they say, but Phoebe wasn't, and she teased Kyrle about being a wimp until he said he'd keep going. So they went to the swamp, and they saw some nice swallows. But when it was time to leave, the car was sitting in a pool of mud, as Kyrle had feared it would be. He started the car, but instead of moving forward, it began slipping backward, toward the water. By this time, it was covered with mud.

Someone ran a short distance to a pay phone to call a tow truck while the rest of the group vainly tried to push the car away from the water. The truck came quickly, but, to everyone's dismay, it, too, got stuck in the mud. Finally, a bigger tow truck came and pulled the car and the first truck out of the mud. Meanwhile, Kyrle drank from his Bloody Mary thermos anxiously. "Phoebe," he said at one point, "when we get out of here, I'm gonna make you clean my car with a toothbrush."

Phoebe also stood out in the nature society because she had a phenomenal memory. She seemed to store all the pictures and text from the Peterson guide in her head, which enabled her to identify species she'd never seen before whether or not one of the old-timers was around. She'd sometimes talk about how a certain bird was lighter or darker or bigger or smaller than another bird of the same species that she'd seen a couple of years earlier. It helped, too, that she had great eyesight—it was 20/13, so her distance vision was even stronger than what is generally called "perfect."

She was widely admired and beloved in the club, despite the single-mindedness that sometimes made her inconsiderate. "Everyone knew she was very bright, very observant . . . very scientifically minded," says Marjorie. At the same time, "She never bragged about anything. She quietly learned things." As she gained more expertise, she mentored other members of the club, just as she'd been mentored when she first joined. She usually carried a telescope in the field that she'd set up for everyone to look through, and when she saw something good in her yard or her neighborhood, she'd invite her friends over for a tour. People started calling her for help when they were stumped. "I'd ask Phoebe questions, and she'd invite me over, have books laid out, and explain it all," says her friend Ron Goetz, who was just a teenager in the early 1970s.

She was a good friend to her WGNSS pals when they weren't birding, too. When Claudia got divorced and moved to a new house, Phoebe showed up with a pan of brownies. When Ron was diagnosed with Hodgkin's disease, she drove to the hospital in Chicago where he was being treated to give him a card signed by all his birder friends. After Marjorie's husband suddenly died, Phoebe went over to her house again and again and made her get in the car and go birding. In her grief, Marjorie was comforted by being in nature, she says, and by Phoebe's warmth and friendship.

LIFE LIST

As Phoebe spent more and more time birding and with her
WGNSS friends, Dave took up a hobby, too. He'd always liked doing simple magic tricks for the kids, like pulling quarters out of
their ears, but he gradually started devoting more time to magic.
He joined a club for amateur and professional magicians, started
teaching himself to juggle, and learned ventriloquism on two dolls
he had made: a chicken, which he named Henrietta, and a pig,
which he called Chester White. He put on lively shows for his kids
and their friends and at the office. Performing seems to have freed
him from his shyness, just as birding freed Phoebe from hers.

He found community in the neighborhood. One summer night,
he rented a film projector and a popcorn machine and hosted a
neighborhood movie night on the lawn. At Christmastime, he took
the kids out caroling—Phoebe either stayed home or came along
reluctantly—and he helped run the annual block party each summer. While he was getting the grills going, setting up the games,
and putting up badminton nets to block off the street, Phoebe and
another misfit mother on the block would drive off together to a
diner, only to return when the festivities were over.

On June 7, 1971, Leo Burnett, who was still working full time at age
seventy-nine, told a friend at the office that he hadn't been feeling
well and thought he'd start coming in just three days a week. In the
afternoon, he bought some newspapers and a pack of Marlboros in
the lobby, was driven home by his chauffeur, and did some work in
his study. Naomi looked in on him at one point and asked what he
wanted for dinner. The next time she went to talk to him, he was
slumped over his desk, dead. He'd had a heart attack.

In the four years since Leo had left the CEO position, the company had opened offices overseas, but it hadn't gone public, as he'd
feared it would. When he died, the agency had two thousand employees in twenty-five countries and was billing almost $400 million

a year. "Leo Burnett, who built a Chicago advertising agency from a bowl of apples and three accounts to the fifth largest in the world in 35 years, is mourned by all who knew him," the *Chicago Tribune* editorialized. *Time* wrote, "He was a short, stout, balding, rumpled, plain-speaking man who viewed the world through black-rimmed bifocals and generally liked what he saw. He was, in brief, the antithesis of the popular conception of the sleek, cynical advertising man. Yet when Leo Burnett died at 79 after a heart attack last week, he was one of the ad world's giants."

Phoebe, Dave, and the children went to Chicago for the funeral, which was held the day before Phoebe turned forty. Afterward, she tried to process her dark feelings by writing a flurry of poems, as she had when she'd been gravely depressed the previous year. One poem mourned the disconnection between her and her father; others contemplated her own death. She wanted to fade away quietly and peacefully, like a glow in the night, she wrote one day. Her body would dissolve, but she'd continue to exist, as a river does when it meets the sea. Other days, however, she thought about death less serenely. At the end of June, she wrote that she hadn't had enough of spring, but it was already gone, and summer would soon be over too. She likened the seasons to the stages of life and said she hoped "to see full winter," by which point her memories would be piled up like heaps of snow. Dying then would be acceptable; what she feared was a premature end.

That same week, she compared herself to a mayfly, an insect that spends most of its short life as a larva, in a shell underwater. After about a year, the mayfly grows wings, sheds its shell, and swims to the surface. It flies about and mates for a day or two, then dies. Phoebe predicted, boldly:

> *Someday I'll have my mayfly day,*
> *when inner growth bursts out the cramping shell*

and I can cast the hollow hull away
that housed me once too well.
From this stodgy, graceless, larval time
will emerge the adult form I sense,
and I will have at length that day sublime—
one final flight as recompense.

About a month after Leo died, Phoebe, Dave, Joe, and his wife took a canoeing trip in Minnesota, on some lakes in the wilderness called the Boundary Waters. You can't drive up to most of these lakes; you have to carry a canoe through the woods to one of the less remote ones, paddle across it, carry your canoe to the next one, paddle across that, and so on. You share the water with moose and loons. When night falls, you set up camp on shore and look up at a dazzling sky. "We went . . . for the total wilderness experience, which is rendered so precious by the contrast with our daily civilized lives," Phoebe wrote in *Nature Notes*.

The trip, she wrote, was "glorious," giving them "a tantalizing taste of utter loneliness, the physical do-or-die challenge of paddling furiously into a strong headwind and finding more strength than we thought we had, and the enticement of the shimmer of blue through the birches and pines, indicating the end of a portage and another beautiful lake to explore." She was also enticed by the "fleeting glimpse into life stripped to its essentials—the food, clothing, and shelter that can be carried in two or three packs in a canoe." She went home, she wrote, "with considerable regret."

At home that fall and winter, Phoebe began to think that if she wanted to be happy, she'd need to reject society. She addressed a poem to a "comfortable pedestrian" who plodded through his or her days, "dulled with riches, food and sleep." The heart of this person beat, but only weakly. "From such a life I stand apart," she declared; "my youth must not be vainly spent." She didn't know how to live instead, however: out of fear, she'd always followed convention, as she wrote in another poem. She'd begun to feel, urgently, a need to chart her own course, and she was trying to figure out what it should be. "I only yearn to find / when faced with blackness closing in / more than just the road behind."

The next summer, on a family camping trip, Penny, age thirteen, noticed a big black mole on Phoebe's back while she was changing into her bathing suit. It was rough to the touch, like a cauliflower, and was bleeding a little from one edge. "I was a precocious child and when I saw the mole I said 'Gee, that's a warning sign for melanoma,'" Penny says. When they got home, Phoebe went to a dermatologist, who said he'd need to excise the mole and some surrounding tissue to perform a test for skin cancer.

During the operation, the doctor used only local anesthesia—a "huge mistake," Phoebe realized when she started to feel pain. When the lab report came back, she found out that she did, indeed, have melanoma, the worst kind of skin cancer: if you don't catch it before it spreads, it's often fatal. On the other hand, melanoma tends to be curable if you catch it before it metastasizes, and further tests indicated that Phoebe's hadn't. As a precaution, the doctor would examine her once a year for the next five years, but he told her he was confident that she'd be fine.

Throughout this ordeal, Phoebe tried to act like she wasn't concerned. When she found out she had cancer, she told the kids, but she also told them it was no big deal. Penny was confused when her best friend's mother expressed concern, and Tom, the second oldest, didn't even know his mother had had a tumor removed. Not even Dave realized that Phoebe might be in danger. "I didn't understand what melanoma meant. I didn't understand how serious it was." He thought that since the cancer was on her skin, it was superficial. She probably didn't actually tell him that;

more likely, he didn't ask what was the worst that could happen, and she didn't say. Maybe she was embarrassed. Back then, cancer was more feared and more stigmatized than it is today, and it was thought that some people had "cancer personalities" that brought the disease on.

At least once, though, Phoebe did her best to open up to Dave. When he was away on a business trip, Marmot saw her crying on the phone to him and telling him she was scared. She must not have made things fully clear, however, because he went on thinking that everything would be okay. So when Phoebe found out, finally, that there was no sign of metastasis, she was the only one who knew enough to be relieved.

According to her memoir, she hardly thought about the close call again.

When Leo died, Phoebe inherited a good deal of money, and Dave's income rose each year at Purina. In 1973, they were able to buy a farm about an hour and a half from Webster Groves, in the Ozark Mountains. The property had an old house, a barn, a lake, and some fields, and was right next to a river and some woods. On the weekends and during school vacations, the whole family spent time there, and everybody found something to do—except Penny, who was in high school, had a full social life, and still disliked the outdoors (and who, incidentally, had turned out to be a top student, like her mother). Phoebe took bird walks, which Tom sometimes accompanied her on, and she and Dave planted trees, flowers, and vegetables together, as they had a decade earlier in Minnesota. Dave also built fences, fixed up the buildings, kept the lawn mowed, and fished. Tom, Marmot, and Sue ran around in the woods and climbed rock faces. The family owned two canoes, and sometimes all six of them went paddling together.

Phoebe also spent a lot of time at the farm alone. On days

when she wasn't going out with WGNSS, she drove there after the kids went to school, spent the day birdwatching and planting, and returned in the late afternoon. By this time, each of the kids was making one dinner a week, which meant that she only had to make three. She kept a "Farm Journal," modeled on the journal Thoreau kept while living in the woods, with notes on the weather, how full the lake and the river were, what was in bloom, what she'd planted, and which birds and other animals she'd seen.

The farm, for a while, gave her the direction she'd been seeking. She treated the land as a canvas, just as her father had treated his land in Lake Zurich, and, like him, she thought big. "Started planting 2000 Shortleaf Pine in blizzard," she wrote in the Farm Journal toward the end of March 1974. The next day: "About 6 inches of snow on the ground and 0 degrees this morning. Heeled in 1800 trees." A week later, she wrote, "Started the garden—onions, peas, corn, carrots" and "Finished planting 2000 pines." She planted wildflowers all over the property that spring, and sunflowers and pansies near the house.

She watched birds differently at the farm from the way she watched them near home. When she was out with WGNSS, she zipped around from park to park, getting quick looks at as many birds as possible, whereas at the farm she got to know a few birds well. She could identify them without any trouble, so in the Farm Journal she focused on their behavior. "First Whippoorwills singing." "Barred Owl in river woods—flying & sitting in tree." "Woodcock doing sky dance on hill at dusk." (In the spring, to attract females, the male woodcock repeatedly flies high into the air, then circles back down like it's an out-of-control plane.) She also set up and monitored nesting houses for bluebirds. "Pair of Bluebirds in & out of house in yard," she wrote, with obvious excitement, in March 1975. Soon, the pair built a nest, and the female laid four eggs in it. In June, Phoebe wrote, "2–3 Bluebird eggs just hatched." Then: "3 baby bluebirds in box—beginning to feather out on wings." Finally, at the end of the month, "Baby bluebirds gone—flown?"

She tended to be in a good mood at the farm. The weather was "lovely"; the night sky was "beautiful"; there was "marvelous fall color everywhere." She liked seeing the kids enjoy themselves there, too. She made entries in the journal when Marmot and Sue decided to turn the old pigsty into their clubhouse (the two of them were "good little buddies," as Sue says), when Marmot caught a two-pound catfish, when Tom saw a Wild Turkey, and when Penny took a long canoe trip with her friends. One fall, the kids collected 650 pounds of walnuts, and Phoebe drove them into town to be sold.

She didn't write much poetry for the first couple of years they had the farm. She was busier and happier than she'd been in a while, and she might not have felt the need to reflect.

In 1967, Joel Abramson, the doctor who got to know the birds of Vietnam while he was fighting in the war there, left the Army, got married, and started practicing internal medicine in Miami. He wanted to see more of the birds of the world, but he thought the tours run by Audubon groups sounded too cushy. "I didn't want to make time for a comfortable breakfast," he says. "In the tropics, it's all over by nine A.M." He didn't want to travel on his own, either. There still weren't many bird-finding books or field guides, which meant that if you wanted to locate and learn the birds of a foreign country, you had to stay for weeks or months.

So, in 1971, Abramson started the first bird tour company, Bird Bonanzas. Every few months, he'd pick a place to go, hire someone who'd already birded there as a guide, and advertise the trip by word of mouth and in *Birding*, charging just enough so he could travel for free. In the meantime, he kept up his medical practice and had kids, whom his wife took care of while he was away. Most of his clients, too, were men with wives, kids, and jobs, though some were retired or independently wealthy, and he had a few women customers, including Phoebe's friend Bertha Massie. The guides he hired were younger men who hadn't settled down; some were getting Ph.D.'s in ornithology.

In the name of finding birds, the tours were strenuous. On a typical day, a Bird Bonanzas group would get up well before dawn; spend eight or ten hours walking in the woods, stopping whenever they saw or heard a bird and perhaps to eat a picnic lunch; return to whatever crummy hotel they were staying in; eat an unpalatable dinner; go over the list of birds they'd seen that day; and go back out to look for owls.

Abramson and his regular customers built up many of the biggest life lists of the day. In 1973, one client, Stuart Keith, was the first person to see 4,300 species—half the birds of the world, according to the taxonomy of the day. At the time, he was forty-one; he'd been birding since he was a teenager and had been one of the founders of the American Birding Association. He'd done some work in finance, but he had an inheritance and spent most of his time birdwatching, both in California, where he lived, and abroad. He was still single.

In an article in *Birding* that he called "Birding Planet Earth," Keith said—truthfully, but with a fair bit of machismo—that getting to "half" hadn't been easy. "How often have I turned to my companions after sloshing all day through some muddy Amazon forest, stepping over inch-long ants whose bite can send you to bed for two weeks, keeping a wary eye out for a Bushmaster . . . , being eaten alive by mosquitoes and ticks, and finally returning to some 'hotel' which should have been condemned years before, and said, 'What kind of maniacs are we to subject ourselves to this?'" Another problem, he explained, is that it's hard to see birds in the tropics. In the

rain forests of the lowlands, where most tropical birds live, the vegetation is thick, and the birds hide behind it. "Anyone can take a series of tropical trips and skim the cream, building a reasonable list
from the easy ones around the clearings and in the nearby treetops;
but to go for the hard ones you have to be just a little bit insane."

He predicted that he'd pass five thousand once he went to Australia, and he hoped to someday make it to six thousand. He didn't
think he'd get much further than that, though. The more birds
you've seen, the less often you see new ones, and when you go
back to a country for a second or third helping, you're generally
looking for the rare, shy, or remote species. Some of the birds
Keith had yet to see could only be found in places he couldn't go,
like the Soviet Union and Tibet. He thought some "young lions"
like Peter Alden stood a chance of making it to seven thousand—
at the time, Alden was just a few birds behind him—but he
doubted it was possible to pass eight thousand, even for a "Mozart
of the birding world" who did nothing but eat, breathe, and look
for birds from age five to eighty-five.

The farm only assuaged Phoebe's restlessness for a little while. In
December 1975, she went to Shaw's Garden, now the Missouri
Botanical Garden, which has flowers and trees from around the
world and is one of St. Louis's biggest tourist attractions. When she
got home, she wrote a poem saying she'd hated it: everything was
too neatly shaped and clipped, and there were too many people, on
walkways that were too carefully built. "[H]ere there is no life for
me." Instead, she wrote, she'd flee to somewhere "wild and weedy,"
like an overgrown jungle. In another poem, she mourned the felling
of some big old trees near the farm, an act she called "barbaric." She
missed the trees so much, she wrote, that she felt like she herself was
wounded and dying.

As she struggled with these feelings of alienation, she decided to go abroad. In the summer of 1974, she and Dave had sent Penny on a summer program in Europe as a sweet sixteen present, and Tom would get to take a trip anywhere he wanted in the summer of 1976, shortly before he turned sixteen. Since he was still interested in nature, Phoebe suggested that they go together to Ecuador and the Galápagos Islands, which, with the rise of ecotourism, were becoming popular destinations. He liked the idea, and they signed up for a general nature tour that was being run by an Audubon chapter. They'd spend a week cruising around the Galápagos and a week on mainland Ecuador, with a stop in the bird-rich Amazon rain forest.

There weren't a lot of books on the birds of Ecuador for Phoebe to study in advance. There was no field guide, and though an encyclopedia of the birds of South America had recently been published, it had few illustrations and said little about how to identify the birds. She bought it anyway, and did her best.

The trip ended up being a mixed bag for her. She had a great time in the Galápagos, where, as she wrote in *Nature Notes*, "humans are totally out of place." The famous archipelago is about six hundred miles off the coast of Ecuador, and, for the most part, the islands are dry, rocky, and stark. She saw one island, Hood, as "a natural world so complete unto itself, the inhabitants so indifferent to our brief passage through their domain, the habitat so hostile to human existence, that one feels very deeply the eeriness of being in a place and time prior to the advent of man."

The animals in the Galápagos have never been preyed upon by humans, so they're not afraid of us. When Phoebe saw a bird, she'd walk right up to it until she was looking into its eyes and was "almost too close to take a picture." She saw, at close range, a Magnificent Frigatebird regurgitate a fish for its chick and a male Blue-footed Booby show off its rubbery webbed feet to a female by kicking them high in the air. She also got close to huge iguanas with sharp spines on their backs, tortoises that were likely more than 150 years old, and fur seals with long whiskers and big, sad eyes.

The snorkeling off the islands was "*marvelous*," she wrote in her notebook. She wrote in *Nature Notes*, "I hesitantly entered the water as a skeptic who thought birds were the most truly beautiful and exciting creatures on earth, and emerged unwillingly, in raptures over the new world of marine life and its unbelievable color and diversity. Alas, life gets so much better as it gets shorter." From the boat, she saw the "incredible night sky," with Alpha and Beta Centauri, the Southern Cross, and other stars she hadn't seen before. The Milky Way was "a brilliant band."

In her *Nature Notes* article, Phoebe said she couldn't summon the words to do her experience in the Galápagos justice, "and it is one I shall never forget."

She didn't have as good a time on the mainland, where the birds were harder to see, especially in the Amazon rain forest. It's not just that there are a lot of trees in the rain forest; there are also bushes and ferns and vines and bamboo stalks, and everything is tangled together. Most birds spend their time up high, in the canopy, so that even if you catch sight of one, you have to crane your neck to see it, swatting at bugs and wiping off sweat all the while. The only way to see any birds at all in a rain forest is to spend a lot of time there, which Phoebe and Tom didn't get to do. Instead, "there was the constant feeling of too much to see in too short a time." The guides weren't really birders, so they weren't much help, and Phoebe had the sense that the big group—about twenty people—was scaring birds off. "Oh, to get back to the rain forest someday for more tropical birding!"

One day, the group took a long train ride from Quito, which is high in the Andes, to the Pacific coast. The scenery was "absolutely fantastic," but they went through it "too fast," and "bird after bird flitted by unidentified." For a while, she and Tom rode on top of the train, with the luggage, where they saw "a few more birds to be frustrated by," but the train was jolting so much that they couldn't get them in focus in their binoculars. "Such tantalizing country, and how we yearned to be able to cover that stretch at a birder's pace!"

Still, during her time on the mainland she got "glorious" views of the Andes at sunrise; she liked the mist and orchids in the foothills; and there were "lovely" butterflies everywhere. Tom, who says he had an "amazing" time, remembers that one night, Phoebe was in such a good mood that she danced to salsa music with one of the guides. Tom had rarely seen her let down her reserve with someone she didn't know well, and he was pleasantly shocked.

By the end of the trip, Phoebe had seen 150 life birds, and her life list had grown to about five hundred.

After the trip, Phoebe suddenly lost interest in the farm. She went to mow the grass and water the garden upon her return, according to the Farm Journal, but then the whole family took another road trip out West, and she didn't write in the journal again until November. (The next year, 1977, she only wrote in the journal twice, and those are the final entries.)

Soon, she was planning to go abroad again. Some of her friends from WGNSS had been to Kenya, and they must have told her that much of the land there is covered with grass or scrub, not trees, so the birds have nowhere to hide. Her WGNSS friends also told her about Burt Monroe, a professor of ornithology at the University of Louisville who led bird tours for small groups in his spare time. Phoebe signed up for a month-long trip around Kenya that Burt was leading in the summer of 1977. Dave, who wanted to see African mammals, signed up for the first two weeks; he couldn't take a whole month off.

Phoebe spent the first half of 1977 studying Kenyan birds. A few years earlier, the first field guide to East African birds had been published. It only covered about a third of the thousand species in Kenya and had no color illustrations, but it was a start. She tried to fill in the gaps by reading academic treatises and talking to friends. (In a scholarly work, you might learn how many eggs a bird lays each spring, but you might not find out what its field marks are.) A friend who'd gone to Kenya with Burt two years earlier gave her a list of all the birds they'd seen, and she figured out which days she was likely to see which species and what sort of habitat each species lived in.

This time, she'd chosen the right tour. The group was tiny— just Phoebe, Dave, Burt, and three others—and Burt, who was about her age, was "the kind of obsessed and knowledgeable leader I'd been dreaming of," she wrote in her memoir. Had she been a man, she might have lived a life much like his, which was probably part of the reason he appealed to her. As a Ph.D. student in ornithology in the late 1950s and early 1960s, he'd done field-work in Central America, Australia, and Africa, sometimes accompanied by his wife and son; afterward, he was hired by the University of Louisville and began leading bird tours abroad.

The group drove a van with a pop-up top all over the country, and everywhere there were birds and mammals in plain view, against a backdrop of green-gold grass and the occasional lonely acacia tree. Some of the common birds in Kenya—the ones you see day after day, and, after a while, even when you close your eyes—are among the most spectacular. The Common Ostrich is eight feet tall and bathes by rolling around furiously in dry dirt. The African Jacana's back shines like newly polished copper. The

Little Bee-eater wears a different shade of green on each feather, or so it seems in the four o'clock sun. The Gray Crowned-Crane stands tall and still, with a "crown" that looks like freshly picked wheat.

In a *Nature Notes* piece, Phoebe couldn't say which birds had been her favorites, because pretty much all of them had left her "ecstatic." "One really has to include the Lilac-breasted Roller, ubiquitous though it is. And how can you compare an Emerald Cuckoo (unbelievable shades of green and yellow) to a group of Madagascar Bee-eaters—or a Paradise Flycatcher—or a Hoopoe—or an Orange-bellied Parrot (unlikely combination of bright orange and green)—or a majestic Verreaux's Eagle-Owl—or that jewel of a

Gray Crowned-Crane

kingfisher, the Malachite? You see the problem . . . I feel like the man in the children's story 'Millions of Cats' who chose them all because they were all the most beautiful."

In general, Burt spotted the birds first and called out their names, but Phoebe didn't add a bird to her list unless she'd seen it well enough to identify it herself; since she was so well prepared, she knew which field marks to look for. "She'd studied and crammed more than anybody I'd ever seen," a man who was on the trip says. "Burt would even ask her a question now and then."

They also saw lions, zebras, rhinos, and most of the other mammals for which Africa is known, but Phoebe made it clear in her *Nature Notes* piece that she thought of them just as a sideshow. The piece ran in two installments over two successive months; in the first installment, there is no mention of mammals, and in the second, there are just a couple of paragraphs about them. "You can see where my prime interest lies," she wrote in the second installment, by way of explanation.

Her only regret, she said, was that she hadn't gone to Kenya earlier. "Politics and habitat are deteriorating with great rapidity— too many people, cattle, and elephants . . . It can be very depressing to discuss East Africa in comparison with the past, but this doesn't necessarily lessen the enjoyment of the present for someone who is there for the first time."

At the beginning of the trip, Burt had given everyone a checklist of the birds they might see, and every night, they gathered to tick birds off. During the first week alone, Phoebe saw 250 life birds, according to her checklist. By the end of the second week, when Dave went home, she'd seen four hundred. By the last day, she'd seen a remarkable 510 lifers, which meant that in one month in Kenya, she'd doubled the life list that she'd been working on for more than twelve years.

The trip was "astounding," she wrote in her memoir. When it was over, "I quite simply didn't want to return home."

On the plane ride home, as she relived the trip in her head, she devised a meticulous system for keeping track of her "complete experience" with each species on her life list. When she returned from an outing or a trip, she decided, she'd go through her field notes and make an index card for each new bird she'd seen. She'd write the scientific and English names of the bird in the top left corner of the card, and the continent where she'd seen it in the top right corner. Below, she'd write the date of the sighting, the exact location, and some details about the bird's appearance and behavior. If she saw that bird again, she'd make a new entry on the card.

As soon as she got home, she made cards for the roughly one thousand species she'd already seen. She was so focused as she worked that her family told her she might as well still have been in Africa, according to her memoir.

She couldn't wait to travel some more. With a couple of friends from WGNSS, she signed up for a trip to Trinidad that a new bird tour company was running in January 1978. She'd heard that the island was a good introduction to the birds of South America: it has a broad sampling of South American birds, but there are only a few hundred species, so it's not overwhelming.

Once again, she'd chosen wisely. The trip was two weeks long, ten days of which were spent in a rain forest, at an old cocoa plantation that had recently been turned into a tourist lodge. The lodge was set in a small clearing full of birdfeeders that were visible from the veranda, and it was also easy to see birds in the trees on the clearing's edge. In addition, the group did some easy birding on the coast and at a vast swamp where there were thousands of Scarlet Ibises, big birds with deep red feathers, dark black eyes, and long, downward-curving bills shaped like the blade of a scythe. In her memoir, Phoebe said Trinidad was "clearly where I should have started" in South America "rather than plunging in over my head with the birds of Ecuador." She saw a hundred life birds and had a "truly magical" time.

When she got home, she wrote a poem that she called "Love Affair With Trinidad." It was gray and dreary in St. Louis, she wrote, but in her mind, she was still in warm, vibrant Trinidad; the sun was burning off the morning mist, and the birds were starting to sing.

The cohesion of the Snetsinger family was fast breaking down, partly because the kids were getting older and partly because Phoebe and Dave were—quietly but surely—growing even more distant. By the winter of 1978, Penny was a freshman at Brandeis University, outside Boston, where she was studying chemistry, as her mother had in college. Tom, who was also a strong student, was in eleventh grade, and Marmot and Sue, who were less studious and more rebellious than their elder siblings, were in tenth and eighth grades and busy much of the time with sports and friends.

Dave was busy with his work for Purina, having become one of the top managers in the poultry department. He still supervised research on poultry feed, and he was starting to get involved in marketing it, which required a lot of travel. He was attending meetings, trade shows, and scientific conventions around the country and the world, sometimes giving speeches to hundreds of people at a time. He took short domestic trips a couple of times a month and went abroad, often to Europe, a few times each year.

Phoebe wasn't home much either. In early 1978, around the time she got back from Trinidad, she decided to try to break the "year list" record for the St. Louis area, which stood at 274 species. She often birded with a male friend from WGNSS, Bill Rudden, a fireman and former hunter who had a knack for spotting. (He recalls that the first time he went into the woods with binoculars rather than a gun, he thought, "Am I gay or something?") He generally worked 24-hour shifts and, consequently, got a lot of days off. Though Phoebe and Bill didn't have an affair, they spent much more time together than they did with their respective spouses, and in Bill's opinion, their friendship was "platonic love."

The Snetsinger family hardly used their farm any more. They still ate dinner together, but when the meal was over, Phoebe would go to her study to read about birds, and Dave would practice magic in the basement. They'd only communicate when one of them answered the phone for the other, and sometimes they'd just yell into the laundry chute.

With Bill's help, Phoebe ended up breaking the year list record in mid-December, with a couple of weeks to spare, but even beforehand, she had the sense that the satisfaction wouldn't last long. When she had just a few birds to go, she wrote a poem saying that she was always seeking out moments of intensity—the sight of a wildflower in full bloom or a mountain cast in the orange light of alpenglow—only to find, a second later, that they were gone.

She did get some recognition for what she'd done, however: a local paper, the *Webster-Kirkwood Times*, was tipped off about the record and wrote an admiring profile of her. She told the paper that her favorite bird was "any bird I'm looking for at the moment. Or seeing a rare bird for the first time . . . if the cardinal were rare and living only in a remote corner of Washington state, I would travel to see it and probably think it was the most beautiful thing I had ever seen."

One of the reasons she liked birding, she said, was because "there is always some surprise. You study and think you know a bird and then you see it in a new area or different stage of development and learn all over again."

"It's an addiction with me."

By this time, she was forty-seven and was considered a sort of elder stateswoman in WGNSS; to share her expertise, she started writing an occasional "birding tips" column for *Nature Notes* with advice on which birds to look for that month and where they might be found. Meanwhile, she was taking little trips around the country, with the goal of bringing her North American list to six hundred. Sometimes she'd just get in a car with some WGNSS friends and drive somewhere; sometimes she'd write to friends of friends in other states and ask them to show her around; and sometimes she took organized tours. (In the late 1970s, there were several bird tour companies to choose from in addition to Bird Bonanzas. The newer companies were modeled on Bird Bonanzas, but were a little pricier, as they had less of a macho ethos and spent some money to keep their customers comfortable.) One of Phoebe's favorite trips from this period was a tour of Arizona led by Rich Stallcup, a birder from California who worked for a company called Northeast Birding. In a *Nature Notes* article, Phoebe wrote of Rich, "This man is as totally enchanted by and knowledgeable about all forms of life as anyone I have ever known." He liked to figure out not just what species a bird was but also what its age and sex were and whether it belonged to a particular "race." "I ate it up," Phoebe's memoir says. "There was a lot more to this identification game than I'd ever realized, and I was learning it from the pros."

She was getting involved, in a quiet way, with the environmental movement. In the late 1970s, the California Condor, a vulture, was nearly extinct, mainly because the mammal carcasses it ate often contained poisonous lead shot. Phoebe tried to see one of the twenty remaining birds, failed, and sent a substantial donation to the Condor Fund. (Today, the condor population is about one hundred fifty, not including birds in captivity.) Once, she took a tour of Arizona where the subject of conservation kept coming up. She didn't say much during these discussions, but at the end of the trip, she gave the leader a check for $500 and asked her to donate it wherever she thought best. She also preserved an acre of the Amazon rain forest by donating money to a land trust.

By the fall of 1979, Phoebe had seen about 590 birds in North America—just ten shy of her goal—and she wanted to start going abroad again. The kids were more self-sufficient than they'd been a couple of years earlier: Tom was in college, at Johns Hopkins, where he was studying engineering; Marmot was a senior in high school; Sue was a sophomore. However, Phoebe was having a hard time with Marmot, who had the sense that her mother was tired of teenagers and couldn't wait until they were out of the house. Marmot was acting out by making things hard for Phoebe. She'd tell her she was going to the library when she was really going out with her friends; she'd tell her she was going out with friends when in fact she was going to the library. In the fall of 1979, Marmot threw Phoebe a curveball by saying she'd decided that instead of going to college, she would get a job and keep living at home. When Phoebe forbade her from doing that, Marmot got furious, and they fought for weeks until, under duress, Marmot agreed to fill out some applications.

Despite all this drama, in February 1980, Phoebe and a friend of hers from WGNSS went to Ecuador on a Northeast Birding tour. The guide, Robert Ridgely, had a background much like Burt Monroe's: He'd been birding in Latin America for more than a decade, had a Ph.D. in forestry from Yale, and had recently published a field guide to the birds of Panama, one of the first good field guides to tropical birds.

The tour covered pretty much the same ground as Phoebe's first trip to Ecuador had, but in four weeks rather than two, and

Bob, unlike the guides on her first trip, knew what he was doing. This trip was also different because the group got to watch birds from high in the Amazon rain forest: a friend of Bob's had recently run a ladder up a huge tree and installed a platform atop one of its branches. When you're birding in a rain forest, a platform like this makes all the difference. There are more birds in the canopy than there are in the understory, because that's where a lot of the good fruit is; and, unlike the birds in the understory, canopy birds spend a lot of time out in the open. Phoebe must have seen toucans, with their huge, clownish, boat-shaped bills; tanagers, which have dramatic turquoise or crimson or green or gold feathers, or sometimes a combination of all of the above; and macaws, which draw attention to themselves not just with their size and color but with loud and persistent squawks that sound like the cries of a colicky baby.

According to Bob, Phoebe stood out dramatically in the group. The others were on vacation; she was an ornithologist-in-training. She'd studied the birds in advance more than anyone he'd ever taken around. In the field, she didn't just wait for him to spot birds but was constantly scanning the trees herself, and she tried to make identifications without his help, too. At meals, she asked a lot of good questions, and in the heat of midday, when everyone else was taking a siesta, she walked the trails by herself. "It was just extraordinary," Bob says. "Most tour participants don't recognize birds. They sit there and wait to be shown them."

She also stood out, he says, because she was ebullient. "She was always asking, 'Are we gonna see this? Are we gonna see that?'" When she saw a good bird, she'd jump up and down and punch the air, smiling so wide that her eyes were little slits. "That's the most beautiful thing I've ever seen!" she said again and again, and sometimes she was almost in tears.

Around the time Phoebe returned from Ecuador, she started coming up with a plan for the future. The trips she was taking were expensive, but she was "totally and irrevocably hooked" on foreign birding, as she wrote later and she valued the safety and structure of organized tours. Thus far, she'd seen about 1,500 birds, which meant there were 7,500 left for her to see. (In the late 1970s, taxonomists had decided that some species of birds needed to be "split" into two, so the total number of birds had officially gone up a little, from 8,600 to 9,000.) She was forty-eight years old. She thought she might like to spend the rest of her life taking two or three foreign tours a year.

She wasn't too engaged with Marmot and Sue at this point, but Marmot was getting ready to go to college—at Beloit, in Wisconsin—and Sue was enjoying being relatively unsupervised. She could come and go pretty much as she pleased, and when her parents were away, she stayed out late and threw parties at the house. After one such party, her parents found beer cans, but neither of them gave her a hard time. "I had a lot of freedom," she says. Marmot puts it a little differently: "Mom let Sue do whatever she wanted. She just sort of gave up after me."

Sue says that her parents "lived almost completely different lives" by this time, which sometimes made her sad, and that she wondered, quietly, why they didn't get divorced. From my talks with Dave, I gather that he felt rejected by Phoebe, and that he wanted to bridge the gap between them but didn't know how, since they'd never been open about their feelings. Maybe, on some level, Phoebe wanted them to be closer, too, but she was planning a life that would drive them further apart.

In the fall of 1980, right after Marmot left for college, Phoebe took another trip with Bob Ridgely, to the swamps and savannas of northeastern Brazil. As in Kenya, the birds were abundant and easy to see. By the end of the year, she had 1,900 species on her life list, and, for the first time, she sent her total to *Birding*. The number-one lister that year was Stuart Stokes, a Brit who had made a lot of money building hospitals and spent much of every year in the field. (At this point, the American Birding Association had members from around the world.) He'd seen 6,150 species, many of them on Bird Bonanzas tours. Phoebe was in 104th place that year.

She was getting ready for her next trip, to Panama, when she noticed a lump in her right armpit. She showed it to her gynecologist, who told her it was nothing to worry about. Neither the gynecologist nor Phoebe seems to have considered a possible relationship between the lump and the melanoma she'd had nine years earlier. For the first five years after the melanoma was removed, she'd gone to her dermatologist, as she'd been told to, and he'd never found anything suspicious.

The Panama trip started in early February 1981 and was two weeks long. The leaders, John and Rose Ann Rowlett, were brother and sister; they'd discovered birds together, when they saw a fiery orange-and-black Northern Oriole on their way home from school one day in Austin, Texas. They were working for a bird tour company named Victor Emanuel Nature Tours, or VENT, and, with some other VENT leaders, they'd devised a technique for drawing birds out of the forest. Birds often come out of hiding when they think other birds of the same species are invading their territory, so the VENT guides made tape recordings of hundreds of birdcalls, which they played back during their tours. The trick "blew me away," Phoebe wrote in her memoir; it was as if the Rowletts had the birds on a string. She liked them a lot personally, too. You won't find anyone jollier than the Rowletts: They call out "Yip, yip!" whenever they see a good bird and "Yip, yip, yip!" whenever they see a phenomenal one, and they call each other by the bird names given to them long ago by their mentor in Texas. Rose Ann is "Grebe," for her long neck, and John is "Peppershrike," because he's cheerful and chunky. "I've seldom had a better, more exciting time on a birding trip," Phoebe wrote many years later.

Throughout the trip, however, the lump in her armpit got more pronounced. She saw another doctor when she got home at the end of February, and this time she was told that the lump could be a sign of melanoma metastasis. The operation she'd had nine years earlier might have come too late, she was told, after the disease had already spread to her lymph nodes. In that case, her prognosis would most likely be poor. She was referred to a surgeon at a hospital, who told her she needed to have the lump removed and tested immediately. She also had to have scans of her brain, liver, and bones. "I went into the hospital feeling that life was suddenly becoming unreal and quite terrifying," her memoir says.

Tom remembers receiving a call from his father at Johns Hopkins, where he was a sophomore, and deciding to come home for spring break, but he says neither of his parents would tell him or Sue exactly what was going on. "I didn't really know how to react, had no sense of what to expect," he says. "Sue and I were both nervous about it, just feeling our way through. We didn't know if we should visit her in the hospital." Sue, who was a junior in high school, says, "I don't think I really understood what was going on. I was really confused and scared, and scared to talk about it."

When the test results came back, at the end of March, Phoebe and Dave returned to the hospital for a meeting with two of her doctors. The cancer had, in fact, spread to some of her lymph nodes, the doctors said. They'd removed those nodes, and there was no sign of metastasis anywhere else in her body, but still, the chances that she'd survive were slim, they said. She pressed them for a more concrete prognosis, and they said that in all likelihood, she would be healthy for only another three months; within a year, she would probably be dead.

The doctors' manner was methodical, like they were delivering a weather report, as Dave recalls. He remembers that Phoebe started crying, and that one of the doctors passed her some tissues. They said there were no proven treatments for metastatic melanoma; unlike many cancers, it didn't seem to respond to either chemotherapy or radiation. But the hospital was conducting a study on a possible new treatment, and they invited Phoebe to volunteer for it. They explained that some needles would be stuck into her hipbone to suction out the marrow, which would be blasted with a massive dose of chemotherapy and injected back into her bone. The bone marrow transplant would be painful, and there was a chance it would kill her. Other treatments were being tested at hospitals around the country, the doctors said, but they had serious side effects, too.

Dave remembers holding Phoebe's hand at the car but that they didn't say much as he drove her home. Understandably, he didn't know "quite what to say with that kind of news." When they got to the house, she wanted to be alone and went upstairs. Dave took Sue into the kitchen to tell her what the doctors had said, and they held each other over the table and cried. The other kids were told over the phone.

In her memoir, Phoebe wrote, "I could hardly believe this was really happening." She kept thinking, "I'm healthy, and I'm not even 50!" As the shock wore off, she began to feel "totally shattered and defeated." She called Peggy Groves, her best friend from college, who was living with her husband, Bob, in Georgia, where he had an internal medicine practice. Bob told Phoebe to come down to Georgia for a second opinion from an oncologist friend of his. She did, and she got the same grim prognosis. Bob's friend strongly advised her against getting the bone marrow transplant: it was too risky, he told her, and the most she could hope for was that it would buy her a little time. He didn't think any of the other studies that were going on were worth signing up for, either.

At the time, Linus Pauling, the chemist and Nobel laureate, was saying that huge doses of vitamin C might slow the spread of cancer. Most doctors dismissed this idea, but Bob figured that Phoebe had nothing to lose, and, at his suggestion, she began a regimen of ten grams a day.

By the time she got back to St. Louis, she'd decided that the vitamin C would be her only treatment. She figured that "a short span of quality living under my control" was preferable to a longer life ruined by "medical incarceration," her memoir says.

At first, Dave felt she was making a mistake. He thought that if the bone marrow study and other experimental treatments were her only hope, she should get them. But on his own, he met with some other doctors in St. Louis, and he came to the conclusion that Phoebe's decision was reasonable. He still thought he would have gotten treatment himself, though. "Most of us have the notion that doctors do no wrong," he says. "Phoebe was much more realistic. This was going to interfere with her life."

It didn't occur to her that she might beat the odds and survive. "I dreaded waking from sleep in the mornings, because reality would strike me with an intense physical blow whenever I did. There simply wasn't much I could do to avoid dwelling on the horror of it all and pondering over how I was going to deal with it."

While she wasn't too interested in birdwatching, she went on a lot of walks to help regain full range of motion in her right arm, and she took along her binoculars out of habit. Sometimes she'd start concentrating on something "beautiful or interesting," and for a moment she'd forget that she was dying. Soon, the spring migration began, and she found herself going out to watch it.

She was already signed up for a tour of Alaska that her good friend Rich Stallcup was leading during the first three weeks of June. She called him to tell him about her diagnosis, and said it was even possible that she'd die on the trip. Rich, who cared about her deeply, encouraged her to come along anyway, and she decided that if she hadn't gotten sick by early June, she would.

On April 9, she wrote a heartfelt and strikingly open letter to John and Rose Ann Rowlett, her beloved guides in Panama:

I wanted to write you both a very special thank-you letter for an extra special trip, but some really catastrophic events have intervened.

In short, I have what all the specialists say is an incurable cancer—recurrent malignant melanoma. I had to have surgery on a lump in my armpit just a few weeks after returning from Panama & the prognosis is not good—nor are the possible treatments, which have ghastly side effects and are at best holding actions . . .

Aside from the emotional impact of all of this, I'm really fine right now. It's a beautiful spring here, and I'm out enjoying it as much as possible. I've decided that the quality of life is much more important to me than trying to stretch out a miserable existence under treatment—and even the doctors say they can't give me any convincing reasons for taking the treatments—so I'm not—and I'll continue trying to live as I want to as long as I can. I'm signed up on the Wings Alaska trip with Rich Stallcup, and hoping very much that I'll be physically able to do it. This is my most-wanted trip at this point and a good goal for me to have right now.

I do want you both to know how sincerely glad I am that I went on your Panama trip while I had the chance. I was not aware that I had a problem at the time, so I was able to enjoy it to the utmost . . .

So—my deepest gratitude to both of you for all the good birds and the good times. I'll never forget any of it. May we do it again, sometime, someplace—

Much love,
Phoebe

Chapter 4

ONCE IT WAS settled that Phoebe wasn't going to get treatment, "she didn't mention the cancer a heck of a lot more," Dave says. He thought she wanted space to deal with it on her own, and he worried that he'd upset her if he brought it up. Neither of them brought it up with the children, either, which left them struggling to cope on their own. Marmot, still a freshman at Beloit, was "eaten up by guilt" because she'd given her mother such a hard time in high school. "I really just wanted to come home," she says, but her parents gave her the impression that she shouldn't. "I kind of got pushed out of the whole thing." Penny, a senior at Brandeis, was choosing between three or four Ph.D. programs in chemistry that spring. Without making a big deal about it, she chose the one closest to home, at the University of Illinois, so she could see her mother when she got sick. "It was really bad. I was devastated."

In retrospect, Sue thinks Phoebe did want to talk about her cancer, and was waiting for someone to give her an opening. As Sue recalls, around April or May, Phoebe went to Lake Zurich for a family party and came back "really, really hurt" because everyone had acted like nothing was wrong.

In all likelihood, Phoebe wanted to reach out to people for support but wasn't comfortable baring her vulnerability, as she hadn't been when she was depressed, in 1970, and when she had her first melanoma, in 1972. She might also have thought that both she and the people who loved her would fare better if she remained stoic.

By herself, she made a monumental decision, which, as far as I know, she told no one about at the time. As she later wrote, she couldn't stand the thought of a long, painful death, and she didn't trust her doctors to keep her from having one. The doctor who'd operated on her in 1972 hadn't given her enough anesthesia; the doctors she'd dealt with this time around had been cold and clinical. She decided that when she got sick, instead of putting herself at the medical establishment's mercy, she'd take matters into her own hands and end her life instantly by shooting herself.

She bought a gun and hid it in a shoebox in her closet. She wrote a draft of a suicide note and put it in a drawer in her study.

On Phoebe's first night in Alaska, the guide, Rich, presented her with a Golden Eagle tail feather that he'd found a couple of years earlier on a roadside in Nevada. In some Native American cultures, he explained to her, eagle feathers were supposed to bring good luck. "I'm not very spiritual," he says, "but I figured, anything that might help." At a time when Phoebe was hungry for people to acknowledge her situation, she must have found Rich's simple gesture touching.

The trip was "an absolute dream of an Alaskan experience," as she wrote in *Nature Notes* afterward. It covered a wide range of landscapes, including the tundra, which was blanketed by "glorious" pink and yellow wildflowers; spruce and fir forests interrupted by "gorgeous" snowy peaks; and some "dramatic" shoreline cliffs where puffins were nesting en masse. In her memoir, Phoebe said she thought less about her cancer than she had all spring because she was so focused on the scenery and birds—which, she wrote, was "emotional salvation." The trip's physical demands were likely a good distraction, too. Since there's so much daylight in Alaska in June, the group stayed out for at least sixteen hours each day, often in wind, rain, and cold. For a week, on an island inhabited only by Inuits, they slept in a one-room cabin with no heat, lights, or water; the "toilet" was a big bucket outside.

Phoebe must have felt well taken care of, however. She had her fiftieth birthday on the trip, and the group celebrated it at a saloon in an old gold-rush town ("and a very fine birthday it was," she wrote in her memoir, "considering that I wasn't supposed to have any more"). Sometimes, she'd see that Rich was looking at her with concern, he says, and she'd give him a thumbs-up to tell him she was okay. Rich thought she was a little subdued at times, but that she seemed to get stronger as the trip went on. "After a week, I said to myself, 'she's not gonna go down here.' "

By the time she got home, three months had passed since her diagnosis, which meant that she could fall ill any day. She didn't want to just sit around and wait to get sick, though, so she decided to take some little trips around the country and to sign up for a tour of Australia in September. "Australia was far away, certainly, and the trip was a month long, but it was also a civilized kind of place from which I could fly home relatively easily if a health problem developed," her memoir says. Dave and the kids all supported the idea.

About ten days after her return from Alaska, she left for a road trip with a friend from New York, Barbara Spencer, whom she'd met on a tour of Arizona a few years earlier. Barbara, who lived on Long Island, was an artist, school psychologist, and mother who had gotten serious about birds when she was going through a divorce. Phoebe and Barbara started in St. Louis and, in about two weeks, covered Minnesota, Manitoba, North Dakota, Wyoming, and Colorado in what turned out to be "a resoundingly successful do-it-yourself trip," according to Phoebe's memoir. When it was Barbara's turn to drive, Phoebe studied a newly published field guide to Australian birds and tried to learn ten or fifteen species a day.

At home, she studied the field guide some more, and she read all the books and articles she could find on Australia and its birds. Since it's an isolated continent, evolution has run an independent course there, which has resulted in some funky "endemic" birds, or birds that live nowhere else. Among the fifteen species of bowerbird, for example, males woo females by building little dens. The walls are made of sticks and vines, and they're covered with all kinds of ornaments, including berries, shells, flowers, and beetle wings. Some bowerbirds even "paint" their bowers by mixing their saliva with fruit or vegetable juice. Once a bowerbird has constructed its lair, it hops around in front of it and calls out to females, hoping to mate with as many as possible. Australia also has lyrebirds, whose males try to outdo one another as mimics. To attract females, the male lyrebird throws its white tail feathers forward so they cover its face like a veil and belts out an original medley, mimicking the calls of dozens of other bird species in turn. Lyrebirds that live near people often add imitations of burglar alarms, welding machines, and other electronic sounds to their medleys.

Phoebe found that getting ready for a trip distracted her almost as much as taking one did. During the tour, she saw bowerbirds, lyrebirds, and several hundred other lifers—many of which she was able to identify without the leader's help—and once again, she had a great time.

When she got home, she signed up for some tours in early 1982, including a long, rugged, and strenuous one in the Indian and Nepalese Himalayas. "Obviously I'm doing well in spite of the dire predictions by the doctors last spring," she wrote to John Rowlett. "I decided as long as I was feeling well I'd do the things

I really wanted to do—so I've really had one hell of a great six months . . . I'm gaining some confidence about living for another year or so & maybe more."

She spent most of the fall of 1981 taking short trips with friends, working on her index card file, and getting ready for her upcoming tours. It had become standard practice for tour guides to send out species "checklists" in advance, and, in an attempt to study more systematically, Phoebe started setting aside a spiral notebook for each upcoming trip and filling it with accounts of every species on the list. "Writing something down has always been the most effective way for me to learn it, and once written down, the information was there for review, or for double-checking during the trip," she wrote in her memoir. She backed up all her notes with references and grouped the birds according to family and genus, as a scientist would have. (A genus is a group of similar, closely related species, and a family is a group of similar, closely related genera. For example, a Blackburnian Warbler is a species that belongs to the *Dendroica* genus, which has twenty-eight other warbler species, too, most of them colorful and vocal. The *Dendroica* genus is one of about a dozen in the New World warbler family, or Parulidae. All bird families belong to the same class, Aves.)

Around New Year's, Phoebe set her first numerical goal in a while. In an interview with the *St. Louis Globe-Democrat* in January 1983, she said she'd seen about 2,500 birds and was hoping to get to three thousand; she also said she had cancer and had to "go fast." She added, "Birdwatching isn't a hobby; it's more than that . . . It colors my whole existence."

On her tour of the Himalayas in the spring of 1982, Phoebe made a good friend, a Canadian woman in her early sixties named Elizabeth Wright. The two of them had a lot in common. Elizabeth had also been a tomboy growing up; when she was little, she'd started calling herself "Joe" because she thought Elizabeth was too girly, and that was still the name she preferred. Like Phoebe, Joe had studied science in college (her major was geomorphology, the study of landscapes), but she, too, had ended up staying home to raise four children, in a small town outside Montreal. Joe had taken up birding when her kids were young, as Phoebe had, and she'd helped start a birding club that was comprised largely of housewives. She'd started taking bird tours as soon as they were widely available, in the 1970s. Her husband had died suddenly in 1980, and she was still grieving when Phoebe met her in 1982.

The guide was Ben King, the Navy veteran who spent the 1960s hitchhiking, teaching ballroom dance, and birding around Asia. Since then, Ben had been a tour guide for Bird Bonanzas, written a field guide to the birds of Southeast Asia, gotten a master's degree in ornithology, and, in 1981, started his own company, King Bird Tours. To the chagrin of some of his customers, he ran his trips like combat operations over which he, of course, was the commander. You were not to try to influence the day's itinerary, but to trust that he would advance your best interest. You were to dress in brown and green, so as not to scare the birds, and you were to be quiet at all times in the forest. You were not to expect an afternoon siesta, but if there was time for one, you were to rest as he did, atop a large plastic garbage bag on the ground. To illustrate his determination, Ben went around saying—hyperbolically, one hopes—that he wore his binoculars every moment of the day, even when he was making love. He was about Phoebe's age but had never married.

In her memoir, Phoebe called Ben "the most indefatigable birder and tour leader I'd yet run into." The group did a lot of hiking at ten to thirteen thousand feet above sea level, where, compared to lower elevations, you get less oxygen so your body has to work harder. They didn't get much sleep; there were long, tortuous drives; and some of the hotels were "unbelievably awful." "Nonetheless, if you had the stamina and drive to stick with Ben through it all, there was nearly always a payoff." Over the course of the tour, which started in early April and was six weeks long, she saw "a simply incredible array of Himalayan birds," and the scenery awed her, too. Out the window of one of her hotel rooms in Nepal, she could see "huge pink magnolias," she wrote in her notebook, and, in the distance, the "sheer southeast face" of Mount Everest, which was flanked by sister mountains Lhotse and Nuptse. The peaks looked "close & awesome."

On May 1, about four weeks into the tour, Phoebe sent a post-card to her family. "Back to elec. & running water after 2 weeks of living in rather awful hotels—*very* primitive but compensated for by superb view of Everest, etc. & hillsides aflame w. red rho-dodendrons, to say nothing of excellent birds . . . Still eager & feel great." At that point, the group was making its way to New Delhi, from which almost everyone would fly home. Only Phoebe and Joe had signed up for the final leg of the tour in northern India.

At the beginning of this last leg, in Kashmir, both women picked up a "debilitating" stomach bug, which was all the more inconve-nient because they were taking some strenuous walks at about ten thousand feet. Simultaneously, Joe started waking up in the middle of the night with heart palpitations, a common response to altitude. They were both "wiped out," Phoebe wrote later, but they found Kashmir "lovely—somewhat reminiscent of the N. Am. West" and were glad to be doing the whole trip. In any event, they soon got a reprieve, a few days on a "sumptuous, really unbelievably luxurious houseboat" on a lake at four thousand feet, a comfortable altitude. They were both taking tetracycline and both feeling better, and the walking they did around the lake was "relatively easy."

The group flew over the "awesome mountains" of the Tibetan plateau to their last stop, Leh, a desert city just west of China.

Though they were high up again—about 11,500 feet above sea level—they weren't planning any serious hiking, and "both of us seemed in fine health and spirits."

They spent their first morning in Leh, May 9, taking a slow downhill walk. "Did not seem to be at all fatiguing, and I was surprised at lunch when Joe told us she'd been fighting nausea off and on that morning," Phoebe wrote later. "She'd *seemed* okay—covered it well. Again we all passed it off as typical altitude symptoms. She ate lunch and enjoyed it and we all napped." When they woke up, Ben took them on another leisurely walk, during which Joe reported that she was once again feeling fine. The group ate an early dinner, went over the day's bird sightings, and, around nine, went to bed. They'd wake up before dawn and spend a little time in the field the next morning before flying back to Delhi and home.

However, Joe didn't show up for breakfast, and there was no answer when Ben knocked on her door. He broke in through the bathroom window and found her lying under the covers, dead. A coroner later said that the causes of death had been dehydration and altitude sickness.

A couple of hours after Joe was found, Phoebe wrote a tender, thoughtful letter to Joe's children that shows not just how much she cared about her, but how determined she was to make the most of the time she had left and to make her own death as painless as possible. The note also affirms that she could express her emotions well in writing, even if she was generally too shy or awkward to reveal them out loud.

Dear John, Abbott, Eleanor, and Jane,

I'm starting this letter the morning after your mother's death. It's difficult to write of this to people I don't know and who are so deeply affected by the situation—but I do want you to have a more personal picture of what happened than you could get from official communications . . .

From my point of view it was a *good* death, though obviously premature for such a vibrant, vital woman.

She had had, as have I, a truly marvelous trip . . . She clearly loved this sort of experience . . . and her life was better and richer for having done it all. Ben and I and the others in the group all loved her, admired her stamina and vitality, and her wide range of interests—she was so *aware* of all aspects of this trip—birds, flowers, people, costumes, comparative cultures and languages of the different areas—an amazing woman—and we all learned much from her. As you know, she was so responsive to and interested in people—conversing on a personal level with the local guides and drivers, interested in and deriving enjoyment from it all. She taught me a lot about how to live—in just a few short weeks.

Phoebe mentioned some of the highlights of the trip and chronicled Joe's last couple of days. When she was found, "[s]he was lying peacefully in bed as though in deep sleep . . . *No* sign of struggle, discomfort or trying to get help. Must have hit her suddenly in the early A.M. and she probably never knew it—Anybody's first choice of a way to die. The doctor appeared shortly thereafter and pronounced her dead—maybe up to 2 hours before." Phoebe said that Ben, who'd taken Joe on a trip the previous year, too, thought in retrospect that he'd noticed "a slow decline in her vigor—a general loss of her normal ebullience and enthusiasm over the past 2 weeks or so. I had not really noticed this—hadn't known her before this trip. I knew I was feeling tired from time to time and that she was too, so really thought nothing of it."

The letter concluded:

She talked about Eleanor's forthcoming visit with the baby and was obviously looking forward to returning to her gardening and other activities at home. As I am, she was delighted to have made the trip, felt successful (she was a *terrific* spotter) and satisfied with what she'd seen and done.

Joe gave us all the impression she was going to live forever. Our shock and dismay and sorrow over her unexpected death is of course nothing compared to yours. Ben and I both feel just awful about this—for all of you—But speaking for myself, if I could have a death like hers—and could live life so fully and with so much spirit up to the very end, I would find such an end truly acceptable.

Joe talked about Eleanor (or Jane?) joking about her dying in some god-forsaken place with her binoculars on. Well, kids, she did. Be proud of her. We sure are.

My love and sympathy to all of you—

Sincerely,

Phoebe

By the time Phoebe got home, thirteen months had passed since her diagnosis, so she was already supposed to be dead. She'd seen about a thousand life birds during that time, and her life list was just under three thousand.

The biggest, baddest eagle in the world is the Harpy. It's more than three feet tall, with a stocky build and a seven-foot wingspan. It flies through the jungle at fifty miles per hour and kills monkeys with a swipe of the talon. The females are a little bigger than the males, and they tend to make bigger kills. In Greek mythology, Harpies were female monsters who took the shape of birds; the eagle got its name from them.

In the summer of 1982, Phoebe would be going to Peru, where

she wanted most of all to see a Harpy Eagle and another massive eagle, the Crested. Despite their size, Harpy and Crested Eagles are hard to find, as they keep a low profile to surprise their prey.

She wanted to see hundreds of other birds on the trip, too, and she decided that since there wasn't a field guide for Peru, she'd make her own. Somehow, she and her friend Barbara Spencer, who would be her roommate, got access to the bird skin collection at the American Museum of Natural History, which is stored in specimen trays in the museum's back rooms and includes most species that can be found in South America. Late in the spring, Phoebe flew to New York, and she and Barbara spent "many happy hours" photographing and taking notes on skins.

There were two leaders on the tour: Phoebe's jolly buddy John Rowlett and Ted Parker, the birder from Pennsylvania who'd founded the "IDIOTS" club and had gone on to set a new Big Year record. Since the mid-1970s, Ted had been leading bird tours—he was one of the original Bird Bonanzas guides—and doing ornithology fieldwork for Louisiana State University. A couple of times a year, he and his LSU colleagues would go somewhere remote, usually in the Amazon rain forest, and roam around for weeks with binoculars, notebooks, a tape recorder, and a tent. Mostly, they were collecting birdsong, trying to figure out which species lived where, and Ted's ability to identify calls had become legendary. It was said, for example, that he could stand anywhere in Amazonia with a blindfold on and identify all the birds that were calling within a mile. Around the time Phoebe met him, he discovered a new species, the Orange-eyed Flycatcher, simply because he'd heard an unfamiliar song in the forest. He was a hippie-ish, likable guy who was also obsessed with college basketball and liked to talk and listen to music around a campfire late into the night.

According to an article Phoebe wrote in *Nature Notes*, the first two weeks of the tour covered a variety of terrain, including the coast, where there were "overwhelming numbers of boobies and cormorants"; the "truly awesome" Andes and their foothills; and some "staggering" high-altitude grasslands. The group ended up at one of the first tourist lodges in the Amazon rain forest, the Explorer's Inn, which was remote and accessible only by boat, and where they were to stay for the tour's final week. In the few years that the inn had been open, a stunning six hundred bird species had been recorded in its vicinity, roughly the same number that had been recorded in all of Texas.

In the thick forest around the inn, the birding was "difficult, often very frustrating, and yet vastly rewarding." In the mornings and late afternoons, Ted and John led the group around the forest; right after lunch, while everyone else was napping, Phoebe and Barbara walked around by themselves. Despite all their studying, they had a hard time identifying a lot of the skulking species they saw on these walks, and sometimes they'd spend a whole hour on a single bird.

By the second-to-last morning of the trip, Phoebe had seen "a treasure chest" of about two hundred life birds, and she'd long since passed three thousand on her life list. But there had been no sign of either eagle she wanted.

At daybreak, Ted took Phoebe and a few other people on a boat ride around a lake. At first, they didn't see much, but then he started paddling fast toward the shore, where there was a huge bird in a tree that "became more obviously a Harpy Eagle the closer we got," Phoebe wrote. "Utter silence fell" as they took in the bird's features: its "enormous head"; its legs "as thick as tree branches"; its "deep, dark, hollow-eyed stare." "I was quite overcome. This was my number one most-wanted bird in the entire world, one I'd never realistically expected to see even briefly, and we'd had these stupendous, heart-stopping views of it."

Harpy Eagle

The next day after lunch, while the rest of the group took a siesta, Phoebe and Barbara took one last walk by themselves. As they made their way down a trail, Phoebe saw a huge eagle fly into a tree about fifty feet away. It looked a lot like the Harpy she'd seen, but this bird's chest was lighter, and it had a longer tail. There could be no doubt: it was a Crested Eagle, as rare and reclusive as the Harpy. The sighting, she wrote, was "almost a religious experience," as if "a divine presence had manifested itself just for us." She seemed to take particular pleasure in having found the bird herself, without the leaders' help.

It had been "the ultimate bird trip"; when she took into account the birds, the leaders, the logistics, and the scenery, the tour came out "well ahead" of every other she'd taken. She'd seen "the two biggest and best raptors in South America," about 230 other lifers, and more than seven hundred birds in all. "I can't wait to go back—that's not quite *half* the birds of Peru!"

There had never been a better time to look for birds around the world. For one thing, the bird tour industry was exploding. New companies were opening every year—with names like Wonder Bird Tours and Birdquest and Wings and Sunbird—and new destinations were being offered all the time, particularly in the very birdy tropics. Many bird tours were rugged and strenuous, as Phoebe's trip to the Himalayas had been, but travel in the world's wildernesses was getting easier all the time: there were more flights to more places, roads were being built and improved, tourist lodges were opening in rain forests and on mountaintops.

There was an explosion in knowledge about birds, too. As tour guides and researchers spent more time abroad, they learned which species lived where (sometimes down to the exact tree in which a rare bird nested), how to identify them, what their calls were, and at what times of day and year they were most active. Field guides to tropical birds were finally being published, and in 1982 Peter Alden, the veteran tour guide for the Massachusetts Audubon Society, published *Finding Birds Around the World*, which was modeled after the bird-finding guides for North America that had come out three decades earlier.

All this made birders start to say that a "Golden Age" had begun, but they always added that it wouldn't last long. According to scientists, hundreds of birds around the world were in danger of going extinct, mostly as a result of habitat destruction and other human blunders. An alarming 150 species had been lost over the previous few centuries, even though fossil records show that birds are supposed to die out at a rate of only one species every hundred years. In the early 1800s, for instance, British sailors brought mosquitoes to the islands of Hawaii, and with the mosquitoes came the diseases they transmit to birds, such as avian malaria and bird pox. Since Hawaiian birds hadn't been exposed to these diseases before, they lacked resistance to them, and about fifteen species perished as a result. Similarly, in the 1940s, the Brown Tree Snake, which eats birds, was introduced to the island of Guam, probably from an American warship. The snake proliferated dramatically and, over the course of several decades, killed off virtually all the birds on the island, wiping out three species in the process.

By the end of 1982, Phoebe had seen almost 3,400 of the 9,000 extant birds. Since the beginning of the year, she'd moved up from forty-second to twenty-second place in the *Birding* rankings. She started talking about trying to get to 4,500 or even 5,000, milestones no woman had achieved.

She no longer wrote poetry. She'd used her poems to vent her unhappiness and try to figure out a path; now that she had one, she had only to follow it.

She sent a Christmas card to her childhood friend Peggy Beman, with whom she'd been in touch on and off since getting her prognosis. "Still thriving," the card began. "It has been an astonishing, wonderful year." She told Peggy about each of the trips she'd taken, though she left out Joe's death. "Glorious—really love doing this, & have made such good friends."

A couple of months earlier, Sue had left for college, at the University of Richmond. Phoebe told Peggy it was "grand" to have the kids leading independent lives, but that she'd be glad to see them over Christmas vacation.

"I really appreciate your good thoughts & communications," she wrote in the card. "No further sign of the cancer, so I'm continuing to make travel plans. I know the balloon will burst some day in the next few years, but meanwhile life is *so good*. I'm really as happy as I've ever been."

Chapter 5

O VER THE NEXT year or so, Phoebe got into a rhythm. She'd study for a trip for a few months, take it, update her index card file, and spend a few months studying for her next trip. "Occasionally I thought about all these incredible experiences I'd have missed if my melanoma had behaved according to prediction—which of course motivated me all the more to keep moving," she wrote in her memoir. "I think I began about this time to feel that maybe I was out-running the disease. Somehow I developed a feeling of virtual invincibility once I was on the plane and heading toward new places and birds; I was leaving the threat behind. At any rate, something was working for me, and I was thriving on my new lifestyle of accelerated travel." Once you've done a fair amount of birding around the world, you stop seeing three or four hundred life birds on each trip, but on each of the trips Phoebe took in 1983—to Brazil, Senegal, Malaysia, and Costa Rica—she saw about a hundred new birds, which brought her life list up to four thousand by year's end and her ranking to four-teenth place.

She was taking more detailed field notes than she had in the past. Until this point, she'd generally just noted the name of each bird she saw and one or two of its prominent features, but now she was keeping the sort of field notebooks a scientist would. She'd say whether a bird was a male or a female; what race it belonged to, if any; what sort of habitat she'd found it in; what it was doing; what it looked like from head to tail; whether it made any sounds; and whether there were any differences between the information in the field guide and her own observations. She learned and used the technical terms that describe the various parts of a bird, such as "superciliary" (the region above the eye), "auricular patch" (the region below the eye), and "tarsus" (the part of the leg just above the foot). She still studied for trips mainly by reading field guides and treatises, but she started listening to cassettes of bird vocalizations and subscribing to ornithological journals as well.

She was figuring out some tricks for making her way through the wilderness. When she was in a rain forest, she carried a small pair of pruning shears, because "it's often nice to be able to snip off a bit of vegetation that's impeding your progress or view." When it rained, she tucked the handle of her umbrella into her bra so both hands would be free for her binoculars. When she had to cross a stream, she put on rainpants over her boots and tied a piece of string tightly around each calf, below the top of the boot. "If you walk across fairly quickly, you can wade in water up to your thighs without getting wet." She wore a vest with big pockets for storing chocolate bars, bug spray, and pencils, and she made a strap for her telescope and tripod so she could carry them over her shoulder.

She wasn't easily rattled. In the mountains of Costa Rica, she was in a major earthquake. She and her group had just gone to bed when the floor of their cabin started heaving, and they staggered outside as fast as they could. The quake soon stopped, but they decided to stay outside for a while as a precaution. Supposedly, Phoebe said to her companions, "Well, we're up. We might as well go look for owls."

She spent as little money as possible. She always asked for a roommate to avoid paying for a single room, and she did her own laundry, in the sinks or tubs of her hotel rooms. Instead of buying souvenirs, she brought home stamps, coins, newspaper clippings, and other pieces of free or inexpensive memorabilia.

On every trip, she made new friends, and she saw some of the same people time after time. The guides were mostly men and mostly a decade or two younger than she; many of them, like Burt Monroe, Robert Ridgely, and Ted Parker, split their time between leading tours and doing academic research. They were invariably impressed and charmed by Phoebe, and vice versa. One guide from this time wrote to her afterward, "Your knowledge of bird distribution amazed me. It was the first time I'd ever been on a trip where I felt a participant knew more than I did and I found it embarrassing . . . You are my idea of the perfect tour participant and should we be on a trip again at some point I would be absolutely delighted." It's possible that Phoebe had crushes on some of these men, but, more likely, she was reproducing the close and innocent relationship she'd had as a girl with her brother Joe. She admired her guides, learned from them, and happily followed them around in the woods in search of adventure.

To be a regular customer on bird tours, you had to have time and money, and a bunch of the regulars had made it big as entrepreneurs. Norm Chesterfield, a Canadian, was a mink rancher; Michael Lambarth, a Brit, owned a company that sold x-ray machines to hospitals; Pete Winter, of Missouri, had a company that mined sand and gravel and mixed concrete. As a kid, Pete had been a hunter, but he switched to birdwatching after serving in World War II because he could no longer stand to kill things, he says. Many other people who took tours regularly were doctors, professors, retirees, and housewives. Most were white, and most were from the United States, Britain, or Canada, three of the countries where birdwatching is most popular. (It's also big in Australia, South Africa, and northern Europe, among other places.) While some people traveled with their spouses, including Michael Lambarth, whose life list only included species that both he and his wife had seen, the tours focused on birds so exclusively—and intensely—that most non-birding spouses stayed home. As a result, some marriages got into trouble, though perhaps—as in Phoebe's case—these relationships hadn't been in great shape in the first place. "It's hard to sustain a relationship when you're on the road," says John Rowlett, the guide, whose first marriage ended when he was still young. "You almost have to marry someone on the inside." There were generally a few more men than women on each tour, in part because women birders tended to avoid traveling until their children were grown or nearly so, while a fair number of men left their young kids with their wives.

The closest friend Phoebe made during this time was Doris Brann, who was in her sixties, had grown children, and had recently moved with her husband from upstate New York to Florida. Like Joe Wright, Doris had a background much like Phoebe's. As a girl, she'd wanted to be an entomologist, and after college she began the graduate program in entomology at Cornell, where she met her future husband, James, another graduate student in the department. After they married, Jimmie finished his dissertation and was hired as a Cornell professor; Doris dropped out of school to raise their kids and, eventually, took up birding with some other faculty wives.

As far as Doris was concerned, Phoebe was "almost perfect": upbeat, energetic, knowledgeable, and kind. "Phoebe was such an inspiration to me," Doris says. She and a lot of Phoebe's other traveling friends say they were struck not just by how well prepared she was for each trip, but by the joy she took in helping the rest of the group, much as she'd helped her friends in the Webster Groves

Nature Study Society. She was often the only person besides the leader carrying a telescope, and she'd always share it with everyone else. She kept track of which birds her friends were hoping to see, even if she'd already seen them herself, and "if you saw a bird you were thrilled about, she'd slap your shoulder," one friend says.

She usually told people she had cancer, but she didn't talk much about it, except to make the occasional joke. A man who was in Malaysia with her remembers that at one point, a huge truck rumbled by the group, spewing toxic exhaust in their faces. Most people tried not to breathe until the truck had passed, but Phoebe said, "I don't have to hold my breath. I've already got cancer." She didn't talk much about her background or her family, either. Mostly, she just talked about birds.

By this time, it had occurred to her that she might not be so different from her father. Around the time she got back from Costa Rica, the *St. Louis Post-Dispatch* ran a profile on her under the headline, "For Her, Birding Is a World-Class Hobby." She told the paper, "You can do it on a local level, or you can go crazy about it like I did. I'm as crazy about this as my father was about advertising."

She also said that she had cancer, "so I'm going to grab these fleeting moments while I can."

In December 1983, as Phoebe was getting ready for a tour of India, Bill Rudden, the friend who says he experienced "platonic love" with her, called to say he'd seen a strange-looking gull by the Mississippi River. He knew how to identify all the gulls that came through St. Louis, but this one, for some reason, had stumped him. Over the next ten days or so, Phoebe drove up and down the Mississippi looking for the bird, to no avail. Bill described it to her as best he could, though, and she suspected it might be a Slaty-backed Gull, which generally migrates between Siberia and Alaska and had never before been seen in the continental United States.

Finally, Bill and Phoebe found the "mystery bird" floating inconspicuously on an ice patch with a bunch of common gulls. At first, it was hard for them to see all its features, but then "the dramatic climax came," according to Phoebe's memoir: "the bird held both wings aloft and stationary for several glorious seconds," revealing some black and white markings that meant it had to be a Slaty-backed Gull. "Our wildest speculation had indeed been true."

She and Bill set the WGNSS telephone tree in motion. At first, their diagnosis was met with some skepticism, but because of Phoebe's reputation, people suspended their disbelief, and as word of the sighting spread, thousands of birders from all over the country converged on St. Louis. The editor of *American Birds*, an ornithological journal, came to verify the identification and had Phoebe and Bill start working on a paper for him. *Nature Notes* called the gull "the best bird ever seen in St. Louis and the entire state"; the *St. Louis Post-Dispatch* ran a front-page story calling it a "once-in-a-century sighting." In early January, the *New York Times* ran a short piece on the bird and the hullabaloo it inspired under the headline, "Rare Gull From Soviet Pacific Is Sighted Near St. Louis." The article noted that Bill had been the first to spot the gull, but it credited Phoebe with the identification.

In *Nature Notes*, Phoebe said the gull was "the local bird of a lifetime." In her memoir, she described the experience as "one of those satisfying triumphs that only birders can fully appreciate." She'd had fun chasing the gull and figuring out what it was, but the recognition she got must have been equally exciting, and it probably made her want to get more.

I've never done acid, but I imagine that when you do, you see things like the birds-of-paradise. The males in this family, which live up and down the mountains of the South Pacific island of

New Guinea, have psychedelic trimmings on their crow-like bodies that they use to persuade females to mate with them: some have tail feathers that look like streamers, ribbons, strips of gauze, or wires; some have "head wires" that look like antennae or vines; some have bits of bright, bare skin around their eyes or atop their heads; some have feathers on their bellies that they can puff up at will, turning them into shields or aprons. When male birds-of-paradise are looking for mates, they try to highlight their trimmings by standing on tiptoe, kicking, quivering, swaying, and contorting themselves into improbable shapes. They're among nature's most flamboyant and bizarre creations, and birders covet them like holy grails.

In addition to providing habitat for the birds-of-paradise, New Guinea's tall, thickly forested mountains have divided the island's people into a thousand tribes that speak 750 languages, some of them as different as English and Chinese, and made it harder for

Red Bird-of-paradise

modernity to infiltrate their cultures. Until a few decades ago, few people had gone farther than a day's walk from their village, used cash or electricity, attended school, or seen a white person. The men wore only loincloths, penis gourds, or "arse-grass"; the women wore thatch skirts and nothing on top. When a man wanted to get married, he purchased his bride with pigs and bird-of-paradise plumes. When two tribes had an argument, it was settled with arrows and spears, and warriors sometimes celebrated their victories by eating the corpses of the enemy.

In the summer of 1984, when tribal ways still endured in all but the bigger towns and cities (though most if not all tribes had stopped practicing cannibalism), Phoebe took a tour of Papua New Guinea, the eastern half of the island, mainly to see some of the birds-of-paradise. One day, her group was driving in the mountains when they saw what looked like massive clouds of dust in the distance. As they got closer, they realized that the clouds were made of smoke, not dust, and that the grass they were rising from was on fire. The guide, Bret Whitney, who had led a tour of the country without incident two years earlier, got out of the van, looked through his binoculars, and, much to his surprise, saw hundreds of men wearing headdresses and war paint, many holding spears twice their height. A few seconds later, the men screamed, charged down a hill, and disappeared, as Bret recalls. The smoke and fire made it impossible to see where they'd gone, but he didn't think they were heading toward the road, and he got back in the van and kept driving.

But in a moment, as they were coming around a curve, they found themselves about thirty feet from a tribal war. The road was the dividing line between the two tribes, with rocks, arrows, and spears flying in both directions. "It looked like a Hollywood movie," a man who was in the van says. "It was unreal." Two Papuan men in Western clothes were also stranded behind the fighting, and they said the battle was being fought because someone from one tribe had recently killed someone from the other. The men assured Bret that no one would hurt them and said the trouble was bound to end soon.

Not wanting to take any chances, Bret barked at the group to tuck their heads between their knees, below window level, and be quiet and still. Stupidly, one man disobeyed and started taking pictures. As soon as he raised his camera, two tribesmen who were standing nearby let out a livid shriek, raised their spears above their shoulders, and charged the van. Inside, everyone screamed. Bret hit the gas. The van was just starting to screech forward when the men thrust their spears into its side, an inch or two below the windows. "It sounded like the van was being pummeled with a baseball bat," Bret says. If it hadn't already been in motion, the men probably wouldn't have missed.

In a second, the van was a safe distance from the two livid men but right in the middle of the battle. Rocks and spears pounded it on both sides. "We were horrified, but we just kept going," Bret says. In a minute or so, they were out of danger, but he "didn't slow down for a hell of a long time."

Phoebe might have been scared in the moment, but she wasn't upset afterward, friends say, just as she hadn't been upset after the earthquake. In her memoir, she called the incident "an interesting cultural sidelight," as if it had been a night at the opera. She also wrote, "I'm not sure how the dents and scrapes in the side of the van caused by the spears were explained to the rental agency—but that's one of the advantages of being part of a tour: it wasn't our problem."

The trip, she wrote, was "simply magnificent." She saw about twenty of the birds-of-paradise, which she said were "extraordinary," and two hundred other life birds. "It was as *different* a part of the world as I'd ever been to, and I could see that one visit, however great it was, would not be nearly enough."

At this point, Phoebe was spending about four months out of every year on the road, and Dave says that even when she was home, she seemed far away. While none of her writings indicate how she felt about her marriage at this point, it appears that she'd pretty much given up on it, and that she was putting the passion that a lot of people put into their marriages into birding and her friendships with other birders. If she had originally fallen for Dave because he was so different from her father, she might have pulled away from him for the same reason: He wasn't formidable, worldly, or daring, as Leo had been—and as she was becoming. Dave, for his part, was genuinely glad that Phoebe was having a great time, especially since she was supposed to get sick soon; on the other hand, he wanted to matter to her far more than he evidently did, and he wished she could be happy, as he was, with their life in Webster Groves.

In the meantime, he was rising even higher at Purina, which must have been a welcome distraction. In the early 1980s, he was put in charge of the entire poultry feed division. Though a lot of other divisions at the company had one head of research and one head of marketing, Dave happily took on both jobs for poultry. He also got involved with some professional societies: For a while, he was president of the Poultry Science Association, and he worked with some meat and dairy researchers to found an umbrella group, the Federation of Food Animal Scientists. In our conversations, it was clear that Dave took a lot of pride in his success, though he insisted, humbly, that it came about through hard work, not intelligence.

The kids say this was a confusing time for them. They were

trying to forge their own lives, but they wanted to be available if their mother needed them. "I always felt a sense of impending doom," Tom says. When he finished college, he applied to the Peace Corps and agreed to a posting in Ecuador, where he'd be building water and sewer systems, but he was nervous about the prospect of being so far from home. (His father didn't approve of his Peace Corps plan, but for a different reason. "He wanted me to get a stable footing in a real-world sense," Tom says. "He wanted me to be financially stable.")

Tom lived at home for a few months in the fall of 1984, while he was waiting to do his training, and one day he was looking for some stamps in his mother's desk when he found the suicide note she'd written a few years earlier. It mentioned the gun, which he found in her closet. He was aghast, especially since he was about to leave the country for two years. "I was worried I wouldn't see her again . . . that she would get sick and I wouldn't get to see her." He didn't feel comfortable bringing the subject up face to face, but when he got to Ecuador he wrote her a letter begging her not to kill herself until he'd had a chance to come home and say goodbye. She wrote him back and said she "wouldn't rush into anything," he says, but, strikingly, she stopped short of promising to wait for him. Having put her children first for so many years, she apparently felt that during these final days, she had a right to be purely selfish.

Early in 1985, Phoebe got asked to join a "strictly invitational" tour of Indonesia that was being run in the summer by Ben King, the intrepid and at times authoritarian guide she'd had in the Himalayas. He wasn't advertising the tour to the general public because it would be "rugged and primitive," involving tough hikes, camping, "grubby" hotels, "hot and sticky weather," and "basic" food, according to a mailing he sent out. However, it would be "the most extensive and comprehensive birding tour ever offered" to Indonesia, with visits to five islands over the course of seven weeks, and the group would probably get to see Wallace's Standardwing, a bird-of-paradise that had been presumed extinct for decades but had recently been rediscovered by a Brit named David Bishop, who would be Ben's co-leader.

Phoebe must have considered Ben's invitation, which she accepted right away, a big honor: she was newer to the world birding scene than most of the other people who made the cut, and there was only one other woman. She was concerned, though, that she was taking on too much for the year. In a letter to Doris that she wrote in March, as she was getting ready for a tour of Mexico, she said that a friend had tried to get her to sign up for a trip in December, "but it's really crowding too much into this year & I just couldn't do it. I'm really pushing it as it is on time, energy & money, with Indonesia in the summer (7 weeks) & S. Africa in the fall." At this point, she was just a few birds shy of 4,500, and she'd decided that five thousand would be her final goal. "I'm looking forward to 'retirement' after 5000—& leisurely birding!" she told Doris.

The first week of the Indonesia tour was taken up with getting to Halmahera, the island where Wallace's Standardwing lives, a journey that involved several flights, some long drives, a few crummy hotels, and a boat ride. Once on Halmahera, they drove for a few hours along a logging road, hiked for two more hours, and, in the end, saw a whole group of male Standardwings showing off for some females. The bird, which was first described by the British naturalist Alfred Russel Wallace, got the second half of its name because the males have long white plumes, or "standards," that hang off their wings like ribbons. When a male wants to attract a female, it perches in a treetop, flies out in front of it, raises its standards above its head as if they're parachute strings, twirls them around, and lets itself fall slowly to the ground. When it lands, it flies back up to the same perch in the same tree, hangs upside down for a while, and parachutes back to the ground. In *Nature Notes*, Phoebe called this spectacle "one of the most exciting and dramatic avian displays I've ever had the privilege of watching."

The trip was demanding, as Ben had said it would be. Most days, the group got up at three in the morning to look for owls; stopped for a quick breakfast after dawn; and birded on hot, buggy, and sometimes steep trails all day. On one tough hike, a man slipped, fell, and seriously injured a rib, though he was able to continue with the trip. The group spent a lot of nights in thatched huts with leaky roofs and often woke up soaking wet and covered with mosquito bites.

Everyone was taking chloroquine pills, which generally prevent malaria. But on Sulawesi, the second island they visited, Martin Edwards, a physics professor from Ontario, came down with a fever and the chills. By the time they got to Bali a couple of days later, his temperature had risen to 103 degrees, and Ben, who still felt terrible about what had happened to Joe Wright on his watch, took him to a hospital. He was diagnosed with a mild form of malaria and given the treatment for it, but his fever only worsened, rising to a dangerous 105 degrees. Ben, horrified, thought he'd been misdiagnosed, and that he actually had the deadly *Plasmodium falciparum* strain of malaria. Though there was a drug for it, Fansidar, the doctors didn't give it to him; it can have serious side effects, and, moreover, they seemed invested in the idea that *Plasmodium falciparum* didn't occur in the region. So Ben and Martin took matters into their own hands: fortunately, Ben had told everyone to bring some Fansidar along just in case, and when the doctors weren't looking, Martin took his. A day or so later, he started to get better, and within a few days he was well enough to rejoin the tour.

As Martin recovered, Phoebe wrote her family a letter in which she showed no signs of being rattled by the close call and seemed to take pride in how well she was faring. "The first section of the trip is over & I survived it nicely." She said they'd been staying in "primitive" huts, surviving on "relatively edible" food, and getting little sleep, and that while one man had probably broken a rib and another had gotten malaria, she'd been "very healthy so far." She hadn't really been suffering, she said, because the birds had been "spectacular" and her companions were "very good birders & most congenial—me & 7 men." (The other woman hadn't joined the trip yet.) The Standardwings had been "marvelous," and the group had found "numerous other species seen by few if any other ornithologists." She described David Bishop, who'd spent most of the previous decade birding in the South Pacific, as "a very engaging fellow & marvelously competent." "All in all some really exciting birding."

It wasn't just Phoebe and the people she traveled with: all around the world, birders were getting into trouble, sometimes because of bad luck, sometimes because of bad judgment, and sometimes because of a combination of the two. Jared Diamond, the scientist and writer, spent much of the 1970s and '80s doing ornithological research in New Guinea. Once, in 1981, he flew into an airport on a small patch of land ten miles off the coast; to reach mainland New Guinea from the airport, you had to take a boat. When he got off the plane, he followed some people from the terminal to a dock, where he saw "a row of long dugout canoes with big outboard motors, flimsy awnings, and pushy young men each trying to hustle newly arrived passengers into his canoe," he wrote later.

The sea was choppy, but Diamond's "cocky" driver went fast anyway, and about halfway to New Guinea, the boat overturned. Two crewmen swam off with the only life jackets. The rest of the group, clinging to the hull, waved and shouted at boats in the distance. Finally, just before dark, they were spotted by two fishermen, each in a small boat. The men agreed to split the group up and take them to shore. The boat Diamond got into was just setting out when he heard screams; the other boat had capsized, probably because it was overloaded. By this time, it was dark. The boat's passengers were never found.

Later, Diamond told this story to a colleague, who said he'd recently flown into the same airport, but that he'd taken one look at the canoes, decided they were unsafe, and looked into other options. He'd ended up in a slow, safe tugboat. "I realized that I hadn't been a powerless victim of that idiotic boatman," Diamond wrote. "There was something simple I could have done to avoid the accident: not get into that canoe."

In 1983, several young British men went trekking in Nepal to look for pheasants. They most wanted to see the Satyr Tragopan, a red bird with white polka dots that lives at about twelve thousand feet above sea level. One afternoon, they were setting up camp in a shepherd's hut when they heard the tragopan calling. They'd been climbing a steep trail all day, and most of them wanted to rest, but one man, Alan Adams, couldn't resist. He went out, alone, into the near-darkness, and no one ever saw him again. In all likelihood, he fell off a cliff.

In the winter of 1985, a British birder named David Hunt led a tour around India. One of the stops was a national park with a big tiger population; to keep safe from the tigers, you get an armed guard, and you're forbidden to walk off the trails. At one point, though, Hunt saw or heard an interesting bird in the thicket and couldn't resist the impulse to try to find it. He told his group to wait for him on the trail. A few minutes later, they heard a godawful scream, and by the time the guard found him, it was too late: he'd been mauled to death by a tiger. When the film in Hunt's camera was developed, it turned out that he'd taken several shots of the tiger with his telephoto lens. In each shot, the tiger is closer, and the final frame is filled with its snarling face.

There's an inherent risk to traveling in remote places, but Diamond, Adams, and Hunt all compounded this risk by exercising poor judgment, perhaps because they were too focused on getting their birds or perhaps because they were trying to be macho—the two main reasons that birders in general make unsafe choices, in my opinion. Of course, Phoebe had a third reason to give danger less than its due: she didn't expect to live much longer anyway, and in any event, part of her probably wanted to die on a trip, quickly and painlessly, as Joe had.

In October 1985, upon her return from a tour of South Africa, Phoebe wrote to Doris that she was "still plugging away toward 5000" and that she thought she'd get there on her next trip, to the Philippines. After that, she wrote, "I'm really planning to relax & take it a lot more casually . . . My health seems fine & I'm beginning to think I'm going to live long enough to get old & decrepit!" A couple of weeks later, however, in November, she found another lump in her right armpit, "and of course I knew immediately what it was," her memoir says. "I went into the hospital feeling very pessimistic but at least grateful for all I'd done since the last time."

The lump was removed and tested, and she learned that the melanoma had again recurred in her lymph nodes. While she was waiting to hear whether it had spread to her organs too, she wrote another letter to Doris. She started out by mentioning that the start date of a cruise they were both planning to take to Antarctica in a year had been changed slightly. "This isn't a problem for me & I hope it's not for you." But, she wrote, "I seem to have a potentially more serious problem." She told Doris about the lump and said she'd soon hear if there had been further metastasis. "I'm feeling fine & there's no reason not to go on planning trips, Antarctica as well as others—but it does make the future seem somewhat less certain. I still plan to send in a deposit in Jan., since it's my top priority for next winter . . . I'd obviously let you know as soon as possible if I had to change plans."

Soon, she got the results of her organ scans. "All came back negative, once again!" she wrote in her memoir. "I couldn't believe my incredible good fortune." It didn't bode well that the cancer had resurfaced, though, and her doctors still thought she wouldn't live long. Since 1981, when she'd been given her prognosis, several studies had shown that a drug called interferon might prolong the lives of some melanoma patients by a few months; her doctors must have told her that, and also about interferon's side effects, which include fever, chills, fatigue, and nausea. She likely didn't even consider it.

She didn't dwell too much on the recurrence. She wrote in her memoir: "From the previous trauma, I had learned to deal emotionally with the threat to my life. Yes, the threat had been renewed. There was certainly a resurgence of many by now familiar thoughts and feelings, but thanks to experience, I wasn't nearly so consumed by it all this time around."

Her trip to the Philippines almost got canceled because it happened to coincide with the downfall of Ferdinand Marcos, the country's longtime dictator. Under pressure from the United States, Marcos was allowing a rival to run against him for president, and the election, which some thought would bring about violence, was scheduled for February 7, 1986, one day before Phoebe's group was due to get there. But by the end of January, only a little fighting had broken out, and Ben King, who was running the tour, decided it would be safe to go. On January 31, Phoebe wrote to Doris, "I'm a little nervous about the potentially explosive political situation at election time, but willing to chance it for the birds. If I get through this one OK, I think I'll try to stay away from trouble spots for a while. With S. Africa & Philippines I may be pushing my luck."

As it happened, the election hardly affected the tour. For the first few weeks of the trip, the votes were being counted, so neither side had reason to protest. When Marcos was declared the victor, supporters of his opponent, Corazon Aquino, accused him of fraud and took to the streets, but peacefully. At the end of February, Marcos was forced into exile and Aquino took power. "The people were very friendly & helpful, seemed happy to be rid of Marcos & optimistic about the future," Phoebe wrote to Doris. "I think they can be proud of what they've done." She saved the newspaper from February 26, with the headlines "Marcos Flees Country" and "Aquino Sworn In As President."

Most of the time, her group was on small, remote islands far from the action. According to her memoir, the "biggest and best" bird of the trip was the Philippine Eagle, which is almost as big as the Harpy Eagle and had nearly gone extinct in the 1960s because the mountain forests it lived in were being logged. In the 1970s, conservationists started working to save the bird, and by the early 1980s its population had rebounded to about three hundred. It had always been known as the Monkey-eating Eagle, but in 1978 Marcos renamed it the Great Philippine Eagle because he thought it would make a good national symbol.

Some researchers gave the group directions to a nest, which they found after "an arduous climb up to a knife-edge ridgetop," and inside, there was a fuzzy white eaglet. They were just getting their scopes focused on the chick when its mother, clutching a monkey in its long, sharp talons, "glided right past us like a 747, almost at eye level, giving us an awesome, heart-stopping view." They watched as the bird tore the monkey into bite-sized chunks and fed them, one by one, to the eaglet. "The total experience was so much beyond what we'd dared dream of; we were all simply stunned."

Her five-thousandth life bird ended up being the Philippine Bullfinch, a little brown bird with white cheeks that also lives in mountain forests. Someone else saw it first, and when he pointed it out to her, she was so excited that she kissed him on the cheek, startling him. At dinner that night, the group celebrated her triumph with a cake. "There was a handful of men ahead of me at this point, and I knew most of them," her memoir says. "A couple of them had even passed 6,000, which seemed impossibly far off to me. I was certainly very pleased to be the first woman to 5,000, and considering my very real health threat, I wasn't seriously thinking much beyond that mark."

After the trip, she got another fan letter, one that surely meant a lot to her. Ben, one of the most accomplished and respected field ornithologists in the world, wrote to her, "Sure enjoyed your company in Philippines. You are my favorite person to be with in the field."

By this time, Marmot had graduated from college and was working as a mountaineering instructor for the National Outdoor Leadership School in Wyoming, and during her vacations she climbed mountains with friends. She'd immersed herself in a culture that was a lot like the culture of birding: just as birders try to see as many species as possible and put a premium on the ones that are rare or hard to find, climbers try to summit as many mountains as possible and value most the ones that are tall and technically challenging. In the spring of 1986, around the time Phoebe saw her five-thousandth life bird, Marmot climbed Mount Aconcagua in Argentina, which, at twenty-three thousand feet, is the highest mountain in the Western hemisphere.

Marmot says that once climbing became the focus of her life, she started feeling close to her mother again. "We had a lot more to connect on. I could understand her passion." They talked about which mountains they'd climbed, which birds they'd seen, and what their goals were for the future. Marmot worried that Phoebe would soon get sick, but she was proud of how she was living in the meantime. On a visit home in April 1986, when Phoebe was on a short trip to Hong Kong, Marmot decided to surprise her by plastering Webster Groves with signs saying "Phoebe Is Over 5,000!" and putting a sign on her car that said, in big block letters, "This Is Phoebe."

In June, *Nature Notes* also heralded Phoebe's milestone. "Never mind that a president was being turned out of office; Phoebe was seeing the Monkey-eating Eagle and some 120 other life birds. The 5000th was a Philippine Bullfinch, not as glamorous as the eagle feeding a monkey to its single nestling, but in the birding game numbers can be as important as glamour. 5000 means well over half of the approximately 9000 species world-wide, and it also means that Phoebe heads the list of all women birders."

She didn't take any trips during the summer of 1986, but she spent a lot of time getting ready for a big one that was coming up in the fall. She and two of her friends from the Indonesia tour, Jim Clements and Arnold Small, had been so impressed with David Bishop that they'd asked him to run a special trip for them to some remote islands in the South Pacific. They'd be seeing hundreds of birds on eight different islands, but they were most interested in the Kagu, which, like Wallace's Standardwing, had disappeared for decades and only recently been rediscovered. The Kagu, the only member of its family, is more funny-looking than beautiful, with a chicken-like white body and a red beak, red eyes, and red legs. Instead of singing, it yelps like a puppy. When it gets upset, it hisses.

Studying for the trip was a "supreme" challenge, Phoebe wrote in her memoir, "with little-known, poorly described and largely un-illustrated birds scattered over the several seldom-birded island groups we planned to visit."

She also spent a lot of time that summer making notes for a friend who wanted to write a magazine article about her. (As far as I know, the article was never published.) She must have liked the idea of having her story told, because she ended up with ten typed pages, single-spaced, and the notes reveal a great deal about her interior life at the time.

She began by describing how she got into birding; the early, occasional trips she took abroad; and the prognosis she was given in 1981. "In retrospect, this death sentence now seems a blessing in disguise (admittedly a *heavy* disguise). It forced me to make some quick decisions, to change my style and develop a 'now or never' approach, to establish my priorities and learn to live for the present moment. Foreign birding provided the perfect mental and physical therapy. I could live from one short-range goal to the next and concentrate fully on this totally absorbing passion."

"Fortune has been with me in many ways: My children at the time were in college or late high school, so I was not needed at home. I had enough inherited money to finance considerable travel as well as my children's education, and I had an understanding and tolerant husband who has accepted the importance of this compulsive approach to birding. And the greatest good fortune of all is that I've stayed healthy for 5 years except for a minor recurrence last winter."

She emphasized that even though she traveled with tour guides and enjoyed learning from them, "my game is trying to be competent in the field wherever I am and to be capable of making my own identifications . . . Even if the leader usually manages to make the identification first, I prefer to know *why* the bird I'm seeing is a Diard's Trogon instead of a Red-naped, or a Pygmy Kingfisher instead of a Malachite . . . If Ted Parker tells me he hears a Warbling Antbird, I want to be able to have an immediate mental image and know what field marks to look for." A lot of "discipline and drudgery" was involved in learning birds in advance, but "I find the payoff immensely satisfying and exciting: It's *fun* to be able to figure out what most birds are on your own."

Some of the trips she'd taken had been "tough," with "long steep" treks, "miserable" living conditions, "uncomfortable weather," "awful food," "little sleep," and long drives in bad cars on bad roads. However, she wrote, "some of the best bird trips I've ever been on had days of various combinations of these," and on most trips, "the compensations vastly outweigh the problems."

She felt "considerable triumph" that she'd reached five thousand, but she wasn't going to try for six thousand or any other number "because I want now to focus on quality and seek some high-priority species . . . [t]here are more than enough of these to last me the rest of my life, be it 1 year or 25." She also wanted to "fill in some gaps in families" (of the 182 bird families, she was missing eighteen) and in "some important avifaunal areas," such as Antarctica, Mexico, New Zealand, the Congo forest, and Madagascar, an island in the Indian Ocean with five endemic families. "So I will continue to take foreign bird trips, but at a somewhat slower pace. I've been averaging 4 per year for the last 5 years, and that means absolutely all my time at home is spent in completing records from the last trip and studying for the coming one."

"If I reach the point where I am unable to travel (for health or financial reasons) but still have time and energy, I'd at least like to learn about the 4000 species I haven't seen. Many of these of course I do know something about—they're the ones I studied but didn't see on the trips I've done. Most of these I never will see, but the names at least evoke an image."

She ended her notes with a section on "dangers and fears." She wrote, "I've been lucky enough not to have been caught in any truly dangerous situations abroad," but then she went on to list some: "hair-raising roads" in the Himalayas, the earthquake in Costa Rica, "some potentially risky walks" in tiger country, Martin's malaria, and Joe's death. She left out the tribal war in New Guinea. "Reading the newspapers could make one reluctant to go anywhere," but she was glad it hadn't deterred her from the Philippines. While she had "no big urge" to go to the Middle East, she'd "probably go to Sri Lanka or Colombia given a suitable opportunity, though admittedly with a few misgivings."

The prospect of dying on a trip didn't bother her. "I'm pretty fatalistic about external events such as air crashes, terrorism, revolutions, etc., and just hope the personal disaster occurs after I've seen the birds rather than before," she wrote. "I don't go out of my way to court danger, but on the other hand, if you're looking for safety and security, there really isn't any—anywhere."

Chapter 6

IN THE MIDDLE of the summer, both of her friends dropped
out of the South Pacific trip—Arnold because he'd had a heart attack and Jim because he'd broken his hip. (Both men were a little
older than Phoebe.) She thought about canceling or shortening the
trip, since without them she'd be responsible for David's whole salary
and all his expenses, but in the end she decided to go forward with it.
"In addition to *wanting* to do the trip as planned, I feel a certain obligation to you," she wrote to David. "We've had you committed to
this five weeks for about a year, and it would be grossly unfair to you
for us all to pull out without significant compensation." She'd also
rationalized the increased cost "as payment for the advantages of a
truly private trip and probably a better chance at a Kagu with just
you and me." The letter ended, "Sure hope *my* health (and yours)
holds out, what with Jim and Arnold falling by the wayside!"

On their first full day of birding in Fiji, someone almost broke
into their rental car. They'd been in some woods near the capital, a
city with a serious crime problem, and as they were walking back
to the car, David saw a man crouched in a ditch with a rock, poised
to smash one of the windows. To startle him, David, who had once

been a policeman in London, said hello politely, whereupon he and Phoebe rushed into the car and "took off like a shot," according to some notes Phoebe made when she got home.

Nevertheless, the birding in Fiji was "very exciting and largely successful," she wrote in her memoir; in a week, she saw about fifty life birds, which she described in her notebook with phrases like "strikingly beautiful" and "brilliantly colorful." At their next stop, the small island of Upolu, part of Samoa, she got another dozen lifers, including the Tooth-billed Pigeon, a chunky bird with a big, hooked bill like a parrot's, except that the lower mandible has two sharp "teeth" that are used to saw through the casings of seeds. She also happened upon the grave of the writer and adventurer Robert Louis Stevenson, who had died of a cerebral hemorrhage in Samoa at the age of forty-four. Stevenson had written his own epitaph, and it resonated with Phoebe so deeply that she later included it in her memoir. It's about living life intensely, and without fear of death:

> *Under the wide and starry sky,*
> *Dig the grave and let me lie.*
> *Glad did I live and gladly die,*
> *And I laid me down with a will.*
>
> *This be the verse you grave for me:*
> *"Here he lies where he longed to be;*
> *Home is the sailor, home from the sea,*
> *And the hunter home from the hill."*

They flew to New Caledonia next, to look for the Kagu. They didn't think their chances were good. Wallace's Standardwing had "disappeared" mainly because no one knew where to look for it, but the problem with the Kagu was that there were hardly any left. Originally, New Caledonia hadn't had any big predators, and the

Kagu, which is flightless, caught insects and built nests on the forest floor. In the 1850s, however, the French colonized the island, and along came dogs, as pets, and rats, as stowaways. The rats made a feast of Kagu eggs; the dogs ate the birds themselves, which, having never been preyed upon, couldn't defend themselves. By the 1970s, no one had seen a Kagu in years, though its yelp was sometimes heard from a distance and was used as the signoff signal on the local radio station.

In the mid-1970s, an enterprising park ranger named Yves Létocart decided to try to save the Kagu by setting rattraps and shooting wild dogs in his park, Rivière Bleue. Soon, he started seeing a Kagu or two occasionally, usually deep in the forest in the middle of the night. Kagus weren't originally nocturnal, but they had apparently become so to avoid dogs. Within a year or two, Létocart was seeing Kagus more often, and by 1986 it was looking like the species might survive. Hardly anyone besides Létocart had seen a Kagu, though. A number of birders and ornithologists had come to Rivière Bleue, but most had left empty-handed; Létocart himself sometimes went weeks without a sighting. So it was "preposterous," as Phoebe wrote in her memoir, that she and David saw not one but two Kagus, and on their first night in the park, after walking just a short distance down a trail. They got within ten feet of the birds—"superb binoc view," she wrote in her notebook—and watched them with a flashlight for "an indelible few moments of magic."

"*Saw* a Kagu in the forest!" Phoebe wrote to her family, on a postcard of a Kagu. "Remarkable good fortune & extraordinary circumstances. Probably the #1 most-wanted world bird by [international] birders, seen so far by only 2 or 3. Big triumph. Healthy, happy & seeing lots of great birds & scenery." She called Létocart "truly remarkable," and before she and David left, she gave him a donation to help him upgrade his taping equipment.

They made a few quick stops over the next couple of weeks and

Kagu

ended up on the tiny island of West New Britain, part of Papua New Guinea, which consists largely of rain forest and, at the time, didn't get many visitors. But David had managed to find them a hotel, and its manager lent them his big blue truck. In a forest a short drive away, they saw some Melanesian Scrubfowl, chicken-like birds that lay eggs in big mounds of soil rather than nests. The soil warms the eggs, making incubation unnecessary. According to Phoebe's memoir, she and David got "great studies" of several scrubfowl near their mounds on three mornings in a row.

As they were returning to the truck at the end of the third morning, they came upon a big group of locals walking in the opposite direction, toward the mounds. Some of them were holding baskets, and it looked like they were collecting eggs for food, as was the custom. But for reasons Phoebe and David couldn't fathom, the group surrounded them and started rushing them angrily out of the forest, as if they were under arrest. At the trailhead, they saw an "alarming-looking" mob of fifty or so men surrounding the truck, looking agitated and waving machetes. "The situation had gone from worrying to frightening." In the pidgin of the region, David tried to explain what they'd been doing, and to illustrate, he pointed to some birds and had a few of the men look through his binoculars. After a while, the mob decided to let them go, though they insisted on following them as far as the nearest village. "We breathed a sigh of genuine relief when they let us go on from there alone."

But when they got to the next village, more men with machetes swarmed the road, and some of them hurled rocks at the car. David tried to distract them by asking what the problem was, "then gunned the motor & got us out & home safe," according to Phoebe's notes. The hotel manager was dumbfounded. Phoebe and David were supposed to fly to their last stop, Port Moresby, the capital of Papua New Guinea, the next morning, but they arranged to get on a flight that day instead. "We knew birding here was over, that anyone driving the blue truck could be killed."

At the West New Britain airport, a policeman found them, apologized, and explained what had happened: there had recently been a murder on the island, and an irresponsible radio announcer had speculated—on the air—that the white man and woman with the blue truck and the weird equipment were the killers.

"Hostile encounter w. villagers & exodus from W. New Br.," Phoebe wrote in her notebook that night.

There were many dangerous cities in the South Pacific in the mid-1980s, largely due to the severe poverty of the region, but Port

Moresby was likely the most dangerous of them all. It hadn't been that way for long. For most of its history, Port Moresby, which is on the southeastern coast of New Guinea and was founded in the 1870s by a British explorer, had been small and sleepy, inhabited mostly by the well-to-do white people—first Brits, then Australians—who claimed to rule over Papua New Guinea. In fact, the colonizers had little influence outside Port Moresby; most native Papuans lived far away, in the mountains, and, for all intents and purposes, answered only to their tribal chiefs, though the Australian administration did put limits on how many natives could move to the capital.

In the 1960s, as Australia prepared to cede power, these limits were lifted, and young native men began moving to Port Moresby, lured by rumors of jobs in government and business and opportunities at the new university. Thousands more young men came to the capital after Australia left—and independence was declared—in 1975. But there were two big problems: first, there weren't enough jobs or apartments in Port Moresby to absorb all these newcomers, and second, many of the men, having spent their lives in small villages with their families and tribes, had trouble adjusting to the unfamiliar environment. Most of the migrants ended up jobless and in slums. Some tried to move back to their villages, but were told they were no longer welcome.

The slums grew and bred gangs—many of them based loosely on ethnicity, as if they were tribes—that broke into cars, houses, and stores and held people up all over the city and its suburbs. Sometimes the gangs left their victims unharmed, but often they beat, raped, and killed them. Over time, the gangs took control of more and more of the city and got increasingly brazen, scaling the razor wire that protected wealthy enclaves and robbing shopping centers in broad daylight. In 1985, not long after a mother and daughter from New Zealand were gang-raped, the government declared a state of emergency. Roadblocks were set up, a curfew was imposed, slums were raided, and for a few months the crime rate went down—only to resurge as soon as the state of emergency was lifted. (Today, things are even worse in Port Moresby, as the gangs now have machine guns. The *Economist* recently ranked the city as the worst place in the world to live.)

Birders and other tourists use Port Moresby primarily for its airport, though there are a couple of popular birding spots not far away. On her first trip to Papua New Guinea, the one where her van got attacked in the mountains, Phoebe had spent two nights in the city without any trouble. This time around, she and David had just planned to pass through for a night as they awaited a flight to Sydney, where David lived and from which Phoebe would fly home. When they bailed on West New Britain one night early, however, they ended up with an extra night in Port Moresby.

As soon as they landed, David called someone from the Papua New Guinea Bird Club to find out if there had been any good sightings around town and if there were any particular places they should avoid. His friend mentioned one park where a woman had recently been robbed, and "we gave up any notion of going there," according to Phoebe's notes. Otherwise, David was told, "things seemed peaceful," her notes say.

In cities, waterfowl tend to congregate at sewage ponds, for lack of any other options. (The stench doesn't bother them, as birds have little sense of smell.) After settling into their hotel, Phoebe and David drove to some sewage ponds about twenty miles outside Port Moresby. The ponds were at the end of a dirt road, far from the nearest village, and unmanned. According to Phoebe's notes, "David said we shouldn't stay till dark. Moresby is much safer now than a year ago—police have really clamped down—but no sense taking a chance. Passed some friendly greetings to a couple of natives near the road on the road out."

The next morning, October 9, they drove to a national park in the foothills of some mountains, where, unexpectedly Phoebe picked up four lifers, bringing her total for the trip to 113. It was, she wrote, a "*great*" morning, but they were finished with the park by early afternoon, and she suggested they go back to the sewage ponds; this time, she thought, they could stay a little later and look for rails, which emerge at dusk. "We spent the afternoon happily enough," she wrote in her memoir, "but we'd run out of new birds, and none of the hoped-for rails appeared at dusk." At around six, as the sun was setting, they got back in their car.

They didn't get far; while they'd been birding, a log had been laid out across the access road to the ponds, and they knew right away that someone was trying to trap them. David started backing up, away from the barricade, but five angry-looking young men with rocks and machetes came charging at the car from behind. One of the men hurled a rock at the back window, smashing it into little pieces.

When the men had surrounded the car, David and Phoebe, hoping to appease them, rolled down their windows and handed them their watches, money, and binoculars. In a calm voice, David tried to convince the gang to let them go: they were on their way out of the country, he said, and they wouldn't make any trouble for them. But the men just got more agitated, screaming at him to give them the keys and at both of them to get out of the car. As David was opening his door, one man lunged at him and stabbed him in the stomach with his machete. It wasn't a deep cut, but it drew some blood.

Some of the men moved the log out of the way while the others shoved Phoebe and David into the very back of the car, a hatchback station wagon. They were practically on top of each other, with bits of glass pricking their arms and legs. The men got into the front and back seats and started driving, fast. It was "an unimaginably awful, terrorizingly rapid ride over rough dirt roads and around curves where we felt sure the driver would roll us over, all the while with clouds of dust and shards of broken glass swirling in," Phoebe wrote in her memoir. "I could hardly bring myself to realize that this was actually happening, that it wasn't either a nightmare or a movie."

David remembers saying to Phoebe, "You know what they're going to do to you, don't you?" and that she replied, "Of course I do." They agreed to continue to try to appease the men however possible; otherwise, they'd surely be killed, they thought.

"After what seemed an interminable time, the car stopped abruptly, and the men forced us out," Phoebe's memoir says. The moon was shining, and she could see that they were at the end of a deserted dirt track, near a lake. Two of the men grabbed David, dragged him around to one side of the car, pushed him down, propped his head against a tire, and held a machete to his throat. The other three guys took Phoebe to the other side of the car, pointed their machetes at her, and made her lie on the ground. Then they took turns raping her. They carried out the rapes methodically, she later said, as if they were fulfilling a perverse obligation. Afterward they switched places with the men who were guarding David so they could rape Phoebe too.

In her memoir, Phoebe said that while she was being raped, "I was afraid that David might over-react and get himself killed, and of course I was afraid that they might kill me. Somehow the actual rape seemed relatively insignificant by comparison." She later told Sue that she had thought of her for part of the time. Not long before, a creepy man had followed Sue when she was taking a hike, and though she'd gotten back to her car safely, she was shaken up and had called her parents. As she lay pinned to the ground, Phoebe thought about how awful it would have been if Sue had been raped, but she decided that since she was more mature, she could handle it.

When all five men had raped Phoebe, they let her get up and

put her clothes back on, and they had her and David sit in the front of the car while they talked, in pidgin, about what to do next. David could understand: they were saying that they could slit their throats, chop their bodies into pieces, and throw them into the lake for the crocodiles to eat. He didn't translate for Phoebe, but she knew that they were talking about killing them, and she thought it was going to be a "terrible, bloody business." It would be better, she thought, if the men had guns. In the meantime, a "cushion of shock" was keeping her from panicking, "and we were both behaving appropriately and not triggering their anger . . . somehow an amazing inner calmness and fatalism prevailed. They were in control, and there was simply nothing we could do, aside from pleading that they let us go."

Outside the car, a disagreement seemed to break out among the men. The conversation got "heated and confused" and then stopped abruptly. The man who appeared to be the ringleader poked his head in the car and said that they were going down to the lake to wash, but that they'd be right back and were leaving a guard. "We sat frozen for 10 min. or so—afraid to move for fear they were just waiting for a reason to attack us," Phoebe's notes say. "Then after 10–15 min. we leaned out—saw no one, heard nothing & figured since they hadn't left a guard, *maybe* they'd decided to let us get away. We were both convinced that if they returned we'd die—slowly and painfully."

Soon, the moon went behind some clouds, darkening the night, and they figured it was a good time to make a run for it. "We crept silently out of the car, kept low, and ran along the dirt track away from the water, which was where we'd last seen them," the memoir says. "We ran and walked and ran again, as fast and steadily as I physically could, leaving the track to dive into the grass and bush to hide whenever we thought we heard a sound behind us . . . We'd long since lost any sense of where we were, but we could see the lights of Port Moresby in the distance, and we headed generally in that direction." At one point, they stopped to rub their T-shirts in the dirt to make them blend in better with the darkness, "aware that at any point we could meet more of these thugs afoot."

An hour or two passed, and they started to think that maybe they weren't being chased. They figured that the men "knew it would be a long time before we could reach help, and that by then they'd be long gone and untraceable." They still felt "totally lost and vulnerable," though, and when they heard men's voices not far off the path, Phoebe panicked, thinking the gang had come to finish them off after all. David found a hiding place for her amid some trees and told her to wait while he investigated; if he didn't come back, she was to stay hidden until morning and then walk toward the city. "Risked his life, but figured there was a fair chance of help," her notes say. In a moment, she heard him talking to the men comfortably, with some women's voices mixed in, too. When she came out from behind the trees, the women put their arms around her and wailed in sympathy. "We were safe and unhurt, and at that point nothing else really mattered," she wrote in her memoir. In her notes, she was a little more forthright, saying she was "unhurt exc. emotionally."

Someone called the police, and they came quickly. With Phoebe and David in the back seat of a cruiser, the police managed to find the spot where she'd been raped. The smashed-up car was still there, with her telescope and a little cash inside. "Bastards didn't want money," her notes say. The police, who were "most considerate and thoughtful," took some fingerprints and had their dogs sniff around but said they weren't optimistic about making any arrests. There were too many criminals in the city, and too few police. Later that night, Phoebe and David were taken to a hospital, where his stab wound was treated and she was examined by a "gentle" doctor. At least one of her rapists had gonorrhea, the doctor found, and he started her on a course of antibiotics. He also gave her and David some Valium. "The doctor was as warm and concerned as the villagers had been, and all in all, I had my faith in the basic goodness of most people restored over and over again that memorable night," Phoebe wrote in her memoir.

David says that as soon as they took their seats on the plane to Sydney the next morning, they put their arms around each other and started to cry. He was touched when she said sympathetically, "You know, you've been raped, too."

By the next day, when she had a layover in San Francisco, she'd apparently decided not to let anyone else know she was in pain. She seemed to want to talk about the rape, but only in factual terms. As she awaited her flight to St. Louis, she called her friend Rich Stallcup, the guide who'd given her the Golden Eagle feather, and told him what had happened in such a matter-of-fact, detached way that he thought she was in some sort of shock, he says. He lived not far from the San Francisco airport, and he told her he was coming to pick her up and take her to his house, but she insisted that she just wanted to go home. In what turned out to be the first of many attempts to minimize the significance of the rape, she said that when she set out to see the birds of the world, she'd known and accepted that there would be hard times.

She told Dave in person, as soon as she got home, but she didn't get emotional with him either. When she'd finished recounting the facts of the attack, she seemed to have nothing more to say. He was deeply concerned about her and proposed that she get some counseling, but she said she'd already decided not to. "She resolved to just go on," he says. "It was strange."

Instead of dealing head-on with what had happened to her, a prospect that must have seemed terrifying, she tried to process it by writing a letter to David Bishop's chief employers, Ben King and Victor Emanuel, ostensibly to clear David's name. The rough draft, the only version I've seen, begins with a catalog of things that had gone well on the trip: she'd seen "over 100 lifers," including the Kagu, which she saw "preposterously well"; David had done a great job with the logistics; he'd been an "excellent spotter" and "skilled" with his tape recorder; he'd been careful in making identifications; and in the "very few instances" when they'd disagreed on one, he'd heard her out "graciously."

She described their close calls in Fiji and West New Britain and said that in both cases, David's actions had saved them. "*In no way* were these David's fault or due to any irresponsible actions or lack of judgment on his part." She also seemed to be defending herself: "We were not being foolhardy or taking known risks . . . When we had any inkling of trouble we *quit* & we left the area."

She said it had been her idea, not David's, to return to the sewage ponds in Port Moresby on the last day, and that it had been her idea to stay late, too. She didn't address the question of whether they should have gone to the sewage ponds at all, which, no doubt, they shouldn't have. Bird tours often stopped at the ponds, but generally in groups of at least ten people, not counting a couple of local guides. "It was ridiculous to go out there [without a big group]," says Bret Whitney, the leader of her first trip to Papua New Guinea. "It was a known risky area."

She figured they'd probably been watched on their first trip to the ponds, and that when they came back the next day, the men had been ready for them, she told Ben and Victor. She was defensive against the possibility that if they'd left the ponds earlier, when it was still light, they might have been okay: "We'd been observed, we were set up, & no matter when we left we'd have been attacked."

She wrote that once they were taken captive, there was nothing David could have done to stop the men from raping her. "Don't resist 5 agitated, uptight, hostile men w. lethal machetes & sheath knives." Afterward, when they were running away, "David could have gone 10x as fast, but he stuck with me every inch, holding my hand, urging me on." She "came out of this w. immense respect for David as a highly capable leader & a fine, decent caring human being. Hell of a *good* man in a crisis."

Apparently fearing that people would suggest she stop traveling, she ended the letter with a passionate defense of her lifestyle— even though, as she did not say, she'd been planning, as of a few months earlier, to "retire" from hard-core birding. "People are attacked & raped in NY, St. Louis & in their own houses. I am cautious within reason. No question in my mind that the rewards of what I do vastly outweigh the risks. I was unlucky, in one way, extremely fortunate to have escaped with my life in another. I have been [extraordinarily] fortunate in all my travels. The impact of the bastards in this world is a real threat—but it's not going to make me stay home & cringe in fear of doing what I've found to be the most rewarding pursuit of my life."

Within a couple of days of getting home, she was turning her attention to the two trips she'd scheduled for the winter, to Chile and Antarctica, both of which she'd signed up for with Doris. On October 14, five days after she was raped, she wrote to Doris, "Checked with the VENT office to make sure the Chile trip was still on. We were getting snatches of disturbing news from there." (There had recently been an assassination attempt against the dictator, Augusto Pinochet, and he'd responded by shutting down some magazines that opposed him.) She also said that she was missing a page of the itinerary for the Antarctica trip and asked Doris to send her a copy of it.

She mentioned but again tried to minimize the ordeal she'd just been through. "Just back from the SW Pacific . . . a really private trip w. just David Bishop and me! 99.9% *great*—including incredible view of a Kagu. The one bad part was a really terrifying incident near Port Moresby on the way home." She said they'd been "robbed, abducted, & assaulted" (she didn't say how) and that they'd been "literally lucky to escape with our lives." She told Doris she'd give her more details when she saw her in Chile, in early December.

Her summer at home had been "peaceful but a bit boring," she wrote. "Really eager about our 2 upcoming trips."

She took two road trips, one to Illinois to see Penny, who was still in graduate school, and one to Indiana to see Sue, who had transferred to Earlham College. She told both of them about the gang-rape in the same factual, detached tone she'd used with Rich and Dave, and she claimed that since she was fifty-five years old, it hadn't affected her much. Sue couldn't stop crying, which seems to have made her mother uncomfortable. As Sue recalls, Phoebe said something like, "Oh, honey, if I'd known you were going to react like this, I wouldn't have told you." By contrast, Penny believed Phoebe when she said the rape hadn't had a big impact on her. "My mother just dealt with things," Penny says.

Over the course of the fall, Phoebe told many more people she'd been raped, including some of her friends from the Webster Groves Nature Study Society and both of her brothers. She didn't tell her mother, who was ninety-two and living in a retirement home, or her childhood friend Peggy Beman, with whom she was in regular touch. She always talked about the attack without much emotion, and she always said it hadn't really affected her. To a certain extent, she was probably out of touch with her feelings; a lot of rape victims go numb to protect themselves. Still, she was surely in far more pain than she was letting on, as she had been when she'd gone through hard times earlier in her life, but was keeping her emotions in a vault, as she had then. She might not have known how to go about sharing her feelings, as she hadn't earlier; she might have been ashamed of having been raped, as is common; and, as her letter to Ben and

Victor indicates, she might have feared that if she gave people an opening, they'd say she was partly responsible and pressure her to be more cautious in the future. She was less scared of facing more trouble on the road, it seems, than she was of being trapped in the suburbs again, in which case, among other things, she'd have to face up to the chasm in her marriage.

At some point in the fall, she wrote a piece for *Nature Notes*—her first in a while—in which she named her ten favorite birds of all time. Nine out of the ten were birds she'd seen abroad; the exception was the Slaty-backed Gull, the bird that had earned her a mention in the *New York Times*. All ten were birds she'd seen in the previous five years—the years since she was told she was dying.

Within a month of the rape, she was impatient to go away again. On November 9, she told Doris in a letter, "I've done very little birding & it has been a slow fall. So I'm getting eager about Chile and Antarctica." In her continuing effort to convince herself and the people around her that the rape had been no big deal—an effort that was belied by the frequency with which she mentioned it—she told Doris that she was already thinking of eventually going back to Papua New Guinea and encouraged her to go too. "If you're interested in New Guinea, do plan on Victor's trip w. David Bishop next summer. He knows it *very* well & a group would be safe enough, I think. I'm very fond of David & find him a tremendously effective leader . . . I'll tell you all about our 'event' when I see you, but don't let it scare you off . . . Believe me, David will be plenty careful about safety after what happened to us." She conceded that while she planned to return "someday," she wouldn't bird around Port Moresby "with just 1 or 2 people again."

She went to Chile in December, at the peak of the austral spring, on a tour led by her friend Bob Ridgely that covered desert, shoreline, mountains, and lakes. After about a week, she sent her family a

Phoebe Burnett in grade school outside Chicago, circa 1941.

Naomi Burnett

Leo Burnett

The Blackburnian Warbler, the first bird Phoebe noticed.

Phoebe as a teenager, while building a sailboat with her brother Joe.

Phoebe and Dave in the late 1960s, at the Burnett farm.

The Snetsinger family around 1966, at the Burnett farm in Illinois. From left, Phoebe, Sue (in Phoebe's arms), Marmot, Penny, Tom, and Dave.

Phoebe at the Burnett farm, 1969, at age thirty-eight. She started writing her poetry the following year.

Phoebe and Dave at their farm in the Ozarks in the 1970s.

Phoebe at home in the spring of 1981, not long after she was told she would likely be dead within a year.

The Curl-crested Aracari, a small toucan of South America.

The Blue Bird-of-paradise, endemic to Papua New Guinea.

In a rain forest in Cameroon, 1987.

The White-necked Rockfowl, a reclusive bird of West Africa.

Showing a Colombian boy a bird, 1995.

The Marvelous
Spatuletail,
a Peruvian
hummingbird.

On a cruise with Dave to Antarctica, 1997.

A family vacation in Utah in the late 1990s. From left, Christina Herrmann (now Tom's wife), Tom, Nancy Siegel (now Marmot's wife), Marmot, Penny, Dave, Phoebe, Rich Fredrickson (now Sue's husband), and Sue.

The Helmet Vanga, the bird Phoebe most wanted to see on her final trip to Madagascar.

LIFE LIST

postcard saying she'd just seen five albatrosses and three petrels on a
boat ride in the ocean. "Best pelagic trip I've ever had." In general,
she was having "good fun" with a "good group." In her memoir, she
described the trip as "a grand, good time": "I loved the country, the
mountains and scenery, the birds, and my companions." The experience was "exactly what I needed to get over the traumatic experience of PNG," she said, not too credibly.

When Tom and Marmot next visited home, Phoebe told them
about the rape in her usual detached tone. She'd sent Tom a cryptic
letter about having something to tell him, but he hadn't guessed that
she'd been raped. "It all felt very surreal," says Tom. "She had developed some distance from the incident, and she talked about it
very factually." Marmot, who had also been cryptically forewarned,
says she was "just really shocked," and that she got very emotional,
even though her mom insisted she was absolutely fine. It occurred
to Marmot, with horror, that if Phoebe had been killed that night,
"she just would have disappeared, and we wouldn't have had a clue
what had happened."

Dave wanted to talk with Phoebe more about the attack; in addition to wanting to know if she was recovering, he wanted to
know if being raped had affected her feelings about him and their
relationship. But she didn't bring it up, and he followed her lead, as
he had six years earlier, when she'd gotten her "death sentence."
He says, "I was always surprised that we didn't talk about it more.
I don't understand how she got over that."

Instead of scaling back on travel, as she'd been planning to since
she reached five thousand and as many people might have in the
wake of such a trauma, Phoebe decided to dramatically increase her
pace. Maybe she was trying to distract herself, or maybe she was
trying to prove, to herself and the world, that she wasn't psycholog-
ically wounded. At the end of 1986, she booked enough tours for
the next year—to the Caribbean in April, to Japan in June, to the

Ivory Coast and Gabon in July, to Madagascar in October, and to New Zealand in December—to keep herself on the road for a total of six months out of twelve, far more time than in any previous year.

Nature Notes was in the midst of running a series of personal essays by club members, and as she made her plans for 1987, Phoebe decided to contribute one. In the piece, which she called "Survival," she talked about how she'd gotten "hooked" on birds, when she had four small children "and badly needed some mental and physical diversion," and about her early years with WGNSS. Most of the essay is about her travels, though. "I took my first foreign bird trip ten years ago, and found even more stimulation, excitement and challenge than I'd discovered in North American birding—so the world was the inevitable new horizon. Five years ago, I was told time was running out fast for me due to cancer. I stepped up my pace drastically and lived from one short-range goal to the next, which seems to have provided the perfect mental and physical therapy. Birding has meant a variety of things to many different people, but for me it has been intricately intertwined with survival."

At the end of the essay, she acknowledged, tacitly, that she was no longer planning to retire from hard-core travel or from thinking about numbers. "There's enough left for me to see and learn to fill ten lifetimes. Even though I've reached some major goals, I hope to continue the game as long as my good fortune holds out."

She took her cruise around Antarctica in February, when there's continuous daylight and the weather tends to be warmish and clear. "I absolutely loved it," she wrote in her memoir. Every day or two, the ship would anchor, and the group would wander around the snowfields and icebergs amid thousands of penguins and fur seals raising their young. "*Awesome* King Penguin colony," she wrote in her notebook one day, after walking among ten thousand pairs of squawking birds and their chicks. At sea, she kept "many early morning hours of solitary vigil" on deck, according to her memoir, "not only watching seabirds, but just absorbing the majesty and grandeur of this starkly black-and-white part of the world." As usual, she tried to help fellow birdwatchers, and she picked up two new fans on board, a businessman from Texas, Bob Braden, and his wife, Myra. "Certainly we consider that the finest 'Lifer' of this trip was one Phoebe Snetsinger," the Bradens wrote to her afterward. "You are indeed the epitome of dedication, exceptional skill, and remarkable intellect. We salute you!" They thanked her for her "guidance, support, and patience" and warned that they planned to follow her around in the future and generally make a "nuisance" of themselves. "Remember: noblesse oblige!"

The fast pace she'd set up for the spring and summer seemed to energize her. In early May, she wrote to Doris, "Back from the Caribbean a week ago, & I've been working furiously on Japan & W. Africa." The trip had been "great." Stuart Stokes, the Brit who'd seen more than six thousand species, had been along, and Phoebe said she'd "*loved*" him. He had "such an eager, youthful attitude & such *vast* experience. Makes me feel like I haven't done any birding at all!" Her next trip, to Japan, was "simply *wonderful*," she wrote to a friend afterward. "Got 63 lifers & really saw *superb* creatures," including the endangered Blakiston's Fish-Owl, an "enormous, glowering, dark-visaged owl with piercing yellow eyes." She hadn't expected to see the owl; it's secretive and well camouflaged, and its population had declined to just a few hundred, mainly because the riverine forests it lived in were being logged and turned into farmland. The sighting put her "in a state of absolute euphoria."

She came home to some bad news in a letter from Doris: her husband, Jimmie, had been diagnosed with cancer. It had been caught early enough that the doctors were optimistic, but he would have to endure some painful treatments. Phoebe responded with kindness and concern, as she had when Marjorie Richardson's husband had died almost twenty years earlier. "I'm *awfully* sorry to hear about Jimmie's cancer, and surely hope they can do something about it at this early stage. I wish you both all possible strength in a very difficult situation. Do keep me posted on events, prognosis, etc."

Phoebe had also gotten some mail from another friend she'd made on a tour, Aileen Lotz, who wanted feedback on a manuscript she'd just completed, *Birding Around the World*. The book was about how best to take advantage of the "Golden Age"; there were sections on how to get started as a birder (including a glossary of common birding phrases such as "Rare Bird Alert"), how to keep a life list, where the "hot spots" were on each continent, and the pros and cons of taking organized tours. Lotz wrote, "For some people, traveling is a way of life. For some people, birding is a way of life. For people who catch both the traveling and the birding bug, the world has virtually unlimited horizons. Just remember to take your binoculars."

In her response to Aileen, Phoebe was clearly trying to think through her feelings about both the rape and her decision to keep traveling. She told Aileen that while she'd done a great job in the book of conveying the "joys & triumphs" of birding around the world, she hadn't spent enough time on the pitfalls. "Probably most of us who have done extensive foreign birding have from time to time been in dangerous or frightening situations," she wrote, without elaborating. "One can reduce risks with common sense, but a lot are simply unavoidable." Some health problems were hard to prevent, too, she wrote, among them drug-resistant malaria and digestive bugs, and physical strain was virtually inescapable. "Depending on our personalities & circumstances we have varying limits to our tolerance for hardship & stress, but we have surely all, at one time or another, been driven to the ragged edge of physical & emotional endurance."

But she made it clear, as she had to Ben and Victor, that she was willing to put up with whatever hardships came her way, and she said that in a sense she even welcomed them: "Success in birding (as in everything else) is gained at a cost of the blood, sweat & tears that we have all shed in profusion. Part of what makes the triumph so sweet is the background of anguishing misses, bitter disappointments & frustrations that seem to be an inescapable part of this game. Surely everyone, at some nadir of the spirit (say when arising at 2 A.M. after little sleep to face an arduous day and fortified at best by a hard-boiled egg), has heard that small internal voice query, 'Why am I doing this?' The answer seems to be that in the end, the rewards vastly outweigh the agonies."

She concluded the letter, "So much for the negative side. I don't want to dwell on it, but I think it's important to acknowledge that there is one." She said she was excited for her trip to the Ivory Coast and Gabon, which was coming up in a couple of weeks. "Should be truly exciting & productive birding and I hope not too much of the negative side I've just elaborated on (though West Africa is a prime spot for a lot of hassles)!"

The trip, which focused on the Congo rain forest, was *"glorious,"* she told Doris afterward. "We saw some really wonderful birds," including a lot of "really challenging forest species" and "lesser-known species." A couple of days after she got back, though, she started running a fever, and it rose, quickly, to 103 degrees, much like Martin's fever had in Indonesia. She had the chills, too, just as he had. She'd been taking malaria pills, but she thought she must have contracted it anyway, and she suspected she had the same deadly strain that Martin had gotten. Clearly, she had more faith in this hunch than she did in the medical establishment, because instead of calling her doctor or going to an emergency room, she took some Fansidar that she had on hand, despite the risk of serious and even fatal side effects. "The cure was miraculous and immediate," she wrote to Doris, with a hint of pride. "I was lots better in 2 hours & just fine the next AM!"

At that point, she went to her doctor. As it turned out, she'd been right.

Chapter 7

ABOUT A YEAR after she was raped, Phoebe's urge to see new birds began to take on a compulsive, even desperate, tinge. She should have been thrilled with her trip to Madagascar in October 1987: it's the second-largest tropical island, after New Guinea, and, because it formed about 165 million years ago, evolution has run a wacky, independent course there, giving rise to lemurs, which live nowhere else, and more than a hundred endemic birds. Instead, according to her friend Joel Greenberg, who took the trip with her, she was often frustrated, saying she was missing a lot of the birds she'd been hoping for. (She knew Joel from WGNSS. When he heard she'd been raped, he called her with his sympathies and joked that he wanted to go on a trip with her "before she got herself killed," he says.) One day, the guide was sick, and, as the group set out without him on a walk, Phoebe turned to Joel and said, unsmiling, "I'm depending on you." Some days, she didn't even come in for lunch. "I might have disappointed her in Madagascar," Joel says. "I wanted to see everything, not just the birds. Maybe I wasn't intense enough."

Six months later, in April 1988, Phoebe was getting ready to go to China when she began bleeding heavily from her uterus. She'd known for a while that she had fibroid cysts and would need a hysterectomy, and the bleeding was a sign that the surgery was overdue. But she didn't want to miss her tour of China—even though it was going to be more than a month long and strenuous—so she decided to put off the operation until June, surely to the frustration of her doctor. She was given some medication that was supposed to help control the bleeding in the meantime.

Maybe the pills worked for a couple of days, but by the second night of the tour, in Hong Kong, she was "bleeding really heavily again, & by morning was beginning to experience real discomfort," she wrote to Doris afterward. "My body was clearly giving me strong signals that I'd better get back home soon if I was going to do it on my own two feet." She called Dave, had him get her an appointment at a hospital in St. Louis, and got on a flight home that evening. By the time she landed, the bleeding was "nearly out of control." She had her hysterectomy the next day.

She was told to spend the next six weeks resting. After a few days, she mourned to Doris that China was "down the drain" and described herself as "a lousy convalescent." But she was relieved that she wouldn't have to miss any other trips, since her next one, to the Manu Biosphere Reserve in Peru, was eight weeks away. A few weeks later, she wrote to Doris, "I'm really anxious to go to Manu in a month. Now that I'm nearly fully recovered (stamina maybe not quite up to par), I'm chafing a bit over my lost spring & anxious to be back in the field."

By the end of 1987, Phoebe had 5,672 birds on her life list, and there were only five birders, all men, who were higher than she in the *Birding* rankings. The top lister at that point was Norm Chesterfield, the Canadian mink rancher, with 6,162 birds; John Danzenbaker, a retired Army colonel from New Jersey, was right behind him with 6,048. Joel Abramson of Florida, the doctor and Bird

Bonanzas founder, was also in the top five, as was Phoebe's friend Arnold Small, a biology teacher in California. The youngest member of the group by far was Peter Kaestner, who was in his thirties and worked for the State Department, largely so he could see birds around the world. He'd already been posted in Zaire, where he was a Peace Corps volunteer, and as a consular affairs officer in the American embassies in India, Papua New Guinea, and the Solomon Islands; he was about to be transferred to the embassy in Colombia. He'd grown up birding with his older brother, Hank, who was on Peter's heels in the rankings and had become a spice buyer for McCormick as a way of funding his travels. (Stuart Stokes, the Brit whom Phoebe had met in the Caribbean, would have been in the top five, and maybe even in first place, but he'd slowed down and stopped sending in his list.)

However, a lot of the birders Phoebe most admired—including tour guides like the Rowletts, Robert Ridgely, Bret Whitney, and Ted Parker—no longer took an interest in "the game," as it was called. They still kept life lists and tried to see as many species as they could, but they'd stopped publicizing their totals and organizing their lives around pushing them higher. A lot of them had grown up being fanatical listers, and in mid-life they were more concerned with seeing and getting to know the birds that most interested them—the approach Phoebe had intended to take once she got to five thousand—and with ornithological research and other endeavors. Ted Parker was still doing research for Louisiana State and still discovering new species in South America; Robert Ridgely was working for the Academy of Natural Sciences in Philadelphia, doing fieldwork in Ecuador, and writing a treatise on South American birds. The Rowletts and Bret Whitney, who'd all been leaders with Victor Emanuel Nature Tours, had recently started their own tour company, Field Guides, which they were working hard to get off the ground.

They'd also stopped playing the game because a big list didn't mean what it once had, in the days of such birding heroes as Ludlow Griscom, Roger Tory Peterson, and Dean Fisher. In the Golden Age, you could basically buy your list by signing up for a lot of tours, following your guides around, and ticking off whichever birds they called out, whether or not you'd seen them well enough to make out their field marks or even knew which field marks to look for. Or, if you traveled by yourself or with a friend, you could count birds without knowing for sure what they were; you could even make up sightings altogether. When birding was done locally, in the context of a club, you had to be scrupulous or risk being shunned, but world birding had opened the door to some shenanigans.

Maybe if Phoebe hadn't had cancer, she would have gone back to school for a Ph.D. in ornithology or biology, written a field guide or a scholarly work on birds, or spearheaded some sort of conservation campaign. But the odds were that she wouldn't be around long enough to see any major projects come to fruition, and, increasingly, she seemed to depend on the rush she got from seeing new birds. She was probably also becoming dependent on the recognition she got for being one of the top listers, and for playing the game how it was meant to be played—the sort of recognition that many smart, ambitious people get in their jobs, but that she'd missed out on during her two decades as a housewife. At the end of 1987, around the time she returned from Madagascar, she told a birding magazine that she'd set her sights on six thousand, which, she said, was "a nice, round number."

In spite of how excited she'd been about her trip to the Manu reserve in Peru—her first trip after the hysterectomy—she didn't end up having a good time.

In a different frame of mind, she would have found the reserve, which had just opened to tourists, utterly staggering: it's in a part of the Amazon rain forest so pristine and remote that it takes a whole day to get there, via small plane and boat, and it's home to monkeys, jaguars, and more than a thousand species of bird—about one in ten of the birds on the planet. But Phoebe came home feeling that her time there had been a missed opportunity. For one thing, "the weather was unbelievably *cold* . . . & this kept down bird activity and song," she wrote to Doris. Otherwise, she thought, the fault lay with the tour company, Victor Emanuel Nature Tours, and the guide, Steve Hilty, a well-known expert on South American birds. The company had booked the group on "what they know to be [an] *un*reliable small plane flight to get us there," and when the flight got canceled, they had to drive, "losing us two critical days." In the park, they stayed in comfort in a lodge instead of camping, forgoing "the better birding opportunities upstream." Steve, who had recently published a field guide to the birds of Colombia, was "surprisingly *un*familiar with many Peruvian birds, I thought, & really hadn't done his homework at all. I knew a lot of the species before he did." She also thought he'd been too focused on pointing out monkeys and big, colorful birds like macaws, most of which she'd already seen, at the expense of the little brown and black birds that would have been lifers for her. "We missed some important habitats & species . . . but I was the only one aware of it." She said she would go back to the Manu soon, but with Field Guides, "who have learned quickly how to plan a sensible, bird-oriented itinerary" for the park.

I suspect that if Phoebe had taken the same trip to the Manu several years earlier—with the same bad weather, the same too-cushy itinerary, and the same leader—she would have been thrilled with it. In those days, she knew much less about the birds of Amazonia, so she wouldn't have perceived any shortcomings of Steve's; she would also have been less aware of the birds she was missing, since she would have been seeing a lot of lifers at every turn.

Perhaps most significantly, she'd changed since she first started traveling, probably as a result of the rape, which, two years on, she still hadn't dealt with in an emotionally honest way. She didn't just want to see a lot of life birds in the Manu—she needed to see them, and she suffered when they didn't come through, as she had in Madagascar and after aborting her trip to China. It's also possible that her anger with Steve was an expression of the unresolved anger she must have had toward her rapists, or that, deep down, she had unresolved anger toward David Bishop too.

During the trip, she kept her frustrations to herself, and she put a lot of energy into helping the rest of the group. "She was as excited about our seeing birds as about her seeing birds," says one man who was along. Afterward, he and his wife wrote to her, "Meeting you was one of the best and most memorable aspects of the trip to Peru for both of us."

Tom had been drifting since he finished the Peace Corps. When he came home from Ecuador in 1987, he didn't think he wanted to keep being an engineer, but he didn't know what he wanted to do instead, and he felt pressure from his father to begin a career. Instead, he moved far away, to Seattle, and supported himself with odd jobs such as painting houses, selling produce, landscaping, and driving a UPS truck. Every so often, he'd quit his job and travel around Central America, getting to know the cultures and doing volunteer work.

In the summer of 1988, when he was twenty-eight, a few weeks after Phoebe's unhappy trip to the Manu, the whole family met up in Kenya for a safari. Marmot and Sue were both living there: Marmot was leading trips up Mount Kenya for the National Outdoor Leadership School; Sue, who'd just graduated from college with a degree in conservation biology, was teaching science in a small rural village. Phoebe didn't expect to see many life birds on the trip and approached it instead as a true vacation. "Will be wonderful to see all the kids together again, & in such exciting surroundings," she wrote to Doris before she left.

Tom hadn't done any birdwatching in years, and he hadn't spent time in nature with his mother since their trip to Ecuador in 1976. In Kenya, though, he had "a magical experience," he says. As he watched Phoebe get excited about birds, he remembered his own passion and began paying attention to them again. He was also awed by what an expert she'd become. "She even knew all the little brown birds." When he got back to Seattle, he started taking walks with his binoculars, and "all of a sudden I was noticing things." He had purpose again, and he felt newly close to his mother. "I definitely felt that once I became interested in birds, I became more fascinated with where she was going and what she'd seen," he says. She was excited about his birding, too, and cheered him on.

Sue was also deeply moved by watching Phoebe on the safari. One night, a family of elephants came to bathe and play at a pond just outside their lodge, and all the guests went out on the deck to watch them. Sue later wrote: "Long after most folks had watched for a while, then gone back to bed, I remember my mom still sitting there by herself, knees tucked up under a blanket, watching with fascination. I asked her if she was coming to bed and she said, 'Oh no, it's not every night I get to watch elephants.' I hung back and watched for a while longer before heading to bed myself, and I remember wondering at the time which was the greater pleasure, watching elephants, or just watching my mother watch elephants."

A few weeks after the family vacation, Phoebe flew back to Africa for a ten-week marathon, her longest stretch away from home yet. She'd signed up for three back-to-back tours: one of Zimbabwe and Botswana; one of Madagascar, to make up for her unsatisfying results there the previous year; and one of Zambia, which, like her fateful trip to the South Pacific, was a "private" one that she'd arranged herself. She'd originally planned to go to Zambia with VENT, but not enough people had signed up and the trip had been canceled. Phoebe and two friends, determined to go anyway, had organized their own trip through a Zambian safari outfitter.

In the Okavango Delta of Botswana, a floodplain several times the size of the Everglades and so remote that you have to charter a small plane to get there, Phoebe saw Pel's Fishing-Owl, which perches on tree limbs hanging over the water and snatches fish from the depths with its talons. "As prepared as one may be, it's still an improbable event, watching this massive owl the color of English marmalade, with its extraordinary lifestyle," she wrote after she got home, in some notes on her favorite African birds. She sent Doris a postcard from Zimbabwe: "*Good* trip in all respects. Also a comfortable & easy one . . . Wish you were along." She also had a good time in Madagascar, ticking off a lot of the species she'd missed before.

There was a little time between the end of the Madagascar trip and the beginning of the Zambia one, which gave her a chance to go back to Kenya and visit Sue. (Marmot was in the midst of a mountaineering expedition.) In her memoir, Phoebe recalled that she and Sue spent "a splendid few days together," and Sue wrote many years later that the visit was "some of the nicest time I shared with her." One night, Sue took Phoebe around to some of her students' homes, where they were greeted like family and fed dinner after dinner. "I was a bit apprehensive about the trail we'd have to take back home that night—a long trek, and across one very rickety foot bridge," Sue recalled. When they got to the bridge, Sue barely had time to say anything "before she was already across it, and was coaxing me across, step by step. I remember thinking how amazing it was, this mother of mine who could come out and visit me in this setting, while most other people's parents stayed in Nairobi or nice lodges. I was so proud to have her there, yet she told me during this trip how proud she was of *me*!"

Zambia is birdy, but it's not very high on the "birdability" scale. The country's seventy endemic species are spread out far and wide, in mountain ranges and swampland accessible only by dirt road. The bird Phoebe and her friends most wanted to see, the Shoebill, could only be found in the remote Bangweulu Swamp, which is famous for being the place where the explorer David Livingstone died of malaria and dysentery. The Shoebill is tall and storklike, with a massive bill that looks like a clog and comes in handy for catching fish and baby crocodiles.

To guide the trip, the safari outfitter had enlisted a prominent local birder, Bob Stjernstedt, who was half British and half Swedish but had been living in Zambia for decades and was famous among African naturalists for both his ability and his pluck. Once, in a part of Zambia known for its lions, Bob climbed a tree to inspect a bird nest, lost his footing, and fell to the ground, where he lay, unconscious, for more than twelve hours. When he woke—bloody, dusty, and covered with flies, but, luckily, untouched by lions—he managed to stagger to a nearby lodge. His first request, as the story goes, was a bottle of ice-cold beer. In her memoir, Phoebe described Bob as "an auditory genius in a class with Ted Parker" and a good leader, even if he had some liabilities, chief among them a case of malaria that periodically disabled him. He also had a bad sense of direction and tended to get the group lost in forests, though after this happened a couple of times, their driver, Thomas, took to sounding the horn every hour or two to orient them.

On the other hand, the safari outfitter was "a disaster." The company was supposed to send an advance team to each campsite to set up the tents and cook dinner, but its truck was always breaking down and arriving late or not at all. "At one point when we did encounter them, we simply took some basic survival equipment and food and carried it in our own vehicle. We slept out a lot and ate so much rice and pineapple (available from roadside stands) that it was a long time before I could face either one."

Their expedition to the Bangweulu Swamp, in a Land Rover provided by the outfitter, was particularly disastrous. When they were a couple of hours from the swamp, on a bumpy dirt path better suited to bikes and pedestrians, one of the car's wheels suddenly popped off. They'd been going so slowly that no one was hurt, but they ended up being stranded on the deserted path for the rest of the day and overnight. (This time, the safari truck really had preceded them, and the advance team was waiting at the swamp.) They ate the snacks they happened to have in the car, got some water from a brook, and, until it got dark, did a little birding by the side of the road. It was a "long and worrisome" day, Phoebe wrote, and "tremendously frustrating" to think she might miss the Shoebill. At bedtime, Bob, who had a fever, tried to get some sleep in the three-wheeled Land Rover, along with Phoebe's friend Bill Davidson, who had a bad back. Phoebe slept outside with Thomas and Bill's wife, Harriet, where, she wrote, they felt "pretty vulnerable."

In the morning, they got a lucky break: a boy on a bicycle came along, and Thomas persuaded him to sell them his bike. In spite of his fever, Bob managed to pedal to a fishing camp and talk its owners into lending him their car. The group ended up getting to the Bangweulu Swamp late that afternoon, exhausted but in time for "lengthy, soul-satisfying" views of two Shoebills.

The whole trip "was a rather unbelievable experience," Phoebe wrote to Doris. "Would have been absolute disaster with a regular bird tour—Fortunately the 3 of us were willing to put up with it all in order to do what we'd come to do." Her ten weeks in Africa

Shoebill

had tired her out, however. "I want to slow down to a saner pace than I've done recently."

She reached six thousand in January 1989, on a tour of Ecuador with the Rowletts that focused on the birds that live in the "cloud forests," or high-altitude rain forests, of the Andes. But instead of celebrating—as she had when she'd gotten to five thousand three years earlier—she fretted about the birds she was missing, mostly due to bad weather. As she later wrote to Doris, "The trip was a disappointing one for me, in spite of the fact that I saw over 70 lifers . . . We had *constant* rain, and too many people—16 in a jam-packed bus, & 2 leaders, so that there were always 17 umbrellas in the way of whatever you wanted to see. They had run another section just before we came, which had been very lucky & encountered a lot of really good birds—which we were unable to repeat 3 weeks later. So there was the constant frustration & disappointment of *not* finding my primary target birds, & also not finding compensating or equivalent good species, for the most part." She said John and Rose Ann "did everything right & tried extraordinarily hard, but it just didn't work out well for me."

According to John, Phoebe didn't complain and was "always composed," but he could tell that she was unhappy, and it struck him that she'd changed. "She wouldn't have reacted like this a few years earlier. Earlier, in Panama, for instance, she was really into seeing even birds she could see at home." Her priorities had become "increasingly focused," and she'd generally become "increasingly intense." "I still found her wonderful to be with but a little different."

Notwithstanding what she'd told Doris about adopting a "saner pace," Phoebe had arranged for six months' worth of travel in 1989, the same amount of time she'd been away during the previous two years. In May, she went to the Gobi Desert of Mongolia with a British company, Birdquest, known for its demanding, pioneering tours. The group drove around the desert in a Soviet military truck, slept in tents and yurts, got caught in sandstorms, and relied on wandering tribesmen for directions. None of that was a problem for Phoebe, but for the first time in her birding career, she had to struggle to keep up on hikes—many of the people in the group were far younger than she—and she felt that the guide, Mark Beaman, the owner of Birdquest, should have gone slower to accommodate her. Afterward, she wrote to Doris that while the "bird results" on the trip had been "excellent," Mark had been "inconsiderate" and "needlessly ran the trip as a marathon for those who could or chose to keep up with him. Wouldn't go with him again [except] maybe in the case of an irresistible itinerary that no one else was doing."

It's possible that Mark was inconsiderate, as Phoebe said, but she was likely frustrated with him for other reasons, too. She was getting more irritable in general, as her other letters from this period show; moreover, by blaming her discomfort on him, she didn't have to face the underlying problem—that her stamina was showing the first signs of decline, not because she was sick but because, on the contrary, she'd survived, against all odds, to see her late fifties. In the middle of the trip, she'd turned fifty-eight.

She had almost gotten into a fight with her mother over this trip. For years, the Leo Burnett Company, which was still one of the biggest and most prestigious ad agencies in the world (and was still privately held), had been building a skyscraper in downtown Chicago, and in the spring of 1989 it was finally completed. Naomi, now ninety-five, wanted all her children to come to the dedication ceremony, and in April or so she told them it would be sometime in June. When Phoebe said she wouldn't be returning from Mongolia until June 18, Naomi, who had never understood her daughter's obsession with birds, urged her to skip the tour if necessary. Phoebe said that wasn't an option. About a week before she was to leave, in late May, the date of the ceremony still hadn't been set. "Our goodbyes were strained: our stands were firm," according to Phoebe's memoir. But a couple of days later, Naomi called to say that the building would be dedicated on June 20, two days after Phoebe's return. With "profound relief," Phoebe told her she'd be there.

In the summer, Phoebe made her repeat visit to the Manu Biosphere Reserve, with John Rowlett and Bret Whitney of Field Guides. The weather was better this time, and John and Bret took the group to the remote places VENT had skipped. Unfortunately, however, one member of the tour, Bill, behaved like an attention-seeking child, as far as Phoebe and much of the rest of the group was concerned. He went around imitating birdcalls, even in the forest, where it was important to be quiet. "It's just me, boys!" he'd yell, smiling and waving, when John and Bret turned their heads. When everyone was lining up behind a telescope, he'd elbow his way to the front, whining, "Bill wants to see the bird, too!" When people were looking at a bird through their binoculars, he'd walk right in front of them so he could get a better view.

Bill bothered many people on the trip, including John and Bret, who eventually sent him home, but Phoebe had the angriest reaction to him. One day, the group heard a Black-backed Tody-Flycatcher calling from the thicket. They stopped and listened, trying to place the sound. Phoebe had just spotted the minuscule bird when Bill stepped in front of her, blocking her view. Without raising her voice, she pointed toward her telescope and said, in a sober tone, "Bill, if you ever get between me and a life bird again, I'll break this tripod over your head."

Even as she became more compulsive and irritable, her reputation in the birding world was growing. By this time, most serious birdwatchers had heard of her and knew the basic outlines of her dramatic life story. "A cancer death sentence, a brutal assault in Papua New Guinea . . . how could it all be true?" wrote Peter Kaestner, the birder who worked for the State Department, many years later. In the late 1980s, he knew Phoebe only by reputation. "How could someone keep going on?" Moreover, he wrote, "Her intense preparation and capability to understand the birds was mythical . . . How could she be so focused, so driven, and yet so nice and generous, all at once?" Tall tales circulated about her that were widely believed: it was said, for example, that she had a photographic memory, and that she referred to birds by their Latin names rather than by their common ones. One guide who took her on a trip around this time says it was a "bloody great relief" when the latter rumor proved false.

People would get excited when they found out they'd be on a tour with her and were honored when she took time out to help them in the field. Even catching a glimpse of her was thrilling, as if she was a rock star. One birder she later became friends with, a Swedish doctor named Magnus Aurivillius, says he and some European friends of his were also in the Manu reserve in July 1988 and happened to be in the same lodge as Phoebe's group. One night at dinner, one of Magnus's friends looked across the room and said, excitedly, "I think that's that famous lady!" According to Bret Whitney, "People started to worship her. She was a living legend."

In early 1990, *Birding* published a special issue on "Birdfinding Around the World." "We live today in a Golden Age of Birding," wrote the editor of the issue, Phoebe's friend Aileen Lotz, by way of introduction. "We have access to nearly every corner of the globe, each with its special share of the world's nearly nine thousand birds." Aileen solicited articles for the issue from some of the biggest names in birding, most of whom had become good friends of Phoebe's: Ben King wrote about his quest to see Reeve's Pheasant in China, which involved two years of negotiating with the Chinese government and scheming with scientists, but was ultimately successful ("Yeooow!" Ben concluded); Ted Parker recalled one of his expeditions with Louisiana State; David Bishop wrote about rediscovering Wallace's Standardwing, a memory that still gave him "goosebumps"; and Doug Pratt, a birder and bird artist who had spent a lot of time in the South Pacific, described the devastation of bird life in Hawaii and Guam and on islands around the world. He urged birders to travel the world soon—"ere another island falls silent."

In another sign that Phoebe was becoming a celebrity among birders, Aileen also solicited an article from her. In a piece titled "Birding on Borrowed Time," Phoebe chronicled her journey from backyard birder to cancer victim to world traveler, and despite all her recent frustrations, her tone was upbeat. Again, she called her cancer a "blessing in disguise" because it had forced her to adopt a "now-or-never" approach. Again, she said that birding had been "excellent mental and probably physical therapy."

She noted, as she had before, that she wasn't just a passive participant in tours. "For me, the real challenge and satisfaction lies in being able to figure the birds out for myself," even if the guide was often faster to identify them than she was. By studying in advance and making her own identifications, she got "a truly valid birding experience instead of simply a list of ticks representing birds that I could not identify if I saw again."

She said she'd recently gotten to six thousand, and while she didn't admit to having a higher goal, she said, "Birding has now become a way of life, and, since I am still thriving, I don't intend to change my lifestyle significantly until circumstances so dictate. Obviously I am extremely fortunate in having the health, time, and financing, to say nothing of a most understanding family." She was also lucky, she said, to be birding in the Golden Age, which she described as a "rather small window in history when transportation to remote areas is feasible, when political and social conditions are reasonable (with a few glaring exceptions), and before the entire world has become people, pavement, eucalyptus, and agriculture."

Though she didn't mention the rape, she acknowledged the "negative side" of birding that she'd urged Aileen to write about in her book. "You will encounter situations any sane non-birder would go miles to avoid: living conditions defying description; physical efforts beyond imagination; stressful situations that drive you to the ragged edge; outright risks to health, life, and limb; and occasional anguishing disappointment . . . As in any realistic success story, the road to satisfaction and goals achieved is strewn with hardships, set-backs, and disappointments. So why do it? Every birder develops a personal an-swer. Mine lies in the high peaks of my birding life: the most special experiences watching some of the world's most special birds."

It's true that Dave was "most understanding" when Phoebe first started to travel, but by 1990 he was running low on patience. She'd pretty much ignored him for almost a decade, just as her father had pretty much ignored her when she was young. "We would talk, but our communication was limited," Dave says. At some point, he suggested they go into marriage counseling, but she said she didn't want to. He was sad about how distant they were, and off and on, he was angry, but often he did his best to pretend to himself that noth-ing was wrong. "How difficult it was for me depended on what was going on with me. I was still growing at points."

As usual, he spent a lot of time working. Around the time Phoebe saw her six-thousandth life bird, he was promoted to vice president at Purina. He kept all the responsibilities of his previous post, as director of the poultry feed operation, and was put in charge of the research for cat, dog, swine, cow, and horse feed, too. In this new position, about 160 people reported to him. On week-ends and when he was on vacation, he put on magic shows at sen-ior centers and children's hospitals, worked on the house and the yard, and took trips on his own or with the kids.

Penny, who'd been hired as a chemistry professor at Sacred Heart College in Connecticut, felt distant from Phoebe, too, even though she was beginning the career that her mother had once planned on. As a kid, Penny had been equally close to both parents, she says, but in adulthood she was having a hard time relating to her mom. Though she had her own obsession—ballroom dancing—she thought being obsessed with birds was "a little bizarre." She also had a hard time with the way birding had taken over her mother's life. "I admired her determination," she says. "Nothing was going to stop her . . . [But] that was also her detriment. That was her life and everything else was sort of second to it."

The other children, for the time being, could relate better to Phoebe's choices. Marmot was still leading mountaineering trips and was talking about trying to climb Mount Everest; Tom was doing more and more birdwatching in Seattle and had taken a volunteer job at a wildlife rehabilitation center. Sue had returned from Kenya, moved to Washington state, and, inspired by her mother, taken a job doing ornithological fieldwork. At the time, there was a huge controversy surrounding the Northern Spotted Owl: logging companies were cutting down trees in the fir forests where it lived, which was putting its future in doubt but creating a lot of jobs; environmentalists were fighting to curtail the logging by getting the owl listed under the Endangered Species Act. Sue had been hired by the National Park Service to monitor some owls and their nests. She was spending her days much as Phoebe did—in the woods, trying to be unobtrusive, looking for the slightest sign of movement in the trees and listening for ancient calls.

On some trips, Phoebe still got euphoric. In May 1990, two years after her emergency hysterectomy, she went back to China, on a tour with Ben King that focused on the massive mountains of western Szechuan. According to her memoir, the hiking was "strenuous," the weather was "miserably" cold, and the hotels were "primitive and filthy," but, thanks to Ben, the birds, including eight species of pheasant, "fell marvelously into place," and she had an "incredible" time. Her field notes were more exuberant than any she'd taken thus far. One bird, the Firethroat, had an "*incredibly* striking pure glowing red throat"; another, the Chinese Monal, a pheasant, had "*dazzling* colors" (every one in the rainbow); and she got "full spectacular all-feature views" of a third, Temminck's Tragopan, a pheasant with a blue head, an orange throat, and a blood-red body that is sprinkled with white dots that look like pearls. She sometimes capped off her description of a bird with an exclamation, like "Exquisite!" or "Spectacular!" She took exuberant notes on the landscape, too. At one point, the group drove over an "incredible," "majestic" 13,000-foot pass; a little later, they were in a "fairyland" of fresh snow. She took note of rhododendron blooms, bits of panda scat, yaks, and marmots. She thought the Min River "must be one of *the* premier whitewater rivers of the world," with "hundreds of kilometers of unbroken turbulent whitewater."

Clearly, then, when the stars were aligned, Phoebe had the same capacity for joy and wonder that she'd had when she first started traveling. In China, she was with one of her favorite guides; he'd apparently set a pace she could keep up with; and the weather, though uncomfortable, hadn't kept the birds still. It must have helped, too, that she hadn't been to China before. On her recent trips to South America, she'd had a short list of hard-to-find targets in mind, but in China even the common birds were new.

She'd arranged to meet some friends and a guide in Cairns, on the coast of northern Australia, in early July to look for a Southern Cassowary, a big bird built like an ostrich, only it's six feet tall rather than eight. It has shaggy black feathers; its neck and head are bald and bright blue; and atop its head sits a chunk of bone-like tissue shaped like a blade, which it uses to clear brush in the forest. It's one of the few polyandrous bird species: males incubate the eggs and raise the young, while females, which are bigger and more brightly colored, try to mate with as many males as possible. Nesting cassowaries can be aggressive, and they've been known to kill people with a swift, eviscerating kick to the stomach.

Phoebe was to spend a few days looking for a cassowary, then take two back-to-back tours, one of the rest of northern Australia, much of which is rain forest, and one of Papua New Guinea, which would cover pretty much the same spots as her trip in 1984 had. In all, she'd be gone for eight weeks.

In late June, about ten days before she was to leave, her mother, who was ninety-six, fell down, broke her hip and leg, and had to have surgery. Phoebe drove to Chicago to be with her in the hospital. Her brothers still lived there, but they were both on vacation—Joe in Asia and Peter in Washington, D.C.—so Phoebe was left to manage the situation by herself. Unfortunately, "complications arose" after the surgery, according to Phoebe's memoir (it's not clear exactly what they were), and Naomi's condition steadily deteriorated; she was also in a lot of pain. Phoebe, certain she was dying, wanted the doctors to focus on making her comfortable, but they refused. "I was confronting an inflexible and exasperating medical world that 'knew best' how to treat her—subjecting her to useless and painful tests, refusing to give more potent pain medication 'for fear of addiction,' etc. I was stymied, frustrated, and miserable."

As she watched her mother suffer, she thought about her own death, as she had when her father had died twenty years earlier. In her memoir, she stopped short of confessing her intention to kill herself when she fell ill, but she said that the time she spent in the hospital with her mother "reinforced my already-formed resolve to do whatever I could to keep my own living and dying somehow under my control as far as humanly possible."

Peter got back to Chicago two days before Phoebe was supposed to go to Australia, by which time Naomi was barely conscious. Phoebe, who clearly didn't want to cancel her trip, kissed her mother good-bye and got in the car to drive home. She was reaching across her chest to adjust her seat belt when she felt a hardness near her right armpit that was both familiar and alarming. She wrote in her memoir, "There was no doubt in my mind, not even a glimmer of hope to the contrary, that this represented another melanoma recurrence, and it hit my psyche like a bomb shell."

Later in the day, after she'd gotten home, Peter called to report that Naomi had died. Phoebe didn't tell him, Dave, or anyone else about the new lump. "I needed options." Peter had said he wanted to hold the funeral in six days—after Phoebe was supposed to have left—to give Joe a chance to return from Asia. "The reasonable, adult course of action (which my mother would have advised) was to cancel my travel plans, go back to Chicago for her funeral, and then go immediately into the hospital for surgery and tests." Instead, she packed her bags and told Dave that she'd be leaving, as planned, in two days.

He was "taken aback." "I didn't understand," he says. He knew that she was neither religious nor a fan of big ceremonies, but "it just seemed to me that part of the reason you go to a funeral is to commune with others, sharing in the loss." In one of the only moments of confrontation in their marriage thus far, he told her it was inappropriate for her to skip her mother's funeral, to which she replied, "I've said my good-byes," as he recalls. He got ready to go to the funeral without her, and Sue decided to accompany him.

On the plane, Phoebe wrote a remarkable letter to Dave and the kids in which she opened up to them emotionally more than ever before, probably because she felt she owed them an explanation, but also, I suspect, because she was lonely and scared and craving a connection with them.

Dearest Family,

I'm starting this letter in the aftermath of Mother's death, on my way to Australia. I want you to know all of the reasons I'm leaving before her burial. I did spend those intensely painful days with her before & after the operation, when all I could do was hold her hand & stroke her head when she was crying out with pain. And I said goodbye & told her I loved her while she was still alive & aware of me.

Not very credibly, Phoebe claimed that since she'd organized the hunt for the cassowary and had gotten some friends to come along, "I just about *have* to be on the initial flight."

> But primarily—because I fear this may possibly be my last trip. I'm feeling good, no problem there, but on my way back home after leaving Mother, I became aware of a distinct & fairly large lump in my right shoulder—not far from the melanoma site. It's large enough so that if it is another melanoma, it has probably already metastasized to internal locations.

She said that in two months, when she got home, "I will agree to have the necessary surgery, and I will consult with whomever necessary about treatment possibilities. Again, I may make the choice to do nothing, but I can hardly expect to be so lucky a second time." (She must have been thinking of her recurrence in 1985 as the first time.) In any event, she wanted to use as much as possible of the time she had left "doing what I love best," rather than waiting to die in a hospital.

She told her family, for the first time, about her suicide plans, which had changed a little since 1981, and laid out her philosophies of life and death:

> I don't fear death as such, whatever it is—oblivion, limbo, or another life. That's something I can't do anything about. What I do fear is a slow and painful death (and even a few days of severe pain is *very* slow, as Mother could attest). So I plan to spare myself

and all of you considerable agony by taking my life quickly and peacefully before the situation is taken out of my control by doctors & hospitals. I have a stockpile of strong sleeping pills & even a gun if the first choice fails. I may have to use some subterfuge, and I may have to do it a bit prematurely (so as not to be too late), but I'll arrange it so I'm not found by someone I love. I thought this all through pretty carefully in 1981, & my basic thoughts & feelings haven't really changed.

Meanwhile, I've had the best years of my life. I want to thank you all, & most of all Dave, for understanding and accepting my need for developing my own independent lifestyle. You can't know what it has meant to me. I feel I've helped set some standards & made a contribution to a pursuit I care deeply about. And I've had immeasurable fun & satisfaction while doing it. I think I've packed more enjoyment into these past years than most people have in a lifetime, and I feel tremendously privileged. Sad, sure, whenever it ends, but not devastated and unfulfilled as I was in '81.

The last time I saw Mother in good health (on my 59th birthday) she commented that she'd finally figured me out: "Phoebe is a bird, afraid of being caged." Pretty good, I thought. In line with that, I'd prefer not to be boxed & buried after death. Please have my body cremated, & then what I'd like best is for all of you kids & Dave to go somewhere really wonderful together & spread my ashes in some beautiful natural spot. Maybe the Wind Rivers (I never got there in life) or the Amazon Basin (where you could leave me in my "acre of rain forest"), or the Olympic rain forest (I've never seen the *Northern* Spotted Owl) or Kenya—or Ecuador or Guatemala (never made it there either) or even the Ozarks (find a yellow Lady's Slipper—leave me there). Your choice—but have a wonderful time together, see some great birds, and leave me there. I'd die really peacefully if I could "look forward" to something like this.

Southern Cassowaries live in dense forests and generally aren't easy to find, but in June and early July of 1990, there had been a drought in northern Australia, and the birds, which eat fruit, were coming out to look for food. Phoebe, her friends, and their guide got "marvelous, *too* close views" of a male as soon as they parked their truck on the edge of a forest, according to Phoebe's field notes. The bird was "coming out of forest & approaching aggressively—doubtless for food . . . quite alarming as [it] lowered head & charged us around & into truck." She noted the bird's "huge thick legs," "long rapier-like inner claw[s]," "hairy black body plumage," "large blade-like casque," and "incredible head-neck colors." The experience, she wrote, had been "wonderful."

Two days later, Naomi's funeral was held in Chicago. "I woke this AM at 1 o'clock, which is 10AM 13 July at home, so I was very much with all of you in spirit at Mom's funeral," Phoebe wrote to Dave, a bit defensively, on a postcard. She was still holding on to the long letter. "Hope Sue & Joe got there OK. Trip is going well, & as always it's great therapy for getting over trauma. Great luck with Cassowaries. Love, Phoebe."

Doris was supposed to join her for the Papua New Guinea leg of the trip, but early on in the Australia leg, the guide got word that Doris had canceled because her husband had died, of the cancer he'd had for several years. Phoebe wrote to her right away. "How awful for you—I'm so dreadfully sorry to hear about Jimmie . . . I wish you all possible strength and peace during this ordeal, Doris." She also told her about her mother's death and about her new lump. Again, she seemed to be defending her decision not to go to the service: "I really felt I'd done what I could for her while she was living & decided to come on to Australia instead of waiting for the funeral." As for the cancer, "I really don't know what to think, or what may happen—but meanwhile I'm having a grand time."

At the end of July, she sent Dave another postcard. "Aust. trip now over—a highly successful one. We're back in Cairns, & three of us leave for New Guinea in the morning." She suggested that she had some apprehensions about that: "Will be a shift of gears, mentally & physically. Aust. is *so* comfortable & familiar-feeling."

I don't know how she felt about being back in New Guinea for the first time since the rape. In her field notes, she mentioned that her group even spent an afternoon at the sewage ponds outside Port Moresby—the place where she and David Bishop had been attacked—but there's no sign that she thought this was either unwise or momentous; perhaps by going back to the ponds without making a fuss, she was trying to show how little the rape had affected her. In her memoir, all she said about the tour was that she "scooped up numerous high-priority species" that she'd missed on her two previous trips to the island. A lot of her field notes were effusive, as they'd been in China and when she saw the Southern Cassowary, which suggests that she was having a good time. She got a "fabulous scope study" of the Blue Bird-of-paradise, which is black with flashes of electric blue, and "spectacular views" of another bird-of-paradise, the Black Sicklebill, which has two ribbon-like tail feathers twice the length of its body. A mossy forest the group visited was "stupendous."

About halfway through the trip, however, they had a close call. They were flying in a small plane to a little airstrip in the mountains, but it couldn't land because there was too much fog. "Finally a last-minute pre-dusk landing with full power for emergency takeoff," Phoebe wrote in her notebook. During the descent, there were "15–20 minutes of dead silence" among the group "& many misgivings for all of us."

A few days after that, she saw her 6,500th life bird, the chunky, noisy, and bright-colored Large Fig Parrot. She put an exclamation mark in the margin of her field notes.

She wrote in her memoir that throughout her time in Australia and New Guinea, the lump got bigger, causing "an undercurrent of serious concern." By the end of the trip, in late August, it had grown from "the initial barely palpable hardness beneath the skin" to "an obvious swelling." She never stopped having fun, though. The group had a layover in Fiji on the way home, during which they stayed at a beach resort near a coral reef. When the guide, Bret Whitney, suggested they take an afternoon off from birding and snorkel instead, Phoebe was resistant, saying she preferred to rent a car and go birding on her own. But Bret talked her into coming along, and once she got in the water and saw some fish—neon and metallic, striped and speckled—she started screaming with excitement through her mask, he says. At one point, he led her to a lionfish, which is covered with sharp, needle-like, venomous spines. "She just went nuts!"

On the plane the next day, Phoebe and Bret sat next to each other. At one point, he says, she turned to him with tears in her eyes, hugged him, and said she didn't think she'd ever get to see him again. She told him about the lump and said she had "a really bad feeling about it," he recalls. "We talked about how important it was for her to get positive again. She bounced back quite quickly. She could really steel herself."

On the last leg of her trip home, she finished the letter to her family that she'd started in July.

I know I've taken a big gamble with this probably malignant lump, but whatever happens I'm glad I've done it. If this turns out to have been my last trip it couldn't have been a better one, or with better people. I had a simply great time & passed another major threshold—6500. Naturally I would love to have more time to do this kind of thing—but if I don't, I feel an awful lot better about impending death than I did in 1981. This has unquestionably been the best 10 (nearly) years of my life, so I figure I've come out way ahead of what anyone has a right to expect. I've set some major standards in this birding game & received some very satisfying recognition for it. I feel really good about that. It's the greatest gift of all to be able to work intensively at what you love best, do it well & have your peers acknowledge & recognize your contributions & success. I know you have had this same kind of satisfaction, Dave, and the best thing I can wish for all you children is that you can experience the same sort of thing at some time in your life.

As Joe says, it's probably best to go out when you're on top—or nearly—so if my end is truly approaching fast, the timing is not too bad after all.

As soon as she got home, she had the lump removed and tested. Once again, the melanoma was in her lymph nodes, and once again, she underwent tests to see if it had spread elsewhere. "And totally unbelievably, one by one, the reprieves came: bone scan, negative; liver scan, *negative*; brain scan, NEGATIVE!" she wrote in her memoir. "I was free to live my life—one more time!!" She wrote to Doris, "It was malignant melanoma, as I'd feared . . . All tests & scans are okay, so it seems not to have spread. I'm sure hoping it's another non-aggressive one." There had been "no good developments" in treatment in recent years, "so I don't plan to do anything about it—except recover from the surgery, which should be no major problem." She was "definitely continuing with all travel plans," though she'd gotten cancelation insurance for an expensive cruise that was coming up in the fall, around some islands just north of Antarctica.

She told Doris, "Back to square 1—living day to day."

Chapter 8

WHILE HER ARM was healing, she made some plans. She and a friend had been thinking about going to the Persian Gulf in late January 1991, mainly to see the Hypocolius, a little gray bird that, like the Kagu, has no close living relatives and is in its own family. In the spring of 1990, she'd written to a birdwatcher in Bahrain, Erik Hirschfeld, to see if he could show them around for a day or two, and in July, while she was in Australia, he'd written back enthusiastically. In the meantime, though, Iraq had invaded Kuwait. The United States and other countries were threatening to go to war to liberate it, and the State Department was telling Americans to avoid the Gulf.

It's a measure of just how fearless Phoebe had become that none of this deterred her. In September, she made plans to stay in Bahrain for a night, look for the Hypocolius and some other birds, and fly to India, where she'd be taking a tour. She wrote to Erik, "Stopping in Bahrain doesn't worry me as long as it is logistically possible for me to get there (i.e., get a visa and a flight in and out). Things of course could get better (or worse) by January . . . I hope it works!" Around the end of September, Phoebe's friend decided "not to risk it," she wrote to Erik, but she told him she would still go "unless a war or the State Dept. stops me." "I can't see that it sounds very risky unless things change."

She'd long ago booked up the fall with three back-to-back trips—the cruise of the sub-Antarctic islands and tours of southern Australia and New Zealand—all of which went off without a hitch. The trips comprised a total of three months, the longest period she'd ever been away, and yielded her seventy-five life birds. The International Ornithological Congress, which brings together academic ornithologists from around the world every few years, was meeting in New Zealand during her time there, and though she didn't attend the proceedings, "birders from all ilks and from literally everywhere were scattered over New Zealand or were assembled on the cruise ship [in the sub-Antarctic]," she wrote in her memoir. "Such fun! I met several friends from a British tour at the base of Mt. Cook, companions from Malaysia while watching Royal Albatrosses, and numerous friends and acquaintances from the U.S., Africa, Europe, and Australia on shipboard."

In all, Phoebe had spent almost eight months on the road in 1990—about two months more than she'd spent in the previous few years, and five months more than she'd spent in the mid-1980s, the era just before she was raped, when she was saying she wanted to slow down and focus on quality over quantity. At the end of 1990, she had 6,600 birds on her life list, a gain of about six hundred from 1989, and she'd climbed from fifth to third place in the *Birding* rankings, having passed Peter Kaestner, the State Department official, and Norm Chesterfield, the mink rancher. She was right behind John Danzenbaker, the colonel from New Jersey. The birder in first place was a Brit, Harvey Gilston, who was almost at 6,800. Gilston had made a lot of money as an entrepreneur, had retired to Switzerland, and, since at least the mid-1980s, had been spending much of every year on bird tours. Some of his peers didn't think he was as knowledgeable or skilled as they were, however, and they thought he depended too much on his guides. "He was just into birds for the collection aspect," one man told me.

As far as I know, Phoebe was always polite to Gilston, but behind his back she criticized him passionately, whether or not her criticisms were justified. "He got into this game relatively late in life (as did I), is an obsessive and compulsive lister, but knows absolutely nothing about what he's seeing, doesn't really enjoy it, and doesn't deserve to be called a birder," she wrote to a friend around this time. "He's never been able to identify anything at all and his 'list' is the result of numerous leaders having shown him everything and told him what it was. Any kind of glimpse at all will suffice, as long as the leader has identified the bird!" She contrasted Gilston with Kaestner, who was right behind her in the rankings and whom she'd recently met during a tour of Malaysia, where he was posted. She seemed to admire him much as her father had admired the hardworking "lonely man" he described in his retirement speech: "My money is on Peter Kaestner for the ultimate winner. He's young, determined, *very* competent and knows precisely what he's doing. He's the only one of us who's doing it right: Since he works for the US State Dept., he is based in one area for at least two years and can really learn it and bird it thoroughly, then move on. Besides being an excellent birder and having seen in the high 6000's before age 40, he's thoughtful, considerate, and just an extremely nice guy . . . So justice will be served in the end. Peter will be, and deserves to be, first." While she stopped short of admitting any desire to win "the game" herself, she'd clearly gotten intensely invested in it.

She no longer had to worry about running out of money, at least not for many years; when her mother died, she'd inherited the rest of her share of her father's fortune. She scheduled another eight months of travel for 1991.

In the end, of course, she didn't get to go to Bahrain. The Gulf War started on January 17, 1991, a week and a half before she was supposed to fly there, and travel to the Gulf became impossible. She was on the road pretty much constantly for the rest of the winter and the spring, though. Her moods were all over the place, as they had been ever since the rape. When she got back from her trip to India, which had been led by her good friend Ben King, she wrote to Doris that the tour had been "poorly planned & not well run . . . Got about 40 lifers, but I'm not really happy with our coverage." She had even "had words" with Ben. For his part, Ben thought Phoebe was "pissed off before she even got there—pissed that we weren't going certain places she wanted to go," he says. "I thought, if she's so unhappy about the itinerary, why is she here?" In the spring, she went to Turkestan and the Caucasus, which were still part of the crumbling Soviet Union, with Birdquest, the company that had run her difficult Mongolia tour. "Back from the USSR," she wrote to Doris in early June. "God, what a miserable place, and *awful* food, mostly cucumbers. Birds were good, but we had to work for them—Long, steep climbs in rugged country."

On the other hand, she seems to have experienced some of the "high peaks" she'd written of in her *Birding* article. In mid-June, during a trip she and Dave took to see Sue in Washington, she had a "fantastic experience" with some Northern Spotted Owls that Sue was studying, according to her notebook. Sue took her into a forest, imitated the owl's hoot, and held out some mice she'd brought along, whereupon a "rising whine-squeal" began sounding in the trees. A female owl with "marvelous large liquid brown eyes" flew from its nest down to Sue, snatched the mice, returned to the nest, and fed them to its "2 fuzzy gray-white young." Phoebe got a good view of one of the young birds munching on its mouse. "After feeding, head disappeared into fuzz-ball, with only bill protruding!"

With the new pace she'd set, she only had a week or two be-tween trips, during which she'd do little besides unpack, pack, work on her index cards, study, and take walks to stay in shape. Her trips followed one another so closely that she had to order an extra copy of her passport; she'd take one copy on the road while the other was getting stamped with a visa for her next trip. During tours, she needed more sleep than she once had, probably due to a combination of her age and her frenetic schedule. She still wouldn't take a siesta, as she didn't want to miss any possible birds, but she often skipped dinner, heated up instant oatmeal or soup in her ho-tel room, and went to bed early. She also caught up on sleep dur-ing plane and bus trips; as soon as she boarded, she'd pop a sleeping pill and put earplugs in. Bret Whitney, the guide, says that while she still got excited about good birds, in general she was becoming less and less "bubbly" and "gregarious" and more and more "me-thodical." He says he was saddened by this, and concerned.

For most of the 1980s, ornithologists had recognized just over nine thousand bird species, but as they gained more knowledge about birds in far-flung places, they began to think that many species needed to be "split" into two. For example, researchers thought that the Rufous-tailed Antthrushes in Venezuela and the Rufous-tailed Antthrushes in Brazil were sufficiently different so as to prevent interbreeding, which meant that the two populations were actually two separate species. In 1990, Burt Monroe, who had led Phoebe's trip to Kenya in 1977 and was still teaching at the University of Louisville, published a thousand-page book, *Distribution and Taxon-omy of Birds of the World*, that assessed all the splits that had been proposed in academic papers, concluded that there were actually

9,700 valid bird species, and gave an account of the habitat and geographic range of each. The book also moved many species to different genera and families, in accordance with DNA testing that Burt's coauthor, Charles Sibley, had been doing since the early 1980s.

Burt's splits were widely accepted by both academics and amateurs, and the American Birding Association told its members to recognize them. For a lot of birders, this was an unwelcome development; they were much further than they'd been before from seeing all the birds in the world. But Phoebe, who made her way through the book when she got back from visiting Sue in Washington in the summer of 1991, had kept such meticulous records over the years that she was able to add many of the new species to her list right away. (Birders call such additions "armchair lifers," since they don't require getting up and going somewhere.) For instance, Burt had declared that the two Rufous-tailed Antthrush populations were indeed separate species, and that the Venezuela population would, henceforth, be called Schwartz's Antthrush. When Phoebe looked up her index card on the Rufous-tailed Antthrush, she saw that she'd seen the bird in both Brazil and Venezuela, so she got to add Schwartz's Antthrush to her list.

In her memoir, she said she found the book "absolutely fascinating." "I could hardly put it down: I'd even wake at night, thinking of something I wanted to look up, and get up out of bed to find the answer before I forgot the question." She ended up with 150 new species, reorganized her index cards to reflect Sibley's DNA analysis, and "found the whole exercise a most pleasurable review of all the birds I'd ever seen." At the end of June 1991, she wrote to Burt, whom she hadn't been in touch with, "What an incredible masterpiece! Couldn't resist writing you a fan letter. I've just spent two solid weeks revising my world list card-file . . . It seemed like a lot of work, but pales into insignificance compared to the years of research, time, and effort you've put into producing this marvelous volume."

She didn't agree with all his decisions, however. "I kept a list of your changes that I know something about and don't agree with; I'd split 16 that you lump, and lump 26 that you split—so not much of a difference really." She was basing her assessments mainly on her familiarity with the research that various friends of hers were doing and on her ongoing review of ornithological journals and treatises. She also enclosed a list of "only about 50" other mistakes she thought she'd found, as Burt was working on an update. In some cases, she'd seen a bird outside the geographic range Burt specified for it; he'd listed some birds as extinct or possibly extinct that she knew had recently been seen; and there were some typos.

She wasn't a professional scientist, as she'd once planned to be, but she knew more about birds than many ornithologists, and, by corresponding with Burt, she was contributing, ever so slightly, to the field. She was also being a perfectionist, as her father had been.

She was happy with the next few tours she took, each of which netted her about twenty or thirty lifers. In July, she went to Christmas Island, south of Indonesia, on a tour led by Ben King, with whom she'd reconciled. In addition to seeing five endemic bird species, she spent hours watching a massive Green Sea Turtle lay and bury its eggs on the shore: "She emerged from the sea after midnight to haul herself up the beach above the high-tide line, laboriously dig a deep pit with her flippers, deposit 80 or so round, rubbery, ping-pong ball eggs, and slowly cover her traces," she wrote in a draft of a *Nature Notes* piece. "Then, 3–4 hours after her initial appearance, she returned to meet the rising tide, lifted her head once toward us and her buried nest site as in farewell and disappeared in the waves. We all felt that night as though we'd given birth." Not long after that trip, Phoebe went to Mexico with Birdquest, the British company, because its itinerary included a part of the Sierra Madre mountains that the American tour companies had deemed unsafe. "This site had received so much bad press in American birding circles from some earlier robberies there that our tours seemed to avoid it like the plague," she wrote disapprovingly in her memoir. "In any case, I *very* much wanted to see the Tufted Jay," which would only be possible on the British tour. She saw the jay, and her group had no problems in the Sierra Madre.

In December, during a period that she'd set aside to be at home, she took an impromptu trip to Morocco with a friend to see a single bird, the Slender-billed Curlew, whose population had plummeted to fewer than a hundred, probably due to hunting and habitat loss, and, as a result, was rarely seen. They went on the advice of a Moroccan friend who had recently spotted the bird in a marsh, and after two days of travel and two days of searching, they found it, then flew straight home. (Today, the curlew's population is estimated at fewer than fifty, and the prognosis for its future is grim.) By the end of the year, Phoebe was just a few birds shy of seven thousand and had risen to second place, ahead of John Danzenbaker. Harvey Gilston was still in the lead, but barely, with 7,069 species.

She got to seven thousand on her first trip of 1992, to Sri Lanka. Few if any bird tours had gone to the island due to a longstanding civil war, but with the help of some local guides, Ben King had put together an itinerary that he thought would be safe. The group avoided the northeast, where an ethnic minority, the Tamils, was trying to secede and form an independent state, and focused on the southwest, where most of the endemic birds were. It turned out to be an "absolute marvel" of a tour that spanned jungle, shoreline, and mountains and gave Phoebe good looks at all twenty-three of the island's endemics, many of them nocturnal and reclusive. Her

Ceylon Frogmouth

seven-thousandth bird was the endemic Ceylon Frogmouth, which has the body of a little owl; a mouth that sticks out like a frog's; huge, hungry-looking yellow eyes; and whisker-like eyebrows that stick straight up in the air. She wrote in *Nature Notes*, "We had a masterful, persistent, and inspired leader in Ben and extremely capable and helpful local guides, but also miraculous good fortune. It was probably the single overall most successful bird trip I've ever done." Afterward, she sent the local guides some bird books to thank them.

The *St. Louis Post-Dispatch* somehow got word that she'd reached seven thousand and ran a short article about her in March. "When it comes to watching birds, Phoebe Snetsinger of Webster Groves is nearly tops in the world," the article said. "It's a tremendous accomplishment," an official from the American Birding Association was quoted as saying. "It's the result of an awful lot of hard work on her part." One of Phoebe's friends from WGNSS told the paper, "Phoebe has got a terrific reputation as being totally honest, and if she doesn't see a bird and know what it is, she won't count it." The paper also interviewed Dave, who remarked, "It seems like every time there's a disaster, an overthrow of a dictator, or an earthquake, she's been there."

The milestone, of course, didn't satisfy her. In her memoir, she said that by this time, she was not only hoping to get to first place in the rankings, but that she wanted to set a "world record" by being the first person to see eight thousand species, a feat she likened to breaking the four-minute mile. Of course, if she became the top lister, she'd set a new record every time she saw a life bird, but she was clearly hoping that by breaking through to the "next thousand," she'd earn a place in history, much as Roger Bannister had.

She may also have been looking for a way to justify several more years of travel—to herself or, perhaps, to Dave. Her annual totals had been going steadily down, since no matter where she went, she'd already seen many of the birds. In 1989, she spent six months on the road and saw six hundred lifers; in 1990, she spent seven months on the road and saw just three hundred; in 1991, she was away for nearly eight months but saw only 250. (Her official total for 1991 was deceptively high—four hundred—because of her armchair lifers.) In 1992, she felt that "given about another five years, 8,000 would probably be possible for me," she later wrote in her memoir.

She wasn't worried that Gilston or Danzenbaker would get to eight thousand first; they were older than she and starting to slow down. But, her memoir says, "I was beginning to feel some hot breath coming up behind me" from Michael Lambarth and Sandra Fisher, the British couple who had a shared list. They didn't publish it in *Birding*, but they kept friends and competitors posted on their progress, and when Phoebe got to seven thousand they were about two hundred species behind her—as they probably told her on the Sri Lanka tour, which they also took. In Phoebe's opinion, they were "very determined," as well as "younger and, seemingly, healthier and wealthier than I."

Michael had made a fortune as an entrepreneur, and he and Sandra lived in the English countryside, where, according to rumor, they kept domesticated geese and falcons on a vast estate. In the field, they wore matching green rubber hunting boots, seemed quite serious, and generally kept to themselves, though they were always polite to the rest of the group. People say that Michael was more enthusiastic about birding in remote places than Sandra was—a man who was with them in China says she was disgusted by the toilets there—but that Sandra had sharper eyes. "She spotted things he couldn't see but would pretend she hadn't seen them." They may well have been highly skilled birders with a passionate appreciation for the natural world, like Phoebe, but they didn't get nearly as much recognition as she did.

In Sri Lanka, Phoebe got the impression that Michael and Sandra, too, had set eight thousand as a goal. She wrote in her memoir, "It was definitely going to be a race, albeit an undeclared one. I certainly was beginning to worry more and to keep closer track of what [they] were doing." At the time, however, she didn't admit to being competitive. The *Post-Dispatch* followed up on its short piece about her with an in-depth interview that was published verbatim. When she was asked if she had a goal in mind, she said, "Nobody's ever going to see them all, and there are many I will never see. But I'm so enchanted with this whole business that as long as I'm able to travel, I will. I may see 7,500, but numbers are unimportant; there are some species I would like very much to see. I could spend the rest of my life looking for them."

Despite her struggles in Mongolia and the Soviet Union, Phoebe had signed up for two strenuous trips within a few months of each other in early 1992: a trek in the Nepalese Himalayas during which she'd go up to eighteen thousand feet above sea level, higher than she'd ever been before, and a tour of Irian Jaya, the western half of New Guinea and a colony of Indonesia, with two steep treks in rugged country to about eleven thousand feet. She'd signed up for the latter tour against the advice of David Bishop, who'd spent a lot of time in Irian Jaya. He doubted she could handle the treks, and he thought Birdquest, which was running the tour, didn't know what it was getting itself into. While Papua New Guinea had begun to modernize in the previous decade or two and had something of a tourist infrastructure, Irian Jaya got hardly any visitors, had few good roads or hotels, and had more villages where ancient tribal ways— such as living in tree houses, believing in sorcerers, and perhaps even practicing cannibalism—endured. Irian Jaya is known to many Americans as the place where Michael Rockefeller, son of New York governor Nelson Rockefeller, disappeared while collecting tribal art in 1961. Some people think he was eaten by a crocodile; others think he was cannibalized.

During her first tour of the Himalayas, the one on which Joe Wright had died, Phoebe had gone up to about thirteen thousand feet above sea level and seen many of the birds that live at that elevation and below. On this trip, which began in Kathmandu in mid-May and comprised a steep eleven-day trek, she had four main targets, all birds that live above thirteen thousand feet.

In the end, the trek was full of both highs and lows for her. On the one hand, she loved the scenery and the birds, as she had when she was in the Himalayas the first time. From a ridgetop at 12,500 feet, she saw "marvelous slopes of blooming rhododendrons" and got "*spectacular* all-morning breathtaking views of Everest, Lhotse & Ama Dablam," according to her notebook. "Worth the climb for this alone!" A few days later, from a peak at 17,300 feet, she had "astonishing, panoramic views" of Everest and Pumori—the latter of which is twenty-four thousand feet high and which Marmot had recently climbed with two friends. Moreover, Phoebe got nice looks at all four of her target birds, including the Himalayan Monal, a pheasant with pretty much every color you could think of and a crest that looks like it's made of green darts. "Stupendous view of male crossing path," she wrote in her notebook. "All gorgeous iridescent colors, crest, golden-rufous tail. Magnificent!"

But the hiking was tough and, on some days, beyond her ability, especially at the higher elevations. "Steep & long uphill," she wrote from eleven thousand feet, at the end of the first full day of the trek. A couple of days later, there was a "*steep, long* tiring climb" to 12,400 feet. By fourteen thousand feet, she found "every step an effort." Many days, the group hiked for four hours, took a break for lunch, and then hiked for four more.

Meanwhile, she was fuming at the leader, who "seemed to be here for his own purposes entirely," she said in a letter to his boss. He was always either way behind or way ahead of his clients, she alleged. When they got to about fourteen thousand feet, she asked him to stick with her the next day to help her find one of her targets, the Snow Partridge. "I think you can understand my dismay & frustration when . . . he streaked by me early on, & when I finally saw him 2 hours later, he'd already had a pair of Snow Partridges some time before—there had been *no* attempt at all to keep his pace to something I could keep up with. When I let him know I was really unhappy that he'd left me behind on a critical day he became very defensive & argumentative & said, 'I know a thing or two about how to bird in the Himalayas.'" She wrote the letter in installments, at the end of each day of hiking, and her criticism got stronger as she struggled more physically and as she began to lose hope of seeing either a Snow Partridge or one of her other targets, the Red-breasted Rosefinch. "[He] came here to do his own thing, bird alone, & not be bothered by leadership obligations," she wrote one night. Later, she called him the "poorest excuse for a leader I've ever had the misfortune to come across." She finally saw the partridge and the rosefinch on the last two days of the trip, by which time she'd filled more than twenty pages of her little notebook with denunciations. (I don't know how long the final draft of the letter was or even if she sent it at all.) She did adopt a slightly more moderate tone in conclusion: "Except for the exasperating & infuriating behavior of the (non) leader on the trail, the trek was one of the best things I've ever done."

While Phoebe was struggling in the Himalayas, Marmot, who was thirty years old, and a friend, Wendy, were in Alaska trying to climb the tallest mountain in North America, Denali, which is twenty thousand feet high and is demanding from both a physical and a technical standpoint. The air is even thinner on Denali than it is in the Himalayas, due to the low barometric pressure near the North Pole; the temperature is rarely above zero, even in the summer; blizzards and avalanches occur year-round; and because of all the snow, you might not know you're stepping into a crevasse or off a ledge until it's too late, though most people attach themselves to a partner or a group with a rope. Only about half of the people who set out to reach the top end up succeeding, and, on average, a few climbers die every year.

Marmot and Wendy got to a base camp and ranger station at fourteen thousand feet on May 12, after a few days of climbing, without any trouble. They intended to rest and acclimate to the altitude for a couple of days, then make their way toward to the summit. Instead, they got caught in a vicious blizzard at the camp and, for the next week, were stranded in their tent. "It was pretty horrendous," Marmot told the *St. Louis Post-Dispatch* when she got home. "I've never been in a storm like that before . . . The winds were 50 to 80 miles per hour, so you couldn't even stand up without bracing yourself against something. Most of the time you couldn't even see the tents right next to you. The days just melded into one another. You'd get up, dig the drifts from the door, and get back in the sleeping bags." Two Italians and three Koreans fell to their deaths during the storm; a Swiss man died of cerebral and pulmonary edema brought on by the altitude. Three Koreans suffering from altitude sickness and frostbite were stranded at seventeen thousand feet without food or fuel, but they were rescued on May 19, during a pause in the storm.

The storm finally ended on May 21, and the climbers at the base camp were told that they had a three-day window of clear weather in which to attempt the summit. Marmot, Wendy, and dozens of other hikers set out. But as Marmot and Wendy neared fifteen thousand feet, Wendy started to feel sick, and Marmot took her back down to camp. The next day, they tried again, and the same thing happened. Wendy gave up on getting to the summit, but Marmot, who apparently approached risk much like her mother did, decided to attempt it alone, which is hardly ever done. "The standard is to use ropes," she told the *Post-Dispatch*. "But from where we were, there's a long knife's-edge ridge to the top, and I was confident I could make it on my own."

She did make it, and, after bearing the cold and wind at the summit for five minutes, began her descent. The *Post-Dispatch* reported: "She acknowledged that given all that had gone before, her judgment could be questioned. 'But I got five minutes on the top of Denali all to myself!'"

In 1991, at age thirty, Tom had gotten an ornithological fieldwork job much like Sue's, but in Hawaii. He'd been hired by the U.S. Fish and Wildlife Service to study the Palila, a little yellow-and-white bird that had once been abundant on Big Island and Oahu but had been devastated by the introduction of alien predators—such as rats, which raided their nests—and by habitat loss. By the early 1990s, just a few thousand Palilas remained. Nearly all of them lived on a single mountain on Big Island, and one of Tom's duties was to relocate some birds to another part of the mountain to try to establish a second population. After a few months, he left that project to set up a new study that was aimed at saving several endangered species in the Hawaiian honeycreeper family, which had been ravaged by avian malaria, rats, and other introduced predators. In his study, Tom was poisoning rats in a forest and watching to see whether bird populations rose.

He got a visit from his mother in June 1992, around her sixty-first birthday, not long after she returned from the Himalayas. He was dazzled by her vigor, as Sue had been when Phoebe visited her village in Kenya. One day, he managed to get them access to a protected forest in Maui where they hoped to find the Maui Parrot-bill, a green and yellow honeycreeper with a hooked beak like a parrot's. It had a population of only a few hundred birds and would be a lifer for both of them. "Almost immediately we both caught a flash of a chunky green-yellow honeycreeper fly[ing] into a dense bush," Tom later wrote. They saw a key field mark—a bright yellow semicircle above the bird's eye—but "[i]t was a poor look for me, poorer yet for my mother—she wouldn't count it," he wrote. "We worked the shrub thoroughly, but the bird had simply vanished."

The rest of the morning and the early afternoon yielded many birds, but no more parrotbills. "By mid-afternoon, I was tiring and beginning to lose hope of finding a cooperative parrotbill," Tom wrote. By contrast, "my mother's hope, persistence, and sheer stamina for looking at every single bird never flagged. She needed to see this species adequately—better yet, well." As dusk drew near, Tom was barely looking through his binoculars anymore, while Phoebe was "actively scanning and putting her binoculars on anything that moved." Finally, she saw a bird hitching its way up a tree, focused her binoculars, and exclaimed, "There's a parrotbill!" They watched it for a good long time and "high-fived in mutual celebration." "We got to the gate at dusk. She had earned her parrotbill."

Phoebe was taking the first-ever bird tour of Irian Jaya, or "Unknown New Guinea," as Birdquest called the territory in its catalog for 1992. "We shall be some of the first birders to visit Irian Jaya, before mass tourism, logging and mining have had a serious impact on the environment," the catalog said. One of the two guides had gone to Irian Jaya to set up the logistics, but neither had traveled there extensively. Since the tour would involve many uncertainties and would include two steep one-week treks in the backcountry, it was appropriate only for the "adventurous" and "quite fit" birder, according to the catalog. In a letter to Doris that she wrote on her return from Hawaii, Phoebe said the trip would be "rugged & exploratory & unpredictable, but I'm hoping for 40–50 lifers," among them several birds-of-paradise. She downplayed the trouble she'd had in Nepal: "I'm encouraged by having been able to handle the Himalayas without undue stress, & have been trying to stay in shape by losing a few more pounds & walking 6 mi. a day." She also said she'd had a great time with Tom in Hawaii. "He took me to some great spots on Hawaii & Maui that ordinary mortals can't get to, & I saw 5 new honeycreepers, more than doubling my Haw. Honeycr. list. Must do Kauai with him while he's still there. I knew this business of having kids would pay off in the long run! (Hope you know I'm joking.)"

It turned out that almost all of the dozen or so other people who'd signed up for the trip were much younger than Phoebe, and there were a bunch of men in their twenties and thirties, including Magnus Aurivillius, the Swede who'd been in the same lodge as Phoebe in the Manu. The group met up in Jakarta in mid-July, flew to Jayapura, the capital of Irian Jaya, and took a small plane to an airstrip in the Snow Mountains, where they met up with their porters and cooks for the first trek. They were members of the Dani tribe, which hadn't abandoned its traditions: the women wore only thatch skirts, and the men were naked except for the hollowed-out gourds that they wore over their penises, tied on so as to remain perennially upright. With the Dani, the group would spend three days climbing in thick cloud forest from about six thousand to about 10,500 feet. In the grasslands above the tree line, they hoped to see MacGregor's Bird-of-paradise, which has a big, orange wattle around each eye that looks like a slice of dried fruit. Getting down would take three days, too.

The way up the mountain turned out to be on "the most awful, steep, slippery, dangerous, muddy trails you can imagine," Phoebe wrote to Doris right after the trip. Often, she was in mud up to her ankles; there were endless fallen tree trunks and streams to navigate; and the trail, at times, was nearly vertical. Each step required "care and concentration," her memoir says. Sometimes the Dani pushed her from behind, and she sometimes got on her hands and knees and crawled. At one point, she took a bad fall. She barely took any field notes, partly because she wasn't seeing many birds (you can't when you're always looking at your feet) and partly because she was so spent at the end of each day. "Hike from 5700 to 8800 camp in forest," she wrote at the end of the first day. "*All day*—long, difficult & slippery, steep—awful, exhausting day." Even the younger people on the trip were having a hard time, Magnus says, though most of the time, they and the leaders were way ahead of Phoebe.

The nights weren't any better, as their living conditions were "utterly miserable," Phoebe wrote to Mark Beaman, the Birdquest owner, afterward. They should have had solid, waterproof mountaineering tents, but instead there was just a tarp that wasn't big enough to cover all of them unless they turned on their sides and arranged themselves like spoons. There were no groundsheets. It rained at night, too, and most mornings the group woke up cold and wet; those sleeping on the edges of the tarp were the worst off, since they generally rolled out into the open a few hours before dawn.

In her memoir, Phoebe wrote, "I'd eat, fall onto our sleeping ground exhausted, often with my muddy boots still on, and wake with the awful knowledge that we weren't there yet—and that we still had to go *back* the same route! Even thoughts of MacGregor's Bird-of-paradise took a back seat to simple thoughts of endurance and survival."

She found the two leaders exasperating and incompetent. One of them had done the whole trek to scout it out the year before, but, she told Mark, he was always cagey about how long each day's hike would be, what the trail would be like, and how much altitude would be gained or lost. "Much of what we were told proved to be fiction." Neither guide had a good grasp on the birds, she thought, particularly when it came to vocalizations. "I could not help but constantly compare the handling of the birding with what I'd experienced on my previous [New Guinea] trips (both with 2 excellent & skilled leaders & full groups of 14), and the difference was often like night vs. day."

Finally, around 10,400 feet, the trees gave way to grass, wildflowers, and a big, clear lake. Phoebe spent a "comparatively easy and relaxing day," and the group had had no trouble finding MacGregor's Bird-of-paradise, whose face wattles were "brilliant" and "incredible," her notes say. She also saw seven other life birds that day, including a group of Snow Mountain Quails that she found herself. According to Magnus, when she spotted them she shouted "Yes!" at the top of her lungs.

She had a wretched time on the descent, though perhaps not as wretched as on the way up, as there are fewer miserable entries in her notebook. "*Long difficult* mostly descending-steeply route," she wrote one night.

There were ten days between the first trek and the second, most of which the group spent happily on Batanta, a small island just off the western coast of New Guinea. The Batantans, who hardly ever got visitors (but who were clothed), serenaded them with song and homemade flutes as their boat pulled up to shore, and they cooked, sang, and danced for them every night. Phoebe wrote in her memoir, "Here we had a perfectly comfortable and spacious thatched hut in which to spread our sleeping bags and only one morning of tough commando exercise necessary to get to the spot for seeing the incredible Wilson's Bird-of-paradise." It's a preposterous-looking bird: its head is bald, blue, and crisscrossed with black stripes, like it's wearing a hairnet; its body is a mishmash of yellow, red, green, and black; its legs are purple; and it has two ribbon-like feathers sticking out of its rump that look like they've been put through a curling iron. On nearby Salawati, another tiny island, Phoebe saw the Western Crowned-Pigeon, whose head is topped with a cluster of fluffy gray plumes that make it look like it's wearing a giant snowflake. "Huge, lacy, filmy, fan-shaped gray crest," she wrote in her notebook. "Exc. scope & binoc. studies." According to Magnus, she watched the pigeon with a "wide, victorious smile."

On the whole, the second trek, from sea level to six thousand feet, wasn't as hard on her as the first one had been. The trails were dry and relatively smooth, she said in her letter to Mark, "and though steep & incredibly demanding, I *could* physically do each step myself with the aid of a stick." Some nights, the group slept in huts, which was more comfortable than crowding together under tarps. "The birds were quite wonderful," she wrote in her memoir, "especially since I could actually look at them." But as on the first trek, she often lagged behind, particularly because the native

Western Crowned-Pigeon

porters didn't help her along as the Dani had, and at times she found the trail "*treacherous*," according to her notebook. At the end of the last day, she wrote, "Long, arduous 8-hr. hike down to 860' & cold beers"—the best beers she'd ever had, she said.

By the end of the second trek, Phoebe had seen almost fifty life birds, far more than she saw on most trips these days. However, in her letter to Mark she said that together, the treks had been "the most truly difficult, exhausting, & unhappy birding ordeal I've ever had, and I feel I probably should have been discouraged from attempting the trip. I'm no stranger to rustic living & do not balk at generally difficult conditions & trails—but I was frankly appalled & shocked by this, and was operating at my physical & emotional limit much of the time. Having enjoyed some quite arduous hiking

& primitive living this year, including a Himalayan trek, I did not expect to feel as utterly defeated by this experience as I was." By the end of the second trek, she was openly feuding with the guides, Magnus says; he remembers that at one point, she said within earshot of them, "We don't have any leaders." Other people in the group were frustrated with them, too, but less vocally. Still, Phoebe was bearing a lot of her suffering stoically, because Magnus's impression was that she "did fine" on the treks. "Phoebe was quite a trooper . . . she did not say much and she never quit." Moreover, "[her] presence was a boost to group morale. If she could do this at her age, then anyone younger should just keep quiet and get on with it."

The group's final stop was another small island, Biak, where they were supposed to spend two low-key days and would be staying in a hotel for the first time since the start of the trip. They spent the first day and the second morning doing "pleasant, regular roadside birding, connecting with most of the endemics," according to Phoebe's memoir. Finally, on their last afternoon, they set out across a bay for a minuscule island to look for a near-endemic bird that Phoebe had already seen elsewhere. The guides had hired a boat that was much like the one in which Jared Diamond had capsized a decade earlier: a long, hollowed-out log with an outboard motor and a long pole, or "outrigger," running parallel to either side of the log for stability. There were no seats, but there was a cabin for luggage halfway between the bow and the stern, and everyone piled onto its roof. There were no lifejackets, and the boat had no lights.

The ride wasn't supposed to take more than an hour, but it was low tide, and the driver had to circumvent a reef. "By mid-afternoon, we participants all sensed that the mission should be aborted, or we'd be returning in the dark, without any lights. I should have spoken up, but didn't—to my later regret—and the 'intrepid leaders' carried on." Around five o'clock, they finally got to the island, but they had no luck finding their bird.

They set out on their return at dusk, again sitting on the roof of the cabin. By this time, the tide was rising, and the driver took the direct route, over the reef. Since it was getting dark, he tried to follow the path of a boat with lights just ahead. Every so often, the bottom of the log would scrape the top of the reef, and the boat would lurch forward "alarmingly," Phoebe wrote. "We finally got across the reef and into open water, where the boat rode more freely, and I breathed a short-lived sigh of relief." The wind and waves were stronger once they'd passed the reef, and the top-heavy canoe began "doing some heavy rocking." Soon, a big wave engulfed one of the outriggers, whereupon the boat rocked to that side, paused for a moment, and overturned, dumping the whole group and their gear into the water.

"It was one of those events that you simply can't believe is really happening," Phoebe wrote. She happened to be on the rising side of the boat, and as it capsized she was able to hang on and land on the upside-down keel, but some of the people on the sinking side were thrown into the water; one was hit on the head by an outrigger and, for a moment, trapped under the boat.

"It was totally dark, and all was chaos." Everyone, it turned out, was alive and okay, and they "shouted, whistled, and screamed" to get the attention of the boat they'd been following. Luckily, the driver heard them and turned around. He said he could safely fit only a few of them in his boat, and the group decided that the eldest among them, including Phoebe, would go with him. When they got to shore, they'd have the police send out a rescue boat. A man who was much older than his wife got into the boat without her, and they parted reluctantly and with tears.

The younger contingent anxiously clung to the hull. "I figured, as long as the boat stayed afloat, we could float through the night and then in the morning we'd be found," Magnus says. "If the boat sank, we would die." At some point, someone made a shark joke, and the response was utter silence. Eventually, the group realized that there was a tiny island nearby, and a couple of people suggested they try to drag the boat toward it. Magnus strongly opposed the idea: he thought there would be crocodiles in the mangroves around the island, and that they would be more aggressive than sharks. In the end, it was impossible to move the boat anyway.

It took Phoebe's group "a long two hours" to get to shore, according to her memoir. At the police station, they were shown a map, and they tried to describe where the accident had happened. It took "another nail-biting hour" for the police to set out. By this time, the wind had picked up, and it was raining.

The group had drifted a little from their original spot, but after an hour, the police found them. They were shaken but fine. The next day, everyone flew to Jakarta and home, except Magnus, who had lost his passport in the wreck and was stranded in Jakarta for three days.

Phoebe had written her letter of complaint to Mark Beaman before the accident, but she added a postscript. "I find it difficult to express my further outrage in regard to the boat accident. Suffice it to say that I feel irresponsible leadership allowed a very dangerous and frightening situation to develop, and that it was by the merest chance that we all escaped as unscathed as we did." The boat was "dangerously overloaded" and the trip "ridiculously overextended." "Both leaders share considerable grave responsibility here, and it would be highly inappropriate for the incident to become a joking matter or simply a 'good story.' "

She didn't face up to her own responsibility for putting herself in danger, however, just as, after the rape, she said she'd been "unlucky" at the isolated sewage ponds without questioning her decision to visit them. When the group set out from Biak for the tiny island, she couldn't have known that the leaders were underestimating the time it would take to get there, but, if she'd been more prudent, she might have decided before the boat left the dock that it was overloaded, and she might have inquired as to whether there were lights or lifejackets. She wasn't acknowledging, as Jared Diamond did after his accident in the same region, that she could have decided not to get in the boat.

From the airport in Jakarta, the guides called Mark Beaman to tell him about the accident, and Mark dashed off a letter that day to the whole group. "I can only say how thankful we are that you are all safe and well." Over the next few days, he talked to some of them, heard how difficult and badly organized the treks had been, and decided to issue a partial refund. Phoebe and the other older clients would get a slightly higher refund than the others, "as we feel you had to battle especially hard," Mark wrote.

He sent Phoebe a long, apologetic letter in response to hers. He was "mortified" at how tough the treks had been, especially for "older participants." "If we had known the true facts we would certainly have suggested that the treks would be too hard for you (and done the same with anyone not under 50 and very fit)." He was "very surprised and concerned" by most of her comments about the leaders, though he took issue—legitimately—with her complaint that they didn't know much about the birds. "I do not think one can expect, when you sign up for what is clearly the first ever tour to a completely new part of the world where only a handful of living birders have set foot and it is clearly stated that the leader has only made a single exploratory visit, to find that the leader is very experienced as regards the local avifauna and particularly vocalizations!" he wrote. "You are pressing at the final frontiers, Phoebe, in your attempt to push that huge list ever higher and you are signing up for trips which are highly exploratory firsts in remote, difficult parts of the world."

In talking about the trip with friends and family, Phoebe didn't try to minimize the seriousness of what she'd been through, as she had after the rape, and she claimed—albeit unconvincingly—to have learned from the ordeal. "Just back from a perfectly AWFUL Irian Jaya trip," she wrote to Doris. "Got 52 lifers . . . this was the only redeeming factor. This was without a doubt the most strenuous thing I've ever done. Made the Himalayas seem like a leisurely stroll around the block." She described the boat accident and said that the whole group "could have drowned." She should have followed David Bishop's advice and not gone on the trip, she said, and she planned to tell him as much in a letter. "I trust everyone has learned some major lessons from this unforgettable experience. I certainly have, and have become very aware of my own physical limitations. (But I *have* seen MacGregor's Bird-of-Paradise!)"

Chapter 9

B URT MONROE HAD been grateful for Phoebe's comments
on *Distribution and Taxonomy of Birds of the World*, and they'd
started a regular correspondence about the update he was preparing.
They'd hardly told each other anything about their personal lives,
but around the time Phoebe returned from Irian Jaya, she heard that
Burt was sick with cancer and wrote to him with concern. "I heard
a most distressing second-hand rumor the other day which I sincerely hope is untrue—that you are going to Bethesda for cancer
treatments? They told me in 1981 that I'd be dead within a year
from malignant melanoma. Since then I've seen all these birds and
had the best 11 years of my life—so if it *is* true, please know that all
may yet be well, and that my most positive thoughts are with you."

He wrote back that he did, indeed, have cancer; it had started in
a kidney a few years earlier and had recently metastasized to one of
his lungs. He'd been considering an experimental treatment that
was being offered in Maryland but had decided against it for fear
that it would incapacitate him. He was getting radiation and other
treatment, however. "The prognosis is excellent; even if they don't
get it all, worst that can happen is I lose a lung in the spring. I got
a spare, anyway . . . Don't worry, it's beaten."

In October 1992, Phoebe took a trip to western Mexico that had been put together by a friend, and, for the first time in a while, she came home ecstatic. She'd liked the "small group of really congenial friends," she wrote later; she'd seen all twenty of her target species; and she thought the guide, Jeff Kingery, was one of the best she'd traveled with. Right after the trip, she wrote a letter to his boss praising him zealously. Jeff had "truly incredible auditory abilities," "excellent visual acuity," and "uncommon perseverance and determination." She'd also liked him "immensely." The trip, she wrote, had been "sensationally successful."

She also went to Israel (for the second time) and Madagascar (for the third) that fall, and by the end of the year she'd passed 7,200. Since January, she'd spent eight months on the road and added 250 lifers, the same, on both counts, as in 1991. She knew from talking to friends that she'd passed Harvey Gilston by this point, which meant that when the rankings for the year came out, she'd be number one. She took little pleasure in that, however, because she was focused on getting to eight thousand first. Michael and Sandra were still hot on her heels, and by this point it was clear that they were determined to beat her. Though she still wasn't talking about the "race" openly, or even admitting that she wanted to get to eight thousand, many years later, in her memoir, she described her thinking around this time: she believed she'd need "three or four more years" of traveling eight months out of twelve to make it to the "next thousand," but she couldn't be sure, as "these were now uncharted waters, and I was quite uncertain that I could continue to find my increasingly scattered lifers at this rate for much longer." Still, "my competition was beginning to face the same problems I was."

To begin charting her course, she tried to figure out which of the 2,500 birds that she hadn't seen were essentially impossible for her. Her "Birds I Won't See" list, arranged in taxonomic order, included about fifty species that had been declared extinct sometime in the twentieth century but were still recognized, perhaps for posterity's sake, in ornithological literature (she marked those birds with an "E"); about twenty more birds were probably but not certainly extinct, such as the Crested Shelduck, formerly of Russia and Japan, a two-foot-tall duck with a Pinocchio-like red bill that, despite its conspicuousness, hadn't been seen since 1964 (she marked the birds that were probably extinct with an "E?"). Hundreds of the other birds she was giving up on were rare, nocturnal, hard to stake out, or all three; the Night Parrot, for example, was seen only every couple of years, in the middle of the night, at various locations in the vast Australian desert. No one knew how many Night Parrots were left, but the number was assumed to be well under a hundred. There were many more birds that she simply couldn't get to: it would have been hard to persuade the Supreme Leader's government to grant her a visa to see the Iranian Ground-Jay; the chaos and bloodshed in Somalia required her to rule out the Somali Lark; she couldn't climb every mountain in the Himalayas or the Andes to see every last pheasant or lapwing. Some birds on the list lived only on tiny little islands—in archipelagos such as the Comoro (in the Indian Ocean) or the Azores (in the Atlantic) or the Cook (in the Pacific)—that didn't have many other endemic birds and therefore weren't worth her time and effort.

She ended up with about a thousand species on her "Won't See" list, which meant that fifteen hundred were "still poss," as she noted at the bottom of the list—roughly half of which she'd need to see to reach eight thousand. Few would be easy. Many of the "still poss" species were secretive birds of the Amazon rain forest that she'd missed one or two or three times already; others had tiny and declining populations; others lived in war zones that were just barely safer than the ones she'd ruled out. They were scattered at every altitude around all seven continents and scores of islands, and, for the most part, she couldn't expect to see more than a handful on any given trip.

As Phoebe was figuring out which birds she could and couldn't see over the course of several more years of hectic travels, Dave, who was sixty-two, was getting ready to retire. Purina had recently been bought by the multinational company British Petroleum, and BP had offered good buyout deals to Dave and some of the other top managers. In his retirement, he figured, he'd spend more time performing magic, do some volunteering, and travel. It had been a while since the whole family had gotten together, and he thought the six of them should take a trip the next Christmas, by which time he would have stepped down.

The kids liked the idea of a family vacation, but Phoebe said she wouldn't be able to make it; she'd already decided to spend the holidays in the Ivory Coast, on a bird tour.

By the early winter of 1993, Burt's health had deteriorated dramatically. "Concerning cancer, the prognosis is mixed," he wrote to Phoebe, optimistically. "[M]y problem is that the cancer has mutated and is now widespread (and rapidly growing)." He had tumors in his lung, in the fatty tissue around his back, in his skull, and in his brain. He wasn't in pain and was still working on the update to his book, he said, and, evidently, he was doing his best to stay positive. "[T]his $@*&% cancer is not going to get me down!"

The reply that Phoebe sent him exemplifies the caring and sensitivity she bestowed on her close birding friends, if not, in recent years, on her husband. "I want you to know how terribly sad I am about your progressing cancer," she wrote. "If there were any justice at all in this world, there are countless people who should have been stricken instead of you. I can't get past the 'angry stage' about what's happening to you. I feel so privileged to have become reacquainted with you since the publication of Sibley & Monroe and to have had such a stimulating and informative correspondence with you. As I hope you know, I'm one of your very many tremendous admirers."

Burt survived to complete the update, which incorporated nearly all of Phoebe's suggestions, and to do a little more teaching and birding. He died in May 1994, at age sixty-two.

Phoebe was conceding Somalia but not Zaire, which was crumbling under the corrupt and heartless rule of Mobutu Sese Seko but contained a huge and tantalizing swath of the bird-rich Congo rain forest.

Since 1966, when Mobutu seized power with the assistance of the U.S., he'd stolen billions of dollars from taxpayers while letting the country's roads, hospitals, schools, police departments, and utility lines rot. In 1990, under pressure from the West, he had agreed to organize elections, but soon afterward he reneged. Protests, riots, and looting ensued. In September 1991, some soldiers, angry over backpay they were owed, mutinied and burned much of Kinshasa; in the fighting that followed, more than 250 people were killed. Most of the foreigners in the country, who, among them, owned nearly all the shops and businesses, fled immediately, leaving their supplies to be looted.

Naturally, there were no organized bird tours of Zaire in the early 1990s, and the State Department advised against going there. Nonetheless, Phoebe went in January 1993 on a trip arranged by a friend. By this time, there were virtually no public services or stores, millions of people were unemployed and hungry, and the majority of the roads had reverted to bush. Various opposition factions were calling for a popular revolt. "Mobutu must go, and now. Christians, arise," declared one rebel in December 1992, a few weeks before Phoebe's small group arrived. They were hoping to avoid trouble by going only to northeastern Zaire, far from Kinshasa, and by flying in and out of neighboring Burundi, which was relatively stable despite growing tensions between the two main tribes, the Hutu and the Tutsi. Just north of Burundi, in Rwanda, Tutsi rebels had been fighting a guerilla war against the Hutu-led government since 1990.

To lead the trip, Phoebe and her friends had hired Terry Stevenson, a Brit. Terry lived in Kenya, had mastered the birds of Africa, and generally led tours for Field Guides. He'd taken up birdwatching as a young boy in northern England but had put birds aside when he entered the prestigious Chelsea School of Art, where he made avant-garde installations consisting of, among other things, furniture, twigs, live animals, and himself. One summer, he took his savings and traveled to Kenya in hopes of being inspired by the tribal art. Instead, his passion for birds was reignited, and a few years later, in 1977, he got a job running a safari lodge.

Terry and Phoebe hit it off. He'd heard about her and started out being a little intimidated, but he found her down-to-earth and kind and was happy to see that she "really enjoyed birds, more than any other top lister." She earned his admiration, too. "She was an incredible worker," he says. "Ninety-nine percent of the time she knew what something was when she saw it. She had everything worked out. I just found it amazing."

It wasn't a physically strenuous trip, but it was audacious. At the beginning, in Burundi, the group stayed at a "really awful" truck stop full of prostitutes and their johns because it was close to good mountain habitat and there were no other options nearby, Terry says. With the help of a safari outfitter, they stocked up on food, fuel, and everything else they'd need for a week and drove into Zaire. For several days, they stayed in a mud hut on the edge of the Congo forest that had been built as a retreat for King Leopold of Belgium and long ago abandoned. The hut was separated from the forest's trails by a river, and the group crossed it every morning and evening via "a truly awesome swinging bridge made of vines and little else," according to Phoebe's memoir. The bridge was rickety and rotting; one day, she lost her footing, one of her legs fell through a hole, and she had to be rescued. The group even drove into Rwanda for a few hours, despite the war. "Beautiful long excellent road thru montane forest," Phoebe wrote in her notebook. "Fabulous habitat." They saw no other tourists anywhere. People pretty much left them alone, Terry says, though in Zaire they got stopped by soldiers looking for bribes and by peddlers trying to sell them snakes, monkeys, and other "bush meat." Over the course of the trip, Phoebe saw forty-two lifers and, she wrote later, had an "absolutely marvelous" time.

On January 28, as the group was heading back to Burundi from Zaire, a faction of Zairian soldiers staged another mutiny in Kinshasa. Over the next few days, hundreds of soldiers, civilians, and diplomats were killed, and in the weeks that followed, riots and ethnic fighting broke out around the country, including the northeast. The ethnic tensions in Burundi boiled over in October, when the Hutu president was assassinated and Hutus took revenge by slaughtering more than 150,000 Tutsis. Six months later, in April 1994, Hutu extremists in Rwanda massacred more than eight hundred thousand Tutsis and moderate Hutus. Zaire descended further into anarchy, largely due to a flood of Rwandan refugees. Phoebe wrote in her memoir, "We did this trip in the nick of time, while the gods were smiling. It was repeated once more the next year, and the participants got out of Burundi with some difficulty, just as the war and all the ensuing human horror tales were beginning."

She'd been lucky to see the birds she'd seen, and lucky to get out alive.

In the late 1980s, Ted Parker, the legendary researcher and tour guide, had gotten more and more worried about habitat destruction in

Latin America, and in 1989, at age thirty-six, he'd quit his jobs with Louisiana State University and Victor Emanuel Nature Tours to found a new initiative at Conservation International that he named the "Rapid Assessment Program." The idea was to take fast but accurate inventories of the flora and fauna in various wildernesses—generally species-rich tropical forests that were at risk of being cut down—and then, as quickly as possible, to write a report that could be used to lobby the relevant government to save the land. In Ted's view, traditional academic studies on biodiversity took so long to research and write that by the time their data could be used for lobbying purposes, it was often too late.

In the first few years of the program, Ted and the other scientists on his Rapid Assessment team catalogued the birds, mammals, amphibians, reptiles, and plants in much of eastern Bolivia, which was largely arid, thorny forest; in a lush cloud forest in southern Belize; and in the dry forests of coastal Ecuador, which they had little hope of saving. "By the time this document is published," they wrote in that report, "much of the forest that we saw during our travels through western Ecuador will have been destroyed." Typically, the surveys comprised a series of low flyovers, to get a sense of the big picture, and a few weeks of camping, bushwhacking, tree-climbing, tape-recording, and note-taking on the ground. There were many occupational hazards: some of the scientists on the team got leishmaniasis, a parasitic disease spread by a biting fly that, left untreated, makes the nose and mouth disintegrate; the mammalogist got bubonic plague from forest rats; and the botanist, Al Gentry, got bitten by a poisonous snake, a Fer-de-Lance, as he collected leaves high in a tree.

In July 1993, Ted, Al, and Ted's fiancée, a Brazilian biologist named Jaqueline Goerck, surveyed the Cordillera del Condor, a mountain range that straddles the Ecuadorian–Peruvian border and was utterly pristine, largely because an intermittent border war between the two countries kept development at bay. "It's the most beautiful place," Jaqueline later told the *Washington Post*, with dense, mossy forest and pink, yellow, and purple orchids. There were no roads, no trails, and only a few Indians; the team had to charter an Ecuadorian military helicopter to take them there and retrieve them.

When they were finished with the survey, they were flown to the city of Guayaquil, where they were to meet with Eduardo Aspiazu, the director of an Ecuadorian conservation group, and two members of his staff before catching their flight home. During the meeting, Eduardo suggested that they all do a quick flyover of what was left of the dry coastal forest that the Rapid Assessment team had surveyed a while back. He managed to find them a plane and a pilot, but at first the pilot insisted that the group of six was too large. Ted, who disliked small planes and tried to ride in them as rarely as possible, volunteered to stay back, but in the end the pilot changed his mind and said everyone could come after all. "Eduardo was so excited," according to Jaqueline.

They flew, low, over the parched brown forest. Then, "[a]ll of a sudden the forest was different and it was a lot richer," as Jaqueline remembered. "Al said, 'This isn't dry forest anymore.'" The group figured the pilot had gotten lost and thought he was starting to turn around when, all of a sudden, they flew into a cloud and hit a mountain.

Eduardo and the pilot were killed instantly. Ted, Al, and one of Eduardo's colleagues, Alfredo, were seriously injured and trapped under the wreckage. Jaqueline was hurt, but she was able to smash a window and crawl out of the plane, along with Eduardo's other colleague, a woman named Carmen. "I said, 'Do you want me to go for help?'" Jaqueline recalled. "And Ted said, 'No, just stay here.'" She agreed, figuring that they'd be missed and found. She talked to Ted and Al into the night, until they lost consciousness. In the morning, when no one had rescued them, she and Carmen set out to find help.

"First there was no trail," Jaqueline said. "The forest was really beautiful forest, ancient, and I had Al's clippers I was using to cut a sort of a trail." She didn't know it then, but she had a broken ankle and two broken vertebrae. "I think after one hour we started hearing people and we yelled back." They'd come upon a village. One of the villagers summoned emergency workers while others rushed to the crash site. Only Alfredo was still alive.

The *Post* reported: "Goerck doesn't believe that, in spite of all the risks they took, [Ted and Al] ever thought that they would die in the jungle. But, she goes on, after considering the question, 'I think it was a good place for them to die. It was beautiful forest, and they were very happy.' There is a long pause before she is able to add, softly: 'Lots of birds.' "

Ted was mourned by conservationists, researchers, and birders around the world, many of whom had long considered him their hero. "His enthusiasm was inspirational and contagious," two ornithologists wrote in an obituary; his experience in the field was "incomparable among contemporaries, and of historic proportion"; his ear was "superior"; and his insights "amazed and intimidated" other scientists. In an obituary in *Birding*, a friend and fellow tour guide for VENT wrote, "Some people have called Ted the Michael Jordan of field ornithology, a rare talent who clearly stood on a higher plane than his contemporaries. Although the comparison is flattering, to me it is not entirely accurate. If Jordan were to elevate his game another notch, he might be worthy of being called the Ted Parker of basketball."

After her success in Zaire, Phoebe decided to put together more private, off-the-beaten-path expeditions. They'd be more expensive than organized tours, but she'd be able to choose the guides and the dates and to orient the itineraries around her increasingly tough target birds. She was thinking one, two, and even three years in advance, and she was starting to talk about "the race" to eight thousand more openly, and in almost militaristic terms. In September 1993, when her list was at about 7,400, she wrote to Jeff Kingery, the guide she'd liked so much in Mexico, "I'm beginning to lay plans for the next few years and develop my strategy for trying to get to 8,000, since I should reach 7,500 early next year. I'll want to do some target-oriented private trips to 'clean up' here and there—and Venezuela still holds a lot of birds for me . . . I have in mind a concentrated effort of 2–3 weeks, hitting several areas." She and David Bishop started writing back and forth about taking a trip together to some Indonesian islands in the winter of 1996. "Based on your prospectus, there are 75 potential lifers there—which probably translates to a 50–60 bird trip," Phoebe wrote. "This would be a most welcome bonus as I'm inching my way toward 8,000."

Simultaneously, she was recruiting friends to come along on the trips, both to make them more fun and to help reduce the cost. "Remember me?" she wrote to Martin Edwards, the Canadian physicist who had nearly died of malaria in Indonesia. "I'm beginning to develop my strategy for the next few years, which is going to include a number of private, target-oriented birding trips, some of them to obscure locations for equally obscure species." She didn't have any trouble getting people to sign on. One friend, an obstetrician from Tennessee named Terry Witt, later wrote that when she sent him a letter inviting him to go to Tanzania with her and Terry Stevenson, the African bird expert, he thought, "Would I be interested in joining Terry and Phoebe for a birding trip to East Africa? This would be like an avid golfer receiving a note from Jack Nicklaus inviting him for a round with Arnold Palmer playing along as well!"

To most people, however, Phoebe still played down both her

goal of eight thousand and the race she was engaged in with Michael and Sandra. In the middle of September 1993, she was invited to give a speech on her career to a birding club outside Chicago. She wrote a lot of notes in advance, and they show that she was planning to present herself as she'd been ten years earlier, when she'd enjoyed every day in the field and was building her list purely for fun and a sense of accomplishment. Her cancer diagnosis in 1981 had given her a "loud and clear" message to "do what you want and need to do and do it NOW," she wrote "Still feeling fine 12 years later—though 2 operable recurrences. Best 12 years of my life. Birding clearly doing me no harm—maybe it's the stimulation, the challenge, the ever-present goals, the jet lag—who knows? I'm doing something that feels *right* and am not about to change my lifestyle until compelled by old age, poor health, or bankruptcy!"

She intended to talk a little about listing toward the end of the speech, but in a light, offhand manner. "Where from here?" her notes say. "Here I am at 7400 species seen—all quite miraculously, I think. Not that I haven't been working at it! So what's possible? 8000 certainly for someone someday, maybe even me, but that's a good 5 yrs. off." (In truth, she hoped to get to eight thousand in three years, by the end of 1996.) After she reached 7,700, she wrote, there would be hardly any "easy or guaranteed ones" left, so seeing three hundred more might not be realistic. "Wish me luck!"

She planned to end her talk with an almost evangelical pitch. "Think how lucky we are to be birding *right now*. Sure, habitats are threatened . . . and we're on the threshold of a major wave of extinctions within the next generation. But *right now* you can still fly for hours over unbroken rain forest in the Amazon basin, over ridge after ridge of unbroken montane forest in New Guinea. *Right now* you can get to more wild places, extraordinary habitats, and incredible birds than has ever been possible in the past, or will be possible in the future. They're all out there somewhere—so do it in whatever style suits you—and ENJOY IT!"

Since returning from Zaire in February 1993, she had gone to Micronesia (for the first time); Hawaii (for the fourth time), where she birded with Tom; Japan (for the fourth time); Kenya (for the fourth time); Peru (for the fifth time); Australia (for the fourth time); and Papua New Guinea (for the fourth time, if you count her disastrous stopover in Port Moresby in 1986). In October and December, she took her sixth and seventh trips to Brazil, the latter of which was a tour that included Michael and Sandra. They were still about two hundred birds behind her, "and it became evident from their comments to me, as well as to others, that they were trying *very* hard to close the gap," she wrote in her memoir.

She only had one day at home—December 16—between her return from Brazil and her next trip, to the Ivory Coast, where she was hoping for forty lifers. She'd be gone for Christmas and New Year's; meanwhile, Dave would take all four kids to an ecotourist resort in Belize.

At some point, probably a bit earlier in the year, when he retired, Dave had decided he'd had enough. He still loved Phoebe, but he was tired of being rejected by her and wanted to find someone who'd be a real companion to him. "I didn't see that there was much for us in the way of a relationship . . . There was caring, but it got lost." Though he "respected" her goal of getting to eight thousand, he couldn't bear the single-minded way she was pursuing it. "I thought, if that's her life, then I want a different life," he says. "To me it was Leo Burnett all over again."

Her decision to skip the family vacation to Belize was the last straw. When she got back from Brazil and was packing for the Ivory Coast, he told her he wanted a divorce. According to her memoir, he said he thought divorce was "the most reasonable and fair course of action" for both of them.

You might think she would have acquiesced right away; for years, she'd been choosing to spend most of her time away from him, and they were emotionally distant even when she was home. Instead, she was furious, partly, she admitted in her memoir, because of his timing. "My ally (as I had thought) had become my adversary, and I was unprepared to deal with it, especially so at this juncture of my life." She was angry, as well, because Dave didn't seem to realize that she, too, had gone through a period of feeling lonely and abandoned, when he was building his career at Purina and she was at home with the four little kids. "Now he was retired, and I was pursuing *my* career, and he was feeling exactly the same lacks that I had. We'd both been guilty of a lack of consideration for the other at different times in our many years together—but was it really too late to recognize this failing and learn from it?" she wrote. She also tried, unconvincingly, to equate his hobby with hers, writing, "He was not interested in sharing my passion for birding, and I felt the same way about his interests in stage magic and ventriloquism." She knew that there had been "a serious lack of communication" between them for many years, but she was "totally and utterly opposed" to a divorce. "There was *so much* to lose, for both of us, and so little to gain."

Dave had a hard time believing that Phoebe still cared so much about their relationship. He thought she might just have wanted to avoid dealing with lawyers, fighting over the house, and splitting their assets, all of which would get in the way of her birding. By this time, he says, she'd spent a good portion of her inheritance, and he had more money than she did. He also figured that she liked the convenience of having him around to maintain their home and take care of other practical matters. "She wanted to get to eight thousand birds, and I was interrupting her life."

Though Dave's explanation probably isn't the whole story, there must be a fair amount of truth to it, as Phoebe's comment in her memoir about "this juncture in my life" suggests. If she was going through a divorce, she could keep taking trips, but she'd no doubt have to slow down, which would give Michael and Sandra a chance to take the lead. It appears that she also equated divorce with failure, which might have made her want to avoid it at all costs. She wrote in her memoir, "Until now, the major challenges in my life had been health related and in no obvious way attributable to fault or neglect on my part. This one was highly personal, with much of the responsibility on my shoulders, and seemed in its own way just as threatening as the cancer."

It's possible, too, that she didn't realize how much she cared about Dave until she thought she might lose him, but that doesn't come across in the memoir. Despite her willingness to take some responsibility for their problems, she mainly wrote about how angry she was.

She had a rotten time in the Ivory Coast. She most wanted to see the White-necked Rockfowl, a secretive, chicken-like forest bird with a bald yellow head and black eyes so big and bulging that they look like they might pop. Her group went to a scientific research station near which some nests had recently been found, but by the time they arrived, the site had been "devastated," as she wrote in her notebook: in place of forest, there were banana and papaya trees, and only the detritus of some mud nests remained. The rest of the day, she wrote, was "*very* slow and quiet."

The next day, the day before Christmas, she decided to go off on her own on the theory that the noise of the group was scaring off any rockfowls. She didn't see one, but when she met up with the group, she found out that they had, and quite well. "*Awful* day," she wrote in her notebook.

She had disappointing results throughout the trip, which mainly consisted of difficult rain forest birding; of the forty life birds she'd been hoping for, she got only twenty-one. "In general, my luck was bad, and whether this had anything to do with my inner state of turmoil is impossible to say," she wrote in her memoir. She had the sense "that my life was falling apart, just as I was on the threshold of my greatest success."

All the same, she impressed the guide. Afterward, he wrote to her: "It was really good to meet you, and I can only thank you for the help and assistance you gave me in the field. Your knowledge is better than resorting to a field guide."

When she got home, she found out that during their vacation, Dave had told the children that he wanted a divorce. "I did resent that the kids had heard a one-sided story, and I felt I needed equal time, so obviously I had long phone conversations with each of them to tell them how I felt about it all, namely that such a move would be wrong, *wrong*, WRONG!—for both of us," she wrote in her memoir. She seems to have thought that if she could get the kids on her side, Dave would be less likely to leave her, but she apparently didn't consider that she was putting them in an awkward position.

In the end, the kids tried to stay neutral, but, for the most part, they sympathized more with their father. Penny says, "I wanted both my parents to be happy. And my dad was not happy." Sue says that when her mother put up a fight, "I thought, why would she want to be with him? The house was just her base for preparing for trips . . . She was irritated with the situation, but she didn't feel a great sadness, I thought."

Dave left town for a while at the end of January, "so I had time and space to pull myself together and think the situation through." She was still angry; she may have been sad, as well, but her memoir doesn't say so. She started thinking strategically, as she had been about the race to eight thousand. "I felt determined to fight what I felt were unfair proposals," she wrote. "I couldn't stop David from moving out if he wished to—but *I* wasn't going to move out and make it easy. If he had to have a different life, then it would be his move." Her plan, she wrote, was to "play a strong defensive game."

She "obviously" couldn't cancel her next trip, a five-week tour of Vietnam, because the arrangements had been made long ago, but before she left, she wrote Dave a "long, emotional letter, trying to initiate a healing approach." According to her memoir, she proposed that they try counseling, as he'd suggested a while back, and she told him that while she wasn't willing to abandon her quest for eight thousand, she'd slow down significantly, for the sake of the marriage, once she got there. She must have reiterated that she, too, had suffered in the marriage, and she must have told him she loved him. "I left the letter for him at home and departed for Vietnam, five birds short of 7,500."

She was with a Ben King tour, the first he'd led to the country, which, until recently, had been off-limits to Americans. During the sixteen-year-long war, most of the forestland had been ravaged by napalm, land mines, and bombs, but in the small patches of forest that remained, Phoebe saw thirty life birds, about the number she'd been hoping for. "I felt better about my situation during this trip," she wrote in her memoir. "I'd done whatever I could do at this point to heal wounds and still be fair and honest with myself and my own needs in life. I knew what I would do, and what I wouldn't do, and initiating any action was simply up to David." Meanwhile, "I managed to concentrate more on the birding than on my own life this time around, so I was once again experiencing the magic healing that birding has always provided for me."

When Dave got home, he read and was moved by her letter. He wasn't sure if her pledge to slow down after eight thousand was good enough for him, but he was no longer certain he wanted to leave her, either, and he decided to find them a counselor. "I was apprehensive enough to be almost physically ill on returning home—because I honestly didn't know what the situation would be with David," Phoebe wrote. But "he was home, and he hugged me!" The counseling route, she wrote, "felt right to both of us," though "it wasn't going to be a quick fix."

At the beginning of 1994, the American Birding Association made a change in the rules of the listing game with which Phoebe and some other members passionately disagreed. Henceforth, if you identified a bird by its call, you could count it on your list, whether or not you'd actually seen it. The change, according to the ABA, was aimed at reducing the amount of stress that birders put on birds. You can listen to an owl or a nightjar without disturbing it, but to get a good look at one you often have to point a spotlight at it. Hearing a Yellow Rail in a marsh is easy, but the bird doesn't like to come out in the open, so to see it you have to "flush" it from the grass. The ABA also argued that since some species sound more distinctive than they look, hearing them is more important anyway.

Phoebe actually stood to gain from the new rule, since she kept a separate list of "heard-only" birds that was about fifty species long, but she thought it was a terrible idea and refused to honor it. To get a real feel for a bird, she thought, you had to see it, and she thought identifications made by ear were less reliable, since avian vocalizations tend to be complex and variable. In other words, she feared a degradation of standards, as her father had when his board wanted to take the Leo Burnett company public. "I consider the ABA ruling allowing 'heard only' birds . . . to be extremely ill advised, opening the floodgates to all manner of spurious 'ticks' and effectively invalidating the competitive listing game," she wrote in a letter to *Birding*, which wasn't published. "I simply won't play it that way, nor will most of the world birders I respect." Michael and Sandra also decided not to count "heard-only" birds, perhaps following her lead or perhaps because they had a problem with the new rule, too.

Phoebe was getting more and more recognition. The 1994 edition of the *Guinness Book of World Records* announced that she was "the world's leading bird-watcher." In March 1994, the magazine *St. Louis Life* published an article hailing her vigor, passion, and "quiet determination." In her interview with the magazine, she was open about the goal she'd set, if not about the intensity with which she was seeking it. The magazine reported, "Now, at an age when most people are looking forward to retirement and social security, Phoebe talks about becoming the first person to ever see 8,000 species of birds in the wild." She also revealed that she'd been attacked in Papua New Guinea, but, surely at her request, what happened to her was described as "horrifying physical abuse," not rape. A book about the ecology of the Midwest that was published in 1993, *Signals from the Heartland*, included a chapter on Phoebe titled "The Bird Woman of Webster Groves." Recalling her early years in town, she told the book's author, Tony Fitzpatrick, "I've seen the world, but I list sitting on that roof at dawn as among my favorite times." The spring migration was bringing fewer warblers to the area than it had when she first moved there, she said, probably because of suburban sprawl. "Bird-watchers in general feel pretty pessimistic about the future . . . But the present is phenomenal."

Bird clubs around the country were running profiles of her in their newsletters. "Top world lister started in Minnesota," proclaimed *Minnesota Birding*. The *Chicago Birder* reported that while her cancer could recur at any time, "[i]n the meantime she has logged over 100 journeys to every conceivable birding locale on the planet." The Los Angeles Audubon Society newsletter, *Western Tanager*, sometimes ran essays by "famous birders"—generally men— and it solicited one from Phoebe early in 1994. "I'm often asked the unanswerable question: 'What's your favorite bird—or trip—or place?' As soon as I decide on one, another immediately springs to mind, and another, and yet another," she wrote. She described a dozen of her all-time favorite trips, including her first trip to Peru, in 1982, when she saw the Harpy and Crested Eagles, and her recent and probably ill-considered trip to Zaire, Burundi, and Rwanda with Terry Stevenson. Her "favorite elevation" was "5–6,000 ft. anywhere in the world . . . At this height the birds, flowers, scenery and temperatures always seem at their best, and it's here where I feel healthiest and most vigorous."

She was getting a lot of fan letters, too. "You are magnificent!" a British friend wrote to her after she'd passed 7,500. "Eighty percent of the world's birds and still fighting. If anyone ever sees more they will never have seen so many in the few years you have used, nor, I doubt, will anyone put as much study and expertise into it as you." A couple of her birder friends wrote to ask if they could be her biographer. "You have a lot of friends and admirers worldwide who would be interested to read about you," pitched one man, another Brit. She replied that while she was open, in theory, to being written about, she didn't have much time to sit and talk.

In the spring, summer, and fall of 1994, she went to Hawaii (for the fifth time, again to bird with Tom), Puerto Rico (for the first time), Turkey (for the first time), Venezuela (for the second time), Ecuador (for the fourth time), the Canary Islands (for the first time), South Africa (for the second time), and Ethiopia (for the first time). The trips added up to seven months away, one month less than she'd been gone the previous year; perhaps she passed up a trip or two as a gesture toward Dave.

In the early years of her travels, Phoebe's main goal had been to enjoy herself, and the number of lifers she got along the way was incidental. After she was raped, she began caring more about how many life birds she saw, even at the expense of her enjoyment, until, by 1994, all she cared about was getting to eight thousand, and any pleasure she got in the process was incidental. Her field notes were no longer punctuated with oohs and ahs; she hardly ever commented on scenery or mammals; and in letters to friends, the highest praise she gave to trips was that they'd been "productive" or "successful," as you might describe a profitable business venture. She'd begun to find her pace onerous, but she didn't see slowing down as an option. "7,620 now," she wrote to a friend in July. "I've promised David (and myself) that I really *am* going to cut way back on birding after 8,000 . . . This verges on insanity." In November, during a brief period at home between her tours of South Africa and Ethiopia, she wrote to a friend that she was going to pack as much as she could into 1995, even though doing so would be unpleasant. "I don't like having to speed up my plans and do all this travel and birding at an even more intense pace than I have been, but it looks like it may be necessary." After she got to eight thousand, which she'd decided was possible by early 1996, "I fully intend to back off from any frantic numerical race and continue more leisurely-paced international birding on a level that I personally find more meaningful." She would "continue to keep track of what I see, but my efforts will be concentrated toward certain priority species with whatever else comes along—*not* toward further [numerical] goals." Her words were almost identical to those she'd used in discussing her impending "retirement" in 1986, right before the rape, when she was on the cusp of seeing five thousand species.

Though she was no longer hiding her competitiveness, she was trying hard to rationalize it, both to herself and to the people she was close to. In her opinion, Michael and Sandra weren't particularly skilled and depended too much on their guides; therefore, she

LIFE LIST

reasoned, it would be bad for the birding community at large if they were the champions. "For better or worse . . . I'm now caught up in this undeclared 'race to 8,000' and plan to see it through with a major push next year toward my last numerical goal—as much as anything, to make the point in dramatic fashion that style, quality, and competence and high numbers on a list need not be mutually exclusive," she wrote to a friend in the fall. She also tried to pretend that Michael and Sandra had instigated the race unilaterally. "Since I passed 7000 in '92, my nearest 'anonymous' numerical rivals have been engaged in an undeclared but obvious 'race to 8000'—[and] I've felt compelled on principle to see this through," she told another friend.

She was haunted by the possibility that they'd beat her, even though she was still ahead by about two hundred birds. At some point in 1994 or early 1995, she wrote a note to herself on the "essential differences" between her and them, probably to calm her nerves. She cared about being competent in the field, she wrote; they just cared about numbers. Lately, to maintain her lead over them, she'd been "doing some high-speed world 'twitching' at a pace I don't like and getting a picture of their style—which I neither like nor admire." (In Britain, a "twitcher" is someone who goes around chasing rarities, often without knowing much about them.) "Anyone w. money can buy birds for their list. What you can't buy is knowledge & expertise, the ability to recognize something surprising when you find it. Only dedication, study, & vast amounts of assimilated experience can lead to this kind of meaningful birding."

She figured that even if she beat Michael and Sandra to eight thousand, they'd pass her eventually, and she came up with a list of three things to say "*when* they have seen 'more.'" One was: "Too bad, since they've gone to the trouble & expense of doing this, that they haven't done it really *well*." The second: "Neither he nor she could have done this alone. It's taken them both—to do a poorer

235

job of it than I have." Of course, they could have argued that working as a team was actually harder, since they could only count birds they'd both seen. Third, Phoebe wrote, "I'll challenge them both to a 'real' contest. Put us in the field anywhere in the world, w. or without a week's prep. time, & I'll put the correct name on more species than the two of them put together."

In this poor state of mind, she found fault with her tour guides more often than ever, even when she saw most or all of her target birds and even when she wasn't under physical stress. During one easy trip in which she saw all forty of the lifers she'd been hoping for, she wrote in her notebook that the guide was "totally w/o initiative or ability to deal effectively w. *simple* logistics"; had "problems with communication"; was "insecure"; and gave "poor directions to birds." She wrote a letter to his boss on the way home saying that though he had showed a good command of the birds, she'd been "frankly uncomfortable" with his lack of "effective management." She accused other guides during this period—often to their deep frustration—of being too focused on recording vocalizations rather than spotting birds; of failing to learn vocalizations in advance; and, ironically, of being ill-tempered. After her trip to Ethiopia in November 1994, she wrote a letter of complaint about a guide that led to his dismissal. When she heard he had been fired, she felt awful.

On the other hand, she was still a patient and enthusiastic mentor to less experienced birders. She'd invited two friends from Chicago who hadn't traveled much, Betsy Fikejs and Melinda Berger, to join her on a private trip to Venezuela in early 1995, and throughout 1994 she wrote them letters about what to expect and how best to prepare. In July, she sent them an official checklist of all fourteen hundred birds that could be found in the country—with some corrections that she'd penciled in—and a list of a half-dozen relevant books. "Don't sweat it—just do whatever you can as long as it's fun and interesting," she wrote. "Believe me, it'll begin to fall into place as we do the birding—and I'm as excited by the whole prospect as you are!" In response to a question Betsy had asked her, she wrote in a postscript, "You should *absolutely*, *definitely* and *positively* go trekking in Nepal in Nov. If there's anything I've learned, it's to seize opportunities first & somehow work in some study time here & there where possible."

When she was home between trips, she and Dave saw their counselor, who, according to Dave, told them that a lot of couples from their generation were "out of sync": the women had waited until the kids were grown to start careers, by which time the men's careers were peaking; just as the women were finding their way in the world, the men were ready to retire. Dave hasn't told me much else about the counseling sessions, though it's clear that he thought they were helpful. In April 1994, Phoebe wrote to Doris, "David and I are going thru something of a crisis in our marriage & are seeing a counselor—a positive step, I think. Too complex to go into here. After 40 yrs, I really hope we can hold together." By summer, according to her memoir, "we were working out our mutual anger and resentment toward a greater awareness of each other's needs." She agreed to take more of an interest in his magic; he agreed to take a birding cruise with her to Tahiti the following year. On a cruise, he wouldn't have to sweat in the rain forest all day, as he would on most of her other trips. He started saying he'd stick with her through her push to eight thousand, with the understanding that she'd cut back dramatically on her travels thereafter.

She had every intention of making good on this pledge, it seems. In August, she canceled a private trip to Japan that she'd been putting together for late 1996. "I'm really sorry, and hate to do this," she told the guide she'd hired, but, she wrote, she'd concluded that the trip would be "low-yield" and "incredibly expensive." "Another factor is problems with David, who is now retired and becoming increasingly unhappy with all my travel without him in pursuit of birds. He knows how important it is to me to reach 8000, which I think I can do in 2 more years. He can accept that, I think, but in return I need to do more with him, and cut back on the solo travel after my last major goal is achieved." She asked the guide if he was still planning to lead a cruise to the "far side" of Antarctica, off South Africa, in late 1995. "This is one David and I could enjoy together, esp. since he's never been anywhere near Antarctica. Let me know if plans for this are coming together."

By the end of 1994, she'd gained some confidence that Dave wouldn't leave her. Around Christmas, she wrote to Doris that they'd had a "good Sept. together" and that all the kids would soon be visiting for about a week, which she hoped would be "a reinforcing family time." Dave seemed to be "accepting" her "last big push to get to (or within reach of) 8000," and she was "optimistic about the future, contrary to a year ago." She wrote to another friend, "To answer your 22 Nov. letter: David and I are okay. Yes, we very much both want to be [okay], and I think we're pulling the marriage out of the fire—for now." The next year would "present challenges," since she had an "over-full birding program." "But remember please (both you and he) that it's my *last big push!*"

At this point, Marmot and Sue felt disconnected from Phoebe, as Penny had for a while. They'd both quit their field jobs, which made their daily lives less like their mother's. Marmot had left the National Outdoor Leadership School and cut back on her own climbing, partly because some friends of hers had died in climbing accidents, and she was getting a master's degree in environmental education in Wyoming. Sue had begun a master's program in conservation biology at the University of Wisconsin in which she was learning to use digital satellite images to assess deforestation. They'd both been "put out," as Marmot says, that Phoebe hadn't come with them to Belize; they were both worried about their father; and they both found their mother harder and harder to talk to. "I'd ask her how a trip was, she'd say what she saw or didn't see," Sue says. "Sometimes I wanted to get past the surface. Maybe I would have wanted more of a feel for the trips, not just a list. Even what continent she was on was hard to keep track of. And I didn't know where all these places were." Marmot says that at this point, her mother "wasn't that easy to engage with" and that she "wouldn't ask you all about your life." She sometimes came to visit them, but usually in conjunction with a bird she was chasing.

By contrast, Tom, who was still doing bird research in Hawaii, felt as close to Phoebe as ever. Since he'd moved to Hawaii in 1991, she'd visited him three times, and each time they'd spent many happy days chasing birds together. On her most recent trip, in March 1994, they'd gotten access, through a friend of hers, to a private ranch that was one of the only places you could see the Hawaiian Crow, the population of which had declined to just eleven or twelve birds. (It was declared "extinct in the wild" in 2002, but there are still a few in captivity.) Tom and Phoebe kept in touch over the phone, too. Recently, Tom and a colleague had devised a new project, the Hawaii Rare Bird Search Team, that involved taking expeditions to remote parts of the Hawaiian islands in search of species that were suspected to be on the verge of extinction, if not already gone. (Most of them were on Phoebe's "Won't See" list.) For the most part, these species were victims of avian malaria, introduced predators, habitat destruction, or a combination of the above. In August 1994, on an expedition to a volcanic mountain on Maui, Tom saw one of the team's target species, the Poo-uli, a chunky, white-and-brown, snail-eating bird that had been recorded only once in recent years and that many ornithologists had given up on. One of the first things Tom did when he got back to his base camp, he says, was call his mother.

He would have liked to see her more and for her to spend more time with the family, but he was far away, too, and, he says, "I would see her decisions as sacrifices—she had to sacrifice time with her family [to reach her goal]. My sisters would say, 'Mom made a choice.'"

Around New Year's, Phoebe wrote herself a note saying that 1995 would be a "Watershed Year." She asked herself some nervous questions:

1) Career—to ~7900+ birds—"safe ground"? (or I'm losing the race)
2) Health—Aug. 95 will be 5 years on melanoma recurrence— Can I pass this?
3) Dave—Will he be content to stick it out thru what I'll do in 95?

She was 230 species short of eight thousand, and, as she wrote in her memoir, "I wanted very badly to win."

Chapter 10

PHOEBE DID BETTER than she'd expected to in the first few months of 1995. She went to Venezuela expecting twenty lifers but ended up with almost forty; she went to the Philippines hoping for fifteen lifers but ended up with more than thirty. The windfall didn't improve her frame of mind, though. When she got home from the Philippines, she wrote a letter to Ben King, who had been the guide, in which she thanked him for some "truly great" birds and "a real boost to my life list" but complained in scorching terms about his "attitude." "Frankly, you seemed as bored, moody, lethargic & negative as I've ever seen you," she wrote. "You were [so] totally uncommunicative & unwilling to talk about birds that it was like pulling teeth to get info. from you. In short, you seemed to be the epitome of the 'burned-out tour leader' & so clearly were not happy with what you were doing that it was a strain on *everyone*." Whether or not her complaints were justified, the letter was a vivid display of her own negativity.

The most important trip she'd planned for the year was to Colombia, which hardly any birders had set foot in, and for good reason. Since the 1960s, the right-wing government and a left-wing guerilla movement, each of which claimed to represent the will of the people, had been waging an increasingly bloody and chaotic civil war. In the 1980s, as the illegal drug trade expanded, drug-lords began asserting their power, too, killing politicians who were tough on crime and fighting guerillas for control of the countryside. Meanwhile, to fund their cause, the guerillas started kidnapping politicians, businessmen, and foreigners, often at highway roadblocks, and holding them for huge ransoms.

Though the State Department strongly advised Americans to avoid the whole country unless they had business there, Phoebe and a couple of equally fearless friends had hired a guide to take them around some mountains near the Caribbean coast, the Santa Martas, which, at the time, were "relatively safe," in Phoebe's words, as most of the violence was farther south. "From there we would go on to Bogotá as circumstances allowed and simply play it by ear as to what we might be able to do," her memoir says. It would be a short trip, from June 23 to July 4. If she saw a decent share of Colombia's seventy endemic birds, she'd probably have the race to eight thousand in the bag, though she was taking nothing for granted. "*Anything* could go wrong at any point in the year," she wrote in her memoir, recalling her thinking at the time, "and I could be standing still just short of the finish line, watching my competitors sail past."

In May, around the time she and Dave returned from their Tahiti cruise and as she was getting ready for a tour of Uganda, her "promising" Colombia plan hit a "major snag" in the form of a "sudden and totally unanticipated announcement" from Penny and her boyfriend, Harlan Tait, that they were planning to get married in an informal ceremony at their house on July 2. They'd met in a ballroom dance class and had been living together in Connecticut for years.

Phoebe had always told Penny, now thirty-six, and her other daughters that she didn't know the first thing about planning a wedding and that they'd be better off eloping; as a result, Penny says, it didn't occur to her to consult her mother before setting the date, and, in any event, she and Harlan didn't have any other free weekends that summer. But, to Penny's surprise, Phoebe was irked that she'd been left out of the planning and upset that she'd have to miss the wedding—unless she skipped her trip, which she apparently didn't see as an option. Penny claims she didn't expect her to change her plans and wasn't mad when she didn't, but Sue says the whole family was ticked off, albeit quietly so. "It was clear there was a choice to be made," Sue says. "My mother knew how all of us felt. It didn't need to be said that we were all upset." In her memoir, Phoebe said she was "surprisingly upset about missing my first daughter's wedding" but that "the notice was too short to change dates for Colombia."

The trip, she wrote afterward, was "truly excellent." "We saw nearly all the Santa Marta endemics and were able to do much more near Bogotá than I had dared hope, even getting as far as some great spots in the central Andes." They had no trouble with the guerillas, who were all over the place; in fact, at one point, near Bogotá, their van got a flat, and a bunch of armed rebels in camouflage came out of nowhere and helped them change it. The rebels even showed an interest in their bird books.

On July 2, while Dave, Marmot, and Sue were watching Penny get married, Phoebe was watching the mating dance of the Red-ruffed Fruitcrow. Two days later, when she got home, she was just seventy birds short of eight thousand.

On the afternoon of July 1, 1995, while Phoebe was in Colombia, Rose Ann Rowlett was leading some birders down a trail in the Manu region of Peru when an eight-foot-long snake emerged from some bushes and attacked the strong young man walking right behind her, knocking him to the ground. Rose Ann's co-leader, John Arvin, who'd been right behind them, beat the snake back into the brush with the tripod for his telescope and recognized it as a Bushmaster, one of the deadliest poisonous snakes in the world. The man who'd been attacked, a Belgian named Peter Boesman, had two bite marks just below the right knee, both of which were oozing blood.

They were hours from the nearest doctor. Peter and John had to take a boat across a river just to get to the group's bus, whereupon they were driven on a rough and windy road to a rural clinic that stocked antivenin. They got there five hours after the bite, by which time Peter's leg was paralyzed, hurting, and starting to swell, according to an account of the incident that was published in a medical journal. He was given antivenin, painkillers, and large amounts of water, but by the next morning, July 2, he felt even worse, and the doctor at the clinic decided to transfer him to a hospital in the nearest city, Cusco. He and John were driven to an abandoned airstrip with overgrown grass to await a small plane that had been summoned. However, after circling the strip several times, the pilot refused to land on the basis that the terrain was too rough, and Peter and John had to be driven to Cusco on a bus. The ride, over bumpy mountain roads, took more than twelve hours. Peter was in great pain and running a fever.

He got to the hospital at around three A.M. on July 3, about thirty-five hours after the bite, and was given more antivenin, more painkillers, and intravenous antibiotics. By nine A.M., he was "alert" and "optimistic," and "the crisis seemed to be over," according to the medical journal. John, who was still with him, radioed Rose Ann and said that the two of them might even be able to rejoin the tour. In the afternoon, though, an ultrasound test showed that there was no circulation in Peter's right leg and that he'd lost two liters of blood internally. He was rushed into surgery, and it revealed vast regions of dead tissue, or gangrene. The doctors arranged for him to fly to a major hospital in Lima, where he'd undergo surgery to remove the gangrene. At that point, he was only given a thirty-percent chance of surviving.

He arrived in Lima on the morning of July 4, but the surgery had to be delayed because the hospital didn't have enough units of blood that were compatible with Peter's blood type—A, Rh negative is rare in Latin America. John and some American and European embassy workers donated their blood, and around five P.M., about seventy-two hours after he'd been bitten, Peter went into surgery. By this time, he was only given a five-percent chance of surviving.

The surgery took all night. In the morning, the doctors gave John some good news and some bad: Peter was alive, but, to save him, they'd had to amputate his leg.

Perhaps Phoebe heard, through the grapevine, about what had happened to Peter, and perhaps that's why, later in July, after her return from Colombia, she gave some thought to what she wanted to happen if she died on a trip. In a letter addressed to Dave and the children, she explained "what I'd like to be done with me after my death (assuming I die in such a way and place that my body needs to be disposed of)." Her sentiments about this hadn't changed since 1990, when she'd first broached the topic with them, though she had more specific instructions this time. "I *definitely* prefer cremation to burial, and would really like to have my ashes spread in some beautiful spot with a vista of snow-capped mountains. Your choice: Rockies, Tetons, Cascades, Alaska, Andes, Himalayas. Use some of your inheritance to go someplace wonderful, throw my ashes to the winds, & then hike, climb, birdwatch & enjoy your time there, wherever it is."

She ended the letter with a poignant acknowledgment of the

difficulty she had in expressing her emotions. "And do remember that I love you all—more than I've ever been able to let you know."

She saw her eight-thousandth life bird on September 26, 1995, a little more than thirty years after she'd seen her first one, on the edge of a buggy swamp in San Blas, Mexico, near the Pacific coast. She'd hired a guide, Steve Howell, author of a field guide to Mexican birds, to take her around the country on a "cleanup," and "one by one, the birds fell into place," she wrote in her memoir. By the end of their last day of birding, her list was at 7,999, and she figured she'd set the record at the beginning of her next trip. But when they got back to their hotel that afternoon, a boatman who'd taken them around the day before had left a message saying that he'd just seen a couple of Rufous-necked Wood-Rails near his dock. Over the years, Phoebe had tried many times to see that bird, without success; it's secretive, and generally stays hidden in reeds and mangroves.

"I had that nice anticipatory feeling that something good was about to happen." She and Steve met the boatman at the dock and scanned the mangrove bushes along the water's edge. "It wasn't long before I glimpsed a furtive movement," her memoir says. "The movement stopped, but I clamped my binoculars on where I'd seen the motion, and there it was, with its red head and neck, green bill, red eye, and red legs standing frozen in the tangled undergrowth: a Rufous-necked Wood-Rail. 8,000!"

She'd achieved her goal much sooner than she'd imagined she would, even in her "most optimistic dreams," and Michael and Sandra were still about two hundred birds behind her. "It had been a comfortable lead after all, and they really hadn't been able to narrow the gap in several years," she wrote. "I drank a lot of Bloody Marys on the flight home."

The word spread fast. The record was announced, to applause, at meetings of bird clubs around the country. *Winging It*, the American Birding Association newsletter, reported: "Phoebe Snetsinger of Webster Groves, MO (who can't possibly spend much time in Webster Groves), has reached a truly remarkable milestone—her 8,000th world species, a Rufous-necked Wood-Rail . . . Her 1993 ABA List Report showed a world total of 7,491 birds; in the intervening 21 months, she saw an amazing 509 new birds. We stand in awe of her continued quest." A story in the *St. Louis Post-Dispatch*, "Birder Peeks At 8,000th Species," was picked up by the Associated Press and published in papers from coast to coast. In her interview with the *Post-Dispatch*, Phoebe announced her retirement from hard-core birding. "It's time to change my pace. I will never see the 9,700 species that exist in the world. It was special just seeing the ones I have."

A couple of days after she got home, on October 3, she wrote a letter to her friend Martin Edwards in which she sounded both triumphant and relieved. "Made 8000 the last day in Mexico—Rufous-necked Wood-Rail, in the mosquito-infested mangrove swamps of San Blas. It was an appropriate one: I'd missed it before, and it took a fair amount of time, effort, skill, suffering, and—as always—luck. Beat the dreaded Brits by over 200! So *that's* over—& now I can go birding for fun!"

At the end of October, she and Dave went to Missoula, Montana, where Marmot had moved, to visit with her and Sue, who was still at the University of Wisconsin. The notes Phoebe took on the trip suggest that she was already thinking more expansively than she had in the thick of her quest. Outside Missoula, for example, she got "dramatic vistas of Mission Mtns, w/ fresh snow, flanked by green pines & brilliant larches, golden in patches of sunlight."

Despite their mixed feelings about many of the choices she'd made, Dave, Marmot, and Sue had put together a thoughtful and generous present for her. When someone retired from Purina, he got a scrapbook commemorating his years there; when Phoebe got to eight thousand, it occurred to Dave that she should get a scrapbook too. Over the few weeks before they all met up in Montana, Marmot and Sue had cut out pictures of birds and birders from various magazines, found some old photographs of Phoebe, and solicited photos and cards from her birder friends. "It is not possible for me to express how much I am indebted to you for all your moral support, thoughtfulness, [and] patience," wrote Doris, who was in her late seventies, was still traveling, and had recently passed five thousand. The time they'd spent together, Doris wrote, "truly has been a highlight of my life." Aileen Lotz, the birder, author, and editor, wrote, "What a fantastic life you have really lived! And how lucky I feel to know you and to have shared a few of those 8,000 with you." According to Bob and Myra Braden, the couple she'd met and impressed on her cruise to Antarctica eight years earlier, "You have been an inspiration to us all."

Tom and Dave wrote sweet notes for the scrapbook, too. "I would love to be able to write a poem or a song or draw a picture in commemoration of this event," Tom said. "Sadly, I have none of those abilities, but I do hope that you can accept this letter and my own meager listing effort as expressions of awe and flattery. Without your presence I never would have become a lister. Without your guidance I never would have found my niche in the birding world. Without that niche I would probably still be back in Seattle managing Paradise Produce."

Dave, who, of course, had been anticipating this occasion for two years, wrote, "It has been an incredible journey . . . You have earned and deserve all the accolades given to you by your peers. You also have the recognition of those who don't really understand about birding at all but know that #1 in the world on anything is pretty special." He said he was "proud to be Phoebe Snetsinger's husband, friend, and sometime birding companion. Just by association that elevates me upward in the eyes of the world." He also said, "in the 'David Snetsinger Book of Records,' you are and will always remain #1."

On the one hand, in the nine years since she'd been raped and changed her mind about retiring, she'd caused her husband a great deal of pain, missed her mother's funeral, alienated three out of four of her children, and missed her eldest daughter's wedding. She'd gotten a deadly strain of malaria, played roulette with her health by postponing two surgeries, taken a trek dangerously beyond her abilities, survived a boatwreck that could have been fatal, and traveled in countries where there was no rule of law. She'd strained her relationships with tour guides, lost sleep over "rivals" who were far behind her, and, increasingly, lost sight of the reasons she'd gotten into birding in the first place.

On the other hand, she'd inspired her kids to travel far and wide and to pursue careers in the natural sciences, and she'd been a mentor and a role model to birdwatchers everywhere. She'd seen birds that had brought her to ecstasy; made dozens of friends around the world; shown, as she'd hoped to, that you could build a big list without letting your standards slip; risen to the pinnacle of a subculture still dominated by men; been feted by her peers, her family, and the press; and amassed a breadth of ornithological knowledge that hardly anyone, amateur or professional, could rival.

No doubt, she'd also kept her mind off the attack in New Guinea that had nearly killed her and the illness that was still supposed to, any day.

Chapter 11

TWO MONTHS AFTER she celebrated her supposed retirement, Phoebe was taken prisoner at gunpoint by a gang of Ethiopian tribesmen.

In 1995, Ethiopia was only beginning to recover from decades of civil war. For years, the country had been ruled by a murderous Marxist dictatorship that depended on billions of dollars' worth of machine guns from the Soviet Union to suppress guerilla uprisings. The guerillas, armed with guns they'd stolen from the army, finally overthrew the regime in 1991, shortly after the collapse of the Soviet Union, and in the mid-1990s a democratic government was being established. The machine guns hadn't gone anywhere, though, and in some parts of the country a culture of guns and violence still prevailed.

Long before she'd gotten to eight thousand, Phoebe had arranged for a guide to take her and a friend to some remote parts of the Ethiopian highlands that her tour in 1994 hadn't covered. When she made the arrangements, she'd thought she'd need the trip to put her over the top, and by the time it was clear that she wouldn't, everything was already set. The group—Phoebe; her friend, a Swedish doctor named Claes-Göran Cederlund; their guide, a Brit; and their driver, an Ethiopian—began the trip in Addis Ababa just after Thanksgiving 1995. They followed dirt roads and tracks up and down mountains and across the high, dry plains, stopping in simple guesthouses to eat and sleep. According to Claes-Göran, Phoebe was noticeably more relaxed in Ethiopia than she'd been in the years she was trying to reach eight thousand, and her field notes appear to bear this out: she got "beautiful close views" of a pair of ducks on a river; she saw "lovely gnarled trees" that reminded her of the magical forest in *The Hobbit*; she saw "sensational" birds as she walked along the edge of an "incredibly beautiful" escarpment.

Toward the end of the trip, when the group was in the lush southern part of the country, they decided to drive to an out-of-the-way forest that no Westerner had been to in years but was supposedly home to some unusual birds. The road to the forest was a windy mountain track, and as they made their way along it in their Jeep, some tribesmen on horseback blocked their path, pointed Kalashnikovs at them, and made them get out. The group's driver tried to explain to the chief tribesman what he and his white passengers were doing, but the chief was "hostile" to them and "irate" that they were trespassing on his land, according to Phoebe's notes.

They were ordered to get back in the Jeep and follow the tribesmen to their village, which turned out to be two hours away on an "incredibly rough road." The village consisted of a few thatched huts and a central square, and the group was made to stand in the square under a brutal sun. All the villagers gathered to stare at them; meanwhile, the driver kept trying to set things straight with the chief. Finally, without explanation, the chief decided to let them go, as long as they swore never to return.

"We were rattled," says Claes-Göran, probably with quite a bit of understatement. In her notebook, Phoebe wrote of the chief: "Omnipotent in his area—Could have been a serious problem."

Overall, the trip was "spectacular," she wrote to a friend when she got back, in a letter that made no mention of the Kalashnikov incident. She told her friend that she'd seen, among many other endemic species, the Prince Ruspoli's Turaco, a big, parrot-like bird that makes loud, raucous calls from the treetops. It's mostly drab green, but it has a crest of fluffy white feathers that stand straight in the air, as if it's an elegant old lady who's just gotten her hair done.

In January 1996, Phoebe was still reveling in her victory, and she was still asserting that it marked a turning point for her. In response to a congratulatory letter from a friend, she wrote, "Glad to have *that* race over—& now I'm going back to being a birder instead of a lister! Yes, Michael & S. tried desperately to beat me to 8,000 & couldn't do it. I realized a couple of years ago that it was a 'serious' race, & decided to go all out for the record . . . However, I'm serious about a more relaxed pace & backing away from the numerical race—for a number of reasons." She went on, however, to talk about the many trips she was taking during the first part of the year, "mostly pre-arranged a year or two ago when I wasn't sure what it would take to reach my target," and several trips she was planning for 1997.

In the meantime, she was getting yet more press. The *St. Louis Post-Dispatch* did another article on her; she was interviewed for a BBC radio show; and *Birder's World*, a magazine, interviewed her on a wide range of subjects and published her answers, verbatim, in a four-page spread. "The one thing that has enabled me, right from the start, to forget about the cancer and not be worried about it is simply the fascination of birding," she told *Birder's World*. "I could absolutely lose myself in preparation for all these fantastic birds that I was going to see and in the birding itself. It has been a way of holding the cancer at bay. I don't know if it's done anything for me physically, but I feel like I'm doing something right." She didn't mention the rape, another dark reality from which birding was a reprieve, of course. She said she was proud of the record she'd set, especially since she didn't expect that anyone would ever get to the "next thousand," but "at this point, I'm not really counting." "I want to de-emphasize numerical competitions and go back to enjoying birds on a more relaxed level . . . I concentrated on breaking the 8,000 record, which I really wanted to do, but I don't want to keep up this rather insane travel pace."

She also told *Birder's World* that while she'd benefited over the previous twenty years from "an explosion of knowledge and expertise in where and how to find birds," she'd also witnessed "rampant logging and forest devastation." She said, as she had before, that the future for birds and birders was grim, and that "at the rate we are destroying our world," the Golden Age wouldn't last more than another twenty years. "We are destroying irreplaceable habitats at an alarming rate. They are *finite*. Some people project the end of the world's rain forests, for example, in the frighteningly near future." Though there was "a slowly growing ecological awareness, at least in the Western world," she saw this as "a finger in the dike—a stopgap measure that will gain us a little precious time."

In some important ways, getting to eight thousand did end up being a turning point for Phoebe; but in equally significant ways, not much changed.

The biggest change was in her frame of mind: by the spring of 1996, she was as ecstatic in the field as she'd ever been. On a trip to Peru in May, for example, she responded to the landscape as if she was seeing it for the first time. (It had, in fact, been a while since her last trip to Peru. In 1990, guerillas from Shining Path had murdered two British birdwatchers, and birders had generally avoided the country for the five or six years that followed.) As Phoebe looked out her window on a flight from the highlands to the coast, she wrote, "Mind-boggling, spectacular, incredible views of Andes.

Close, beautiful, sensational jagged snow-capped peaks, glaciers, & turquoise alpine lakes." The notes she took on the birds bubbled over with excitement. They had "exquisite details" or "stunning plumage" or a "striking, unusual color" or a "beautiful color & pattern"; she got a "super view" or "*beautiful* views" or "*exc.* views" or "incredible close soaring views in exc. light." She was especially excited to see the Marvelous Spatuletail, a hummingbird known from just a few sites. It has a tiny body, like most hummingbirds, but its tail is long and extravagant, comprising two long, ribbon-like feathers, each of which ends with a blob of plumes shaped like a tennis racquet. "Incredible," she wrote.

Contrary to what she told *Birder's World* and many of her friends, she was, in fact, still counting, but she'd decided to stop sending her list to the American Birding Association. In a letter to *Winging It* explaining this decision, she said she wanted to "consciously end this phase of hectic competitive listing" in favor of "a pace which I find more enjoyable, satisfying, & meaningful." (The letter wasn't published; perhaps she never sent it in.) Furthermore, she'd become "disenchanted with ABA listing standards" (she was referring, tacitly, to the ABA's decision to let "heard birds" count) and more aware of the "arbitrariness" of the master list of bird species that the ABA used (she was referring, again tacitly, to the ABA's failure to come to grips with new and valid splits in a timely fashion). "I plan in the future to take the approach of primarily increasing my knowledge & understanding of the world's complex avifauna, rather than my numerical list according to ABA rules." In effect, she was doing what her father had threatened to do, thirty years earlier, in his retirement speech: she was taking her name off the door of an operation that no longer met her standards.

By the end of the summer of 1996, however, she'd quietly come up with a new numerical goal. Having already seen representatives of all the 180 bird families, she decided to try to tick off all but a hundred of the slightly more than 2,100 genera. At that point, she was missing about 130 genera, so she'd need to fill in thirty. As she wrote to one friend, "I think I've probably seen enough look-alike species or splits in the same genus to last a lifetime . . . but a new genus—well that really is something." In a letter to her old friend and tour guide Bret Whitney in September, she said she was having a great year, "especially now that the pressure is forever off species-counting." Yet later in the same paragraph, she wrote, "I *would* really like to see 30 more genera . . . I probably can't do much better than that, and even that will take me another 5 years or so. But I'm (only!) 65, and it's been 6 years now since that last melanoma recurrence that had me so worried, and which I so dreaded facing after our last PNG-Fiji trip in '90."

She probably couldn't picture her life without a numerical goal to give it shape; perhaps she also feared what would happen to her physical and mental health if she wasn't striving for something. She was likely looking for a way to justify more travel, as well. She'd barely slowed her pace since her "last big push" had ended ten months earlier, just as her father, in his "retirement," had worked almost as hard as ever. Since setting the record, she'd gone to Ethiopia, Costa Rica (for the second time), the Bahamas (for the first time), Indonesia (for the third time), Tanzania (for the third time), Peru (for the sixth and seventh times), Hawaii (for the sixth time, though Dave came with her, to see Tom), and Colombia (for the second time, again against the advice of the State Department). In all, she'd been gone for five months out of ten and seen about two hundred life birds. It's true that she'd planned most of these trips before she knew when she'd get to eight thousand, but it's also true that she could have canceled many of them without in-curring a big financial penalty or disappointing anyone. Instead, she disappointed Dave, who was still waiting for her to make good on her promise.

She did spend much of November and December 1996 at home, though that was more an aberration—or "vacation," as she called it—than the beginning of a change in lifestyle; by then, she'd already booked up most of 1997. In November, she wrote to Doris that she'd be taking back-to-back trips to Cameroon, Ireland, and Bulgaria early in 1997 that would keep her away from home for a stretch of six weeks. "That's really too long to be away, but I'm home now for over 6 weeks, so I guess it balances out—?"

During this period, she exchanged some letters with Bret, who was working on a field guide to the birds of Brazil and was looking for financial backing. He sent her a prospectus and a possible budget, and she wrote back enthusiastically and with a generous pledge of $2,500 a year for the next four years. "*Clearly* you're doing the most exciting and groundbreaking bird research and exploration that's being done on this planet right now," she wrote. "I fully expect the project will be accomplished in the same brilliant way you seem to do everything you undertake!" Characteristically, she also gave him some suggestions on how to improve the prospectus and budget and how best to go about soliciting money.

She spent a good part of the fall getting started on a book of her own. At some point since setting the record, she'd decided that she wanted to tell her life story herself instead of handing it over to someone else. She didn't particularly like being interviewed, she told friends, partly because she thought she expressed herself better in writing and partly because she'd been frustrated by inaccuracies and distortions in the articles that had been written about her. She also wanted an opportunity to reflect on her life, as she wrote in an early draft of her introduction. "Life can hardly be considered over at my current age of 65—but an era clearly is, and my psyche is now demanding some evaluation and assessment." The working title of her memoir was *Birding on Borrowed Time: History and Reflections for Family and Friends.*

It's not clear how much of the book she wrote in the fall of 1996, but it's likely that she finished at least the first chapter, "Beginnings," which, to me, is one of the most interesting. While much of the rest of the book is an account of which birds she saw on which trips—without, despite her intentions, a great deal of self-analysis—"Beginnings" is an intimate meditation on why she didn't discover birds earlier, and on how powerfully they changed her life when she did. "Why is it such a rarity for little girls to become intrigued with birds at an early age as compared to little boys?" she began. "The question has been asked many times, and I have no good answer." She described her tomboyish inclinations as a child, her adventures with her brother Joe, and the long walks she took on her parents' farm. "By all reasonable criteria, I *should* have become hooked on birds early on . . . but nothing took hold, and I can't quite explain why." In college, she wrote, she took long walks "in a beautiful wooded area adjacent to the campus" that "must surely have been a truly wonderful spot during warbler migration." She was, however, "oblivious to it all," perhaps because she was "heavily into intellectual pursuits" at the time. She was particularly surprised that birds hadn't gotten a hold on her when she was a science teacher at the Baldwin School and taught a whole unit on them. "Here was a gift-wrapped golden opportunity for catching my attention and interest, if there ever was one. But did it work? In retrospect, I can't believe I never even took those kids outside to see anything they were learning about. I cringe at such memories now."

"So when *did* it finally happen, this awakening that has ultimately let me get the real world in focus and that has given me my bearings for navigating through the best years of my life?" She described how she'd needed "some sort of outlet" as a young housewife and her experience with Elisabeth Selden and the Blackburnian Warbler in the spring of 1965, an event that "quite simply hooked me forever." "Finally, I was ready to see what had lain before me all those years."

While by her own account her best years came later, once she started traveling, she wrote of that first spring of birding with the kind of nostalgia that many people feel for their first love. "Almost every birder has a first magical season of wonder, whether it happens at age five or fifty, during which some of one's most cherished and indelible birding memories take shape. I look back with a bit of envy now at the open-mouthed astonishment with which I entered the world of birding."

At some point during the writing process, she scrawled a note to herself, perhaps to focus her thoughts. It said, "I have been; I have seen and done. I have left children, legacy." In addition to all her stated reasons for writing the book, she must have been motivated by a desire for this legacy to live on.

She also made an overture toward Dave during this period, with mixed results. Since her great experience snorkeling in Fiji in 1990, she'd been thinking about learning to scuba dive, and in the fall of 1996 she convinced Dave to try to get certified with her. He was "willing," she wrote in her memoir, but "probably not as sold on the prospect as I was." Their first few classes were at a nearby Y, in the pool, and they also spent some mornings swimming laps together, "just to get in shape and more comfortable in the water," she wrote to a friend. In December, they flew to the Florida Keys for a second set of classes, in open water. Unfortunately, their trip coincided with a record-setting cold front, and the first day of class was gray, windy, and frigid. The sea was rough, with four-foot-high waves, and Phoebe threw up as they rode out to the reef. When they got in the water, the surface conditions were "turbulent and intimidating, not to mention cold"; underwater, the visibility was bad, which was "disorienting," she told her friend. She and Dave both had trouble with their equipment: her oxygen tank slipped out of its strap; he dropped his weight belt to the bottom. The next day was sunny and a little less rough, "so we completed the necessary dives—but just." While they were diving, Dave had some ear pain; afterward, he realized that he'd lost some hearing ("temporary, we hope and the doctors think"). The whole thing, she wrote, was "more trauma than fun."

When they returned, Phoebe found out, to her shock, that Sandra Fisher had gotten cancer and died. Michael, in grief, had given up birding. In her memoir, Phoebe wrote that Sandra's death was "saddening" and "seemed yet another signal for an end to the competitive aspect of birding in my own life."

Over the next year, Phoebe took a lot of trips and had a ball. She'd already seen so many birds that she could only get a dozen or so new ones—and only one or two new genera—on any given trip, but this just seemed to heighten her appreciation for the ones she did see, and she was passionately appreciative of her surroundings, too. In March 1997, she went to Namibia, which is largely desert but had just gotten unusually heavy rains; as a result, she wrote in her notebook, the land was "green and lush," pink blossoms had sprouted on the teak trees, and the birds, prompted to mate, were in "full song" and "stunning breeding plumage." She got an "exquisite close perched view" of a Shaft-tailed Whydah, a little bird that grows jet-black tail feathers several times the length of its body for the breeding season, and she heard "liquid" and "melodic" and "warbly" and "tinkling" mating songs. She also got "amazing colorful close all-feature views in beautiful light" of a flock of hundreds of storks, beheld "herds of spectacular Oryx," and saw "marvelously wind/sand-sculptured granite formations."

In November 1997, she took another cruise to Antarctica—this time with Dave, and to the "far side," off South Africa. In a

snowfield surrounded by an "amazing," "end-of-the-earth" landscape of still blue icebergs, she saw a colony of thousands of three-
foot-tall Emperor Penguins "in every pose and action": waddling,
bleating, sledding on their stomachs, tending to their "adorable"
fuzzy chicks. The Emperors, made famous by the movie *March of
the Penguins*, are the only penguins that breed during the dark and
punishing Antarctic winter. In May, just as winter is beginning,
each female lays an egg, leaves it with her mate, and goes off to
the sea to feed; throughout the winter, thousands of males huddle
together to keep themselves and their eggs from freezing. Later,
Phoebe's group went to another Emperor colony in a "simply stunning setting" with "magnificent," "castle-like" icebergs, according to
her notes. "Spent 6 hours—several scattered colonies & splendid sce-
nic walk around gorgeous blue icebergs."

   She'd achieved a royal status among fellow birders. During van
rides and at meals, her companions would often keep quiet so they
could listen to her stories, made vivid by her "dazzling" memory, one
friend said. When she took the time to help novices, they were hum-
bled. "Thank you for being so helpful on the trip," wrote a woman
who had been with her on a tour of Brazil. "I know at times you
might well have wanted to be impatient with the likes of me, rank
tyro that I am. But you were always patient and *always* generous, even
eager, to share your scope." A woman on her Namibia trip wrote,
"We certainly enjoyed meeting you and profiting by your expertise
and experience. Your reputation as the world's champion birder had
preceded you and I was happy to find you such a delightful companion." She still had time for members of the Webster Groves Nature
Study Society, too. "I truly appreciate you taking out time from what
must be an incredibly busy schedule to give a struggling newcomer a
boost of confidence," one member wrote in a card. "I can only hope
that in my lifetime I can become half the birder you are."

   She didn't get upset with any of her guides during this period,

Emperor Penguin

and when something went wrong, she tended to take it in stride. On her trip to Cameroon, in January 1997, she got stung by a bee on her eyelid one night, and, while she was sleeping, the whole right side of her face swelled up. Instead of getting upset about it, she turned it into a joke. At breakfast the next day, she played a trick on some friends by turning away as they walked toward the table, then swinging around to face them, in all her swollen glory, when they were a few inches away. In a picture taken that day, her eye is just a little slit, but she's beaming.

She was away for seven months out of twelve in 1997, during which she saw about a hundred life birds and fifteen new genera. By the end of the year, she was barely paying lip service to the notion of slowing down. She wrote to her friend Betsy Fikejs at the beginning of January 1998: "Most of my excursions these days yield a very few but very special birds, and since good health is holding, I'm planning at least a couple of years in advance. Hope to do more in Brazil, Poland, Colombia, the Tibetan plateau, Peru, and Malawi in the coming year, as well as some family things. There are 24 months this year, right??"

When she was home, she continued working on her memoir, with an audience of other birdwatchers in mind. There's little in the book about her early years and her family life, and only a little more about the decade or so she spent with WGNSS; the focus is on her travels and, in particular, on the birds to which they took her. Again and again, she said the years since 1981 had been the best of her life, and she wrote with enthusiasm about pretty much all the trips she'd taken, even those that had been a mixed bag, and even the one on which she'd been raped. As usual, she described the rape, but, as usual, her take on it was factual rather than emotional. Only the trip to Irian Jaya hadn't been "worth it," she claimed, but she managed to end her account of that ordeal on a positive note all the same: "I'd learned something about the physical limits of my own endurance, and the trip had certainly given me a benchmark for all time: no matter how tough a future trip might be or how awful the conditions, I'd instantly feel better by realizing that it wasn't as bad as Irian Jaya!"

She comes across as brave and passionate but lacking in self-knowledge. She claimed that she was "over" the rape within two months; she didn't reflect on why her list and getting it to eight thousand became so important to her; she said she was "flabbergasted" when Dave asked for a divorce; and she didn't acknowledge that she'd broken her promise to him to slow down. Each of these subjects—the rape, her compulsiveness and competitiveness, and the deterioration of her relationship with Dave—might have been too painful for her to give a lot of thought to. In any event, if the book was an attempt to preserve her legacy, she might have thought that there was no point in tarnishing it with her flaws.

She also worked on another ambitious project during her periods at home in 1997: her very own taxonomy of the birds of the world. Since Burt's death in 1994, the coauthor of his *Distribution and Taxonomy* book, Charles Sibley, had updated it to include 9,950 bird species, 250 more than he and Burt had originally recognized. A few of the new species had just been discovered, but the vast majority were splits that had been proposed by ornithologists in the field since 1990. The new version of the book was put out on CD-ROM, and Phoebe learned to use a computer so she could read, annotate, and edit it. She'd been poring over all the ornithological journals and keeping in touch with friends about their research, and, in her opinion, Sibley had overlooked a fair number of valid splits. Her own reckoning, which she completed in the fall of 1997, allowed for 10,030 species of bird, eighty more than Sibley recognized. When she translated her life list to the taxonomy she'd fashioned, she found that she'd seen close to 8,400 of the 10,030 birds. (The American Birding Association still recognized just 9,700 species, of which she'd seen about 8,300, but since she was no longer in "the game," she didn't have to worry about that.) She knew that as ornithologists learned more about previously mysterious birds, they'd propose many more splits, and she intended to stay abreast of this research and update her taxonomy as she saw fit. "I find it very exciting to be birding at a time when the whole question of 'what is a species' is very much open to debate," she told a friend. "It makes so much of what one sees (and hears) potentially very interesting, and a lot more fun than just ticking off x-many birds on a list which may not bear much relation to reality."

To account for the ongoing taxonomic changes, she started thinking of her life list not as a raw number but as a percentage:

the number of birds she'd seen divided by the total number of birds on her master list. With 8,400 out of 10,030 species, she stood at 83.7 percent. By using percentages, she explained in an article for *Winging It* in December 1997, she wouldn't be fooled into thinking she was making more progress than she actually was. "If I should ever see '9,000,' it *won't* be because I've seen 90% of what's out there (which I now consider impossible for anyone), but because [after] a few more years of taxonomic explosion there may have become a total of 11,000 or 12,000 'species' to work from!"

The percentage system was also another means of preserving her legacy, though she probably wouldn't have admitted it. If, in the year 2020, there were twelve thousand valid bird species, her list of eight thousand-plus wouldn't seem too impressive; but if the way people thought of it was that she'd seen 85 percent of all the species that were recognized during her lifetime, that might be another story altogether.

In the early winter of 1998, she was unhappy with a trip for the first time in a while. She'd signed up for a tour of Brazil—her ninth—with roughly the same itinerary as a tour she'd taken in 1993, but she had reason to think she could bag a few new genera this time. Bret Whitney, the guide, had recently discovered a new species that was in its own genus, the Pink-legged Graveteiro, a bird with drab plumage but legs the color of bubble gum. Bret had also gotten special permission to take the group to the protected scrubland, or "caatinga," where the last surviving Spix's Macaw lived. The big blue parrot, which was also the only member of its genus, had been close to extinction for decades, largely due to trapping by pet traders, and since 1990 there had been just a single bird left.

A couple of weeks before the trip, however, the macaw

disappeared, and the scientists who had been monitoring it assumed it had died. Phoebe's group spent a few hours looking for it in the caatinga just in case, to no avail. In a mournful entry in her notebook that she called "Heartbreak of Extinction," Phoebe wrote: "I've known from day 1 that I wouldn't see Great Auk, Carolina Parakeet, Dodo, etc. But not until 2 days ago . . . did I learn that neither I nor anyone from this point on would ever see a wild Spix's Macaw. The guillotine has fallen on the last one. It's been my closest personal brush with extinction and a powerfully moving & depressing one. We spent a day in the caatinga of its former stronghold—and the ghost of the former blue flocks hung like a pall."

They also ended up missing the Pink-legged Graveteiro, which Phoebe took just as hard, but for a different reason. Though Bret had set aside a whole day to look for the bird, he "screwed up," in his words, by taking them to the northern end of its range rather than the center. As dusk neared and it became clear that they weren't going to see it, Phoebe had some tense words with him, fumed about him in her notebook ("Bret spent the day learning how *not* to find the Graveteiro"), and began drafting a letter of complaint to John Rowlett, who still worked with Bret at Field Guides. "I'd never seen her so upset," says her friend Martin Edwards.

Together, she found the two misses devastating, especially because so few other lifers were possible for her on the trip. She wrote in her notebook, "This trip was my most expensive big loss & gamble in terms of time, money & effort & emotion—Virtual total waste of resources."

But she rallied at the end, when the group went to a rain forest reserve near the Atlantic coast that was normally open just to scientists and was accessible only by a nine-hour boat ride up a tributary of the Amazon. The research center they stayed at was a "totally amazing place," Phoebe's memoir says, with comfortable rooms, a generator, and a 150-foot-tall canopy tower from which she finally saw a life bird and new genus, the Golden Parakeet. It's shaped like a macaw, but it's tiny, and it has an "amazing golden color" and green wingtips, as Phoebe wrote in her notebook. She also got "fabulous" views of eight Dark-winged Trumpeters, which, despite being the size of chickens, normally manage to stay hidden in the understory; she'd seen the species before, but not well. The eight trumpeters were "feeding, walking, preening, & wing-flicking" and had "amazing purple iridescence" on their breasts.

On March 23, 1998, shortly before Phoebe was to leave on her third trip to Colombia, four American birdwatchers were kidnapped not far from Bogotá by the country's most powerful guerilla group, the Revolutionary Armed Forces of Colombia, or FARC. The group was one woman and three men: a former nun from Illinois, Louise Augustine, who was sixty-three and whom Phoebe knew well; Peter Shen, thirty-five, a cell biologist from New York City; Tom Fiore, forty-two, a bike mechanic, also from New York City; and Todd Mark, a 32-year-old flight attendant from Houston. They'd been traveling, without a guide, in search of the Cundinamarca Antpitta, a drab olive bird that had been discovered just a few years earlier by Peter Kaestner, when he was posted at the U.S. Embassy in Bogotá. (He'd since been transferred to Namibia.) They'd left their hotel in Bogotá around three A.M., driven for a couple of hours on a highway, and, around dawn, turned onto a dirt road that was supposed to be a good place to find the antpitta. A few miles down the road, they bumped into some FARC rebels who were getting ready to stage a roadblock on the highway. At first, the rebels were friendly to them, but then they took all their equipment, stuffed them in the back of a truck, and drove them to a camp high in the mountains.

The kidnapping wasn't reported until a few days later, on March 27, about a week before Phoebe's tour, with Birdquest, was to begin. (The American companies were still avoiding Colombia, and this was to be the first Birdquest tour there.) Through a spokesman, FARC told the press that they thought the birders might be CIA agents, in which case they would have to kill them; if not, the guerillas would demand a ransom for their release. In response, the State Department urged Americans to postpone all "non-essential" travel to Colombia, an upgrade from its standard warning against going there. "Along with serious concern for my friends . . . the inevitable question arose: 'Did they see the antpitta before they were captured?'" Phoebe asked, remarkably, in her memoir.

"What do you think???" she wrote in an e-mail to Paul Coopmans, who had led her first trip to Colombia, in 1995, and would be leading this one too. He wrote back telling her not to worry: the kidnapping had occurred in a known guerilla stronghold that he'd never considered including on the itinerary; he'd heard (wrongly) that it had taken place at night—when, he said, it was imprudent to be out and about; and he assumed (also wrongly) that the group had been traveling, unwisely, by public bus. "On the tour we are avoiding areas that have regular trouble, and . . . we want to be back in the cities by dusk, since most of these things happen in the middle of the night . . . we should thus be reducing risks to a minimum. Throughout the tour I intend to remain as updated as possible on security situations in areas to be visited, and reserve the right to substitute one area for another if such thing would seem necessary for the group's security."

Paul's case was good enough for Phoebe and five of the other birders who'd signed up for the trip. "Quite frankly, I would tell the State Department that this trip is 'essential,'" Phoebe quipped in her memoir. "You can't get much more 'essential' to a birder than the chance at some of the species (and genera) that we might find in perfectly safe areas on this trip." (Her use of the present tense suggests that she wrote the passage right after getting Paul's e-mail.) Her family didn't try to stop her from going, but Dave, Marmot, and Sue clearly didn't want her to. Dave asked her what he should do if she was kidnapped and held for ransom; Marmot said she was making the same kinds of rationalizations that mountaineers make in the face of danger. Sue wrote her a thoughtful, affectionate e-mail: "I obviously don't know what the risks are, or how fast things are changing, but I know I'll be worried about you. So, just a reminder that I and the rest of your family love you a lot—so whatever you choose to do or wherever you may end up going, PLEASE, be very very safe."

After getting Sue's e-mail, Phoebe sent one to the whole family in which she tried at once to minimize and justify the risk she was taking, and in which she spelled out her philosophy about risk-taking in general:

I do appreciate and understand everyone's input, and your e-mail, Sue, made me realize I really should respond in a serious vein. By the way, I didn't know you were getting your wisdom teeth out. It can be awful, I know, and I sympathize. I'll call you before I leave.

So yes, I do plan to leave Friday as scheduled, unless of course the trip is cancelled, which I now doubt. I do not feel this is a risky venture, despite the US papers . . . The big point is that the 4 birders were reckless and careless, and probably out of touch with what was going on . . . The people I'm going with are neither of these, but extremely aware, in touch and sensitive to any serious risks . . . We'll be extremely careful not to travel at night, not to set any patterns of repeated visits to the same remote areas, etc.

. . . And yes, of course, in any sort of passionate endeavor, such as mountain-climbing or birdwatching, emotion and desire take precedence over reason, objectivity and caution. But I also know and feel that if I had taken no risks in life and followed only the most cautious route, I'd never have done most of what has been most meaningful to me. I can only compare this particular situation to a scenario like this: if I knew someone who went to New York City and was dumb enough to walk across Central Park at night, being mugged and robbed in the process, would that seriously deter me from going to New York? Of course not.

Obviously something bad happened to some unlucky and . . . naïve birders in Colombia last week, and if I had any really good reason to believe it would happen to me, of course I wouldn't go—REALLY! . . . All I can do, as always, is use my best judgment (clouded a bit, of course, by what I want so much to do!). Trust me—it'll be okay. (And as an afterthought, in case lightning strikes, NO RANSOM, please!).

All my love, Mom

It did, in fact, turn out to be okay, probably because of a combination of Paul's savvy and some good luck. The group did a lot of driving, mostly in the cloud forests of the Andes, but avoided the highway where the kidnapping had taken place and other sites that Paul considered unsafe. Contrary to what Phoebe had assured her family, they often traveled after dark, but they got away with it. She saw twenty life birds, three of which were new genera, a haul that was "really excellent, considering this was my third trip to Colombia in the past few years," she wrote in her memoir. In a letter to a friend, she said that "it all turned out more or less as planned—i.e., totally trouble free" and that she saw "some really great and much-wanted species."

However, the trip had exhausted her. "We were never up later than 4 AM, and with the long and frequently arduous drives, often didn't arrive at a hotel till late evening. I skipped about half the dinners, just to get enough sleep to keep from being totally frazzled! . . . Lots of one-night stands, and no let-up at all for 3 straight weeks on the long days." One day, they rode horses for ten hours in the rain on "a steep, very rocky, and incredibly difficult trail," she told her friend. "Walking it would have been impossible for me, and it was nearly that on horseback!" The purpose of the ride was to find a single bird, the Rufous-fronted Parakeet, but in the bad weather, it eluded them. "So it was a grueling pace—and that gets even harder as I get older." Her next big trip, to Tibet, which the Chinese government had recently opened to tourism, would probably be even tougher, she wrote, if only because the weather "could be frightful." "There are those who are convinced I'm a masochist—and they may be right!"

The four hostages ended up getting home safely, too. On April 2, just as the Birdquest tour was starting, one of them, Tom Fiore, managed to escape from the mountain camp where they were being held. He bushwhacked down a slope for several hours and found his way to a small village, where, serendipitously, he bumped into a television crew covering the kidnapping. "Lots of food, no violence," Fiore said, in rudimentary Spanish, on the air. He was flown to Bogotá and back home.

The other hostages were released at the end of April, near the end of the Birdquest tour. It probably helped that the former nun, Louise Augustine, had hurt herself badly in a fall off a ridge as she was being marched from one campsite to another; the guerillas were sensitive to their public image, and, having concluded that she wasn't with the CIA, they wouldn't have wanted her to die on their watch. They'd also concluded that neither she nor the other two remaining hostages, Shen and Mark, could make a significant ransom payment. At a hospital in Bogotá, Augustine was diagnosed with a collapsed lung, a broken pelvis, and eight cracked ribs, though she was expected to make a full recovery. Shen and Mark were uninjured.

A couple of months later, Shen told *Outside* magazine, "Birding is worth it. This particular experience wasn't worth it, but it's worthwhile going and exploring the world and taking calculated risks." Mark, sounding much like Phoebe, said, "You're vulnerable anywhere you go. I'd hate for people to think that just because this happened there, you shouldn't go anywhere. I think if anything we need to fight back as adventurers in the world." But he added, "I'm ready to concede some places, at least temporarily."

Phoebe's trip to Tibet, which began in June, around her sixty-seventh birthday, made her struggles in Colombia seem measly. According to her notebook and her memoir, the hikes, at ten to fifteen thousand feet above sea level, were "strenuous to impossible," and the drives, on rough mountain roads for up to fifteen hours, were "long," "exhausting," "agonizing," and "*agonizing*," depending on the day. There was continual fog, rain, and sleet. The hotels were "miserable," with no heat or plumbing and with filthy outdoor pits in lieu of toilets; the food was disgusting and sometimes covered with fly eggs. The five-week-long tour was led by Ben King, who was Phoebe's age but still indefatigable, and she was much older than most of the other customers. "I certainly got to the 'roof of the world' and back, but as is so often the case, it sounds a good bit more glamorous than the reality of day-to-day surviving and birding there," she wrote in her memoir.

Nonetheless, she fared far better than her younger friend Steve Martin did. One day early on, Steve, an environmental consultant from Colorado, bumped his big toe against a rock, which led to a bruise, which led to a painful, pus-filled infection. In each new town, he would go to the local clinic, usually a small, unlit room with a dirt floor. The "doctors" at these clinics cleaned his wound, carved away the pus, and gave him intravenous antibiotics, but nothing helped. He could have been evacuated, he says, but he didn't want to miss the Tibetan endemics, and he didn't think his condition was getting worse. (He was wrong. Upon his return, he found out that the infection had made its way into his bones, and for a while it looked like his foot would have to be amputated.) He got through the trip, he says, largely because of Phoebe. "Every morning Phoebe would ask, 'How are you?' 'What can I do?' 'Can I carry things for you?'" Though she was struggling, too, she was "a jewel to be with," and she stayed upbeat by focusing on the birds, Steve says.

Indeed, in addition to all the complaints, Phoebe's notebook is full of expressions of wonder: she got "stunning" and "fabulous" and "spectacular" and "*superb*" views of birds; she got "incredible views" of snow-capped mountains, saw "dramatic dolomite peaks emerging from grassy, flowery slopes," and rode through a "lush green valley" of juniper scrub that was bisected by a "rustling clear stream." She wrote about watching two male ibex in a snow-field rear up on their hind legs and charge each other, clashing horns; about seeing wolves, foxes, wild asses, and sheep; and about walking through fields of blue and purple wildflowers.

Her assessment of her longtime friend Ben was mixed. On the one hand, she credited him with helping her find every last one of the seventeen life birds she'd hoped to see, two of which represented new genera; but on the other hand, she blamed him for setting a pace she couldn't keep up with and thought he was too authoritarian. She wrote in her notebook that Ben's idiosyncrasies were "simply becoming more than I am willing or able to cope with as I grow older and the ornithological rewards diminish."

Ben, in turn, thought Phoebe was being a control freak. With her success, he says, she'd developed "Queen Bee syndrome."

While she hadn't slowed down, at least not appreciably, she and Dave were spending more time together during the periods between her trips than they had before she set the record. In addition to their trip to the Keys, they'd taken several vacations with the kids, including one to the Catskill Mountains in New York for cross-country skiing and one to the Salmon River in Idaho, for whitewater rafting. They'd visited the kids at their homes together, and they'd taken a cruise together around southeast Alaska. In March 1998, between Phoebe's trips to Brazil and Colombia, they'd given scuba another try, this time in the warm waters off the Cayman Islands and with a private instructor. "We're both much more comfortable with equipment and techniques now than a year ago, and I saw about 50 lifers—all fish," she wrote to her friend Betsy afterward, though she added that at one point, Dave got attacked by stingrays. Over the summer, Dave bought an RV, and after Phoebe's trip to Tibet he took them on a road trip to see friends, relatives, and sights on the East Coast. Again, Phoebe gave a good review of the trip to Betsy: "Great trip; lots of fun with the new RV 'toy,' and good to see family and old friends, plus some conventional sightseeing of Civil War battlefields and historic spots. Wonderful weather. It was David's trip, so he did all the route-planning and organization, and I was along to help drive and just relax. I was really ready for this total change of pace after Tibet. I think I came home as 'burned out' as I've ever been, badly needing to just do *something else* for a week or so."

For Dave, however, these occasional vacations weren't enough. Phoebe had promised to be a real partner to him once she passed eight thousand, and, nearly three years after the fact, it didn't seem like that was going to happen. They were no longer in counseling, and they'd stopped talking openly about their feelings. "We grew apart again, but I wouldn't have brought up divorce again," he says. Surely, he wanted to avoid a rerun of the fights they'd had when he brought it up the first time. The kids—even Tom—saw what was happening and felt bad for their father. "It was unequal the way things panned out," says Tom. "He went on some [bird] trips with her, but was that really a sacrifice for her?" His mother "didn't hold up her end of the bargain."

Marmot was feeling neglected, too. In the early spring of 1998, when she was thirty-six, she and her longtime partner, Nancy Siegel, announced that they were going to get married near their home in Montana. Though they wouldn't be married in the eyes of the law, they wanted to mark their commitment to each other. Marmot says that they wanted to have the wedding in July, to take advantage of the nice summer weather in Montana, but that Phoebe said she wouldn't miss her trip to Tibet, which was going to take up most of the month. Phoebe did say she'd cancel a short trip to Poland in May, an offer that didn't much impress Marmot. She ended up setting the date for early June—right before Phoebe left for Tibet—but not without some hurt and anger, which still came through strongly when I spoke with her many years later.

In the fall of 1998, Phoebe's body began to break down, surely due to a combination of the enormous stress she'd been putting on it and her age.

In late September, she went with a few friends and a guide to northern Peru to see two species, the Ash-throated Antwren and the Orange-throated Tanager, that had been discovered within the previous few decades but seen by scarcely any birders since. The region the birds lived in had been a Shining Path stronghold, and, moreover, the sites that they were known from were all but inaccessible. To get to the Ash-throated Antwren site, Phoebe and her friends had to drive to a remote town in the mountains and ride ponies for several hours up a steep, muddy trail. Mules, led by camp assistants, took up the rear with their gear. When the group got to their campsite, in a clearing on a ridgetop, they had to go about convincing the local Indians that they weren't out to harm them. At a meeting called by the Indians, the group was asked, among other questions, if it was true that white men kidnapped children and killed them by sucking off their fat. "What I have to do these days for new and exciting birds is increasingly absurd!" Phoebe wrote to a friend later. To see the Orange-throated Tanager, they had to drive over rough mountain roads for several days, enduring several break-downs; persuade the military to let them trespass on restricted land; drive up to a ridgetop on a "muddy road w. various deep holes," according to Phoebe's notebook; and, again, endear themselves to the local Indians, who conducted a "security check" and demanded payment.

They saw both the antwren and the tanager, the latter of which was a new genus for Phoebe. The bird was "simply marvelous," she wrote in her memoir, with a fiery orange throat, a velvety black back, and blue wings that shone in the sun. But while they were looking for it, as they were walking, slowly, down a gentle hill, her knee suddenly started to hurt. Over the next few days, the final stretch of the trip, it swelled up and got so painful that she could barely walk. At home, an orthopedist diagnosed arthritis and osteoporosis, put her on anti-inflammatories, and started her on a program of physical therapy and ultrasound.

The treatment helped, but not much. "So I fussed and I fumed, felt geriatric and miserable . . . and generally railed against my aging body and its increasing vulnerability and slowness in healing," her memoir says. A couple of weeks after her return from Peru, she wrote to the trip's guide, "The knee problem won't entirely go away—arthritis seems to be a factor, according to the doctor—but this is news to me, and I didn't think it came on that quickly, as a result of one easy walk. Surely there was another factor, like a pulled muscle/ligament/tendon, and it's just taking forever to heal—as things do at my age. Whatever it was, the great [Orange-throated Tanager] experience was worth it!" Still, she added, "God, I hate it, feeling like a geriatric—which I clearly am!"

By early November, when she was to leave for her next trip, a private cleanup of South Africa, she was feeling a little better and figured she'd be okay as long as she brought along sufficient "geriatric supplies," as she told a friend: her pills, some topical analgesic, a knee brace, a cane, and a folding stool. She also packed a "Freshette," a portable funnel designed to allow a woman to urinate in the woods standing up, like a man, and thereby to avoid putting stress on her knees.

She was in pain at times, but she managed, even climbing up a couple of nasty hills. She saw most of her targets, and toward the end, according to her memoir, she had a "beyond-my-wildest-dreams" experience with a Buff-spotted Flufftail, a small but plump bird whose black plumage is drizzled with golden polka dots. It's not particularly rare, but it's secretive and seldom seen; the bird she and her guide saw, a "beautiful male," had responded to a tape of a female's voice. When they were finished watching it, they realized that the park they were in had already closed, and that they were locked in behind a fence topped with razor wire. Despite her bad knee, Phoebe scaled it.

By the time she got home, in early December, she was only eleven genera short of her goal. She'd reach it, she thought, but her injury seems to have made her think that her adventuring days might be coming to a close. "Those 'final 11' will take me 2 more years, I think, and I'll never see the last 100," she wrote to Doris. "It's also becoming ever clearer which species I'll never see, and which ones I may still try for." She said she might need to get her knee replaced and suspected that a cataract was forming in one of her eyes, but she said, "I'd really like to avoid *any* surgery until I'm 70 (2 more years), and have pretty much wrapped up the birding goals."

She had about a half-dozen trips planned for 1999, she told Doris, including a tour of some remote parts of the Philippines with Birdquest that would be "intense and rugged, and will certainly be my last time on those islands"; another tour of Madagascar, mainly to see some endemic species on the Masòala Peninsula, a relatively unspoiled part of the island that had previously been off-limits to tourists; and a privately arranged cleanup of Australia. "None of these trips will get me more than 10 species, but there are some new genus targets in nearly all of them. So it should be a busy, interesting and productive year—I hope."

Chapter 12

S HE HADN'T GIVEN up on the White-necked Rockfowl, the chicken-like bird with a bald yellow head and big black eyes that she'd missed—but the rest of her group had seen—in the Ivory Coast in 1994, right after Dave had asked her for a divorce. The rockfowl wouldn't be a new genus for her; but, because it's secretive and striking, it's a bird with a lot of cachet, and she was still frustrated over having missed it the first time. In January 1999, she returned to the Ivory Coast purely to look for it, hiring a guide to take her around a rain forest reserve where it had recently been seen. It was a long haul for a single bird: she flew to London, then Zurich, then Abidjan, where she met up with her guide; spent a night in a hotel; drove for ten hours, four and a half of them on "awful" dirt roads, to the reserve; camped on the edge of it; and hiked for nine hours to a campsite deep in the forest. "Long all-day hike to Bush Camp," she wrote in her notebook. The next morning, they hiked to a hillside where, during the last breeding season, a pair of White-necked Rockfowls had built a mud nest amid some boulders. Within an hour, they heard a harsh call from a White-necked rockfowl that had seen them and been startled, and they spotted it briefly as it flew into a tree. The bird soon perched for a moment on a branch in the open, giving Phoebe "an exquisite view of this astonishing creature," according to her memoir. "Instant, total success!"

She and her guide spent the next few days looking at other birds in the forest. On their final morning, they went back to the hill, hoping for a longer look at a rockfowl. This time, they found an inconspicuous place to sit, and, after about an hour, a rockfowl emerged, perched on a rock not far away, and stayed put. "Spectacular whole bird view," Phoebe wrote in her notebook. Triumphantly, they headed back to camp. As they were walking, they came upon an ant swarm and stopped to see if it was attracting any birds. A short distance away, to their astonishment, they saw two more rockfowls, perched on a log and a branch, respectively, both of them too busy snatching ants and preening to notice them. Phoebe set up her folding stool and, for a half-hour, gazed ecstatically. She noted their "bare golden" faces, their "heavy black" bills, and the "silky lemon-yellow wash" across their otherwise white chests. "Exquisite, stationary or leisurely hopping studies," she wrote. "Totally amazing experience." In her memoir, she said she would remember the morning "forever." The "gnawing void of past frustration" had been replaced with "that wonderful, warm feeling of total fulfillment that all birders know so well."

Despite her differences with the American Birding Association, in the spring of 1999 the editor of *Birding* asked her to write a retrospective on her career. She liked the idea and ended up writing two articles: one on her "Ten Favorite Places Around the World," and one, "Birding Planet Earth: Twenty-five Years Later," that took stock of the changes in world birding since Stuart Keith became the first person to get to "half" in 1974. Keith, who was about

Phoebe's age, was still alive and still birding, with a life list of about 6,500.

Phoebe's favorite birding locale of all time was Kenya, for its "spectacular" and "easily seen" birds—and probably out of nostalgia for the life-changing trip she'd taken there in 1977. In second place was Madagascar, for its high number of endemic birds and endemic species in general. "You really can't get more different than Madagascar in this life." She likely ranked it so high, as well, because she was excited about going there again—for the fourth time—in the fall. Her third-favorite destination was Australia, with its eight hundred species, "a huge number of which are endemic," and many of which can be seen in a month-long tour; her fourth, in spite of what she'd gone through there, was Papua New Guinea, for its "fabled" birds-of-paradise and "other simply wonderful species." Of the remaining six places on the list, three were in South America (Argentina, southeast Brazil, and the Manu Biosphere Reserve in Peru); two were in Asia (Malaysia and India); and the tenth-place finisher was South Africa.

Her "Birding Planet Earth" piece was characteristically upbeat, although, as usual, she made some grim prognostications. For the most part, she wrote, things had only gotten better since Stuart Keith's day, when the Golden Age was just beginning. There were more field and bird-finding guides, many of which were "marvelous"; more birdcalls were known and available on tape; a smattering of new species had been found and described; and there were more tours to take, with more experienced, "highly skilled" leaders. Even if you didn't take tours, she said, you could benefit from the expertise of people who did by talking to them and looking at their field notes. Moreover, the "accessibility and bird-ability" of many parts of the world had improved in recent years. A few birders had gone to Tibet and Iran; Ethiopia and Yemen were safe again, or so she said; Bhutan, with its "pristine Himalayan forests," had recently opened to tourists; "parts of Colombia can be done with care again"; and northern Peru was "open and wonderful."

In his "Birding Planet Earth" piece in 1974, Keith had predicted that it would be impossible—even for a hypothetical "Mozart of the birding world" who birded nonstop from age five to eighty-five—to pass eight thousand, or ninety-three percent of the 8,600 species that were recognized at the time. Despite all the advances since Keith's day, Phoebe made a similar prediction, saying it would be impossible for the hypothetical Mozart to even see ninety percent of the birds of the world. Once you've seen the vast majority of birds, she explained, "adding significant numbers becomes a practical impossibility." She said that while she'd seen eighty-four percent, she'd recently hit a "plateau" and didn't expect to gain more than a percentage point; but she thought Peter Kaestner, who was only in his forties and was still globetrotting under the auspices of the State Department, would eventually see somewhere between 85 and 90 percent of all birds—hopefully, she wrote, during her lifetime. She'd "always admired" his approach of learning the birds of a particular region thoroughly, often over the course of two or more years.

She ended the piece with a call to arms, as she'd ended her speech to the Chicago birding club a few years earlier. "Birding is the best and most exciting pursuit in the world, a gloriously never-ending one, and the whole experience of a foreign trip, whether you see 10 new birds or 500, is simply too good to miss," she wrote. "We are living at the best possible time in the history of mankind to see a representation of the birds of the world," but it was just a "narrow window." Once more habitat was destroyed and more species lost, "the pursuit may become more depressing than it is exhilarating. From Stuart Keith's era through mine and then Peter Kaestner's, we will probably have had the best of it, so don't let it pass without considering taking part in the greatest avian celebration ever witnessed."

Perhaps as a result of the Irian Jaya fiasco, Birdquest had taken great pains to communicate that its tour of the Philippines in April 1999 was going to be more of a boot camp than a holiday. In recent years, so much habitat had been destroyed on the Philippine islands that the birds had been pushed to a few difficult-to-get-to and difficult-to-be-in places. There would be "very early starts to reach the remaining areas of good habitat," "difficult trails," "rough roads," and "basic accommodations," according to the Birdquest catalog. The "epic journey" was only "for those with a strong desire to see the marvelous but vanishing avifauna of the Philippines and a willingness to 'do what it takes.'" Though Phoebe had already seen most of the 185 endemic birds in the Philippines, this trip, which would cover some ground she hadn't before, gave her a shot at another twenty or so, including a couple of new genera. She'd probably signed up for it before she hurt her knee, and when it came time to leave seven months afterward, she evidently decided she could handle it. At this point, she was also having chronic backaches, which she assumed were a function of age.

The group's first stop, and their home for several days, was, of all places, a prison. (This detail, curiously, was omitted from the catalog.) During the previous few decades, while much of the rest of the Philippines was being logged and built up, the vast grounds of the low-security Sablayan Prison and Penal Farm, on the island of Mindoro, had hardly changed at all. There were lakes, streams, some scrubland, and a patch of rain forest, all of which was surrounded by a big metal fence. During the day, the hundreds of inmates, clad in orange jail suits, worked on the farm and in other jobs; at night, they slept in small wooden shacks with no plumbing. One of the shacks was cleared out to house the Birdquest group, though two inmates—

a murderer and a marijuana dealer—would stay with them as their "hosts" and to cook their meals.

On their first day at the prison, the group took an easy walk during which Phoebe saw three lifers, a "promising start," as she wrote in her memoir. On the second day, they were more ambitious: in search of the Black-hooded Coucal, an endemic whose population had been reduced to a meager 250, they climbed up a steep hill in thick forest by following a "rocky slippery streambed," according to Phoebe's notes. She got a decent view of the bird, which looks like a crow, only brown, but then it started to rain, and they began walking back down the rocky streambed. It was drenched and thus even more slippery. At one point, as Phoebe was gingerly making her way from one foothold to another, with her left hand holding her umbrella and her right, dominant hand stretched out for balance, she slipped and started to fall. She put out her right hand to break the fall, and as she landed on it, she heard her wrist snap. "Immediately," she knew that she'd done "something awful" to it, her memoir says. "It dangled at an odd angle and though I could still wiggle my fingers, it was useless, with all strength suddenly gone." The pain, she wrote, was "moderate."

She managed to get back to the shack, where she put her wrist, which was already swelling, into a cooler of beer. She took some painkillers, washed them down with a couple of the beers, wrapped her wrist in an elastic bandage, and succeeded in convincing herself, and the head guide, Pete Morris, that it wasn't broken. She wrote in her memoir, "There were no doctors on this trip, or anyone very knowledgeable to consult, so I was pretty much left to my own conclusions and decisions. I'd never broken a bone before and had always assumed that the pain would be unbearable, so based on that and a lot of wishful thinking, I concluded I'd probably just sprained it badly. I put the 'snap' I'd heard when I landed in the back of my consciousness somewhere." They were passing through Manila the next day, en route to Panay island, but when Pete suggested she get it looked at there, she demurred. "She said a Philippine hospital wasn't for her," he says. "She wanted to get medical treatment at home."

The truth was no doubt closer to what she later wrote to Doris and other friends: "If I'd had it x-rayed and treated in Manila I really would have had to abort this one-shot trip, and I just simply didn't want to do that." She didn't expect to return to the Philippines, and, clearly, she preferred the physical pain of trying to get through the trip with a serious injury to the psychological pain that would come with missing the birds.

The trip, unfortunately, got more strenuous as it went on. On Panay, Phoebe did "an even worse and more dangerous 'hike' " up another rocky gorge in search of the endemic and highly endangered Writhe-billed Hornbill, which has a ridiculously big red beak, on top of which lies a sort of third mandible, a chunky red ornament that looks like a horn. It was the sort of hike where you need your hands for traction and balance, but she "somehow" managed to do it one-handed, she told Doris. At the top, however, there were no hornbills in evidence; the bird's population had plummeted to about 150, which made it an extremely hard get. "Hellacious climb up rocky gorge. 10 stream crossings at beginning," she wrote in her notebook later that day, presumably with her left hand. The writing is shaky and awkward.

That evening, at camp, "my companions all assured me I could not possibly have done what I did with a broken wrist, so it must just be sprained," she wrote in her memoir. "I agreed; I was taking painkillers nonstop." The pills helped her "get by" during the day and sleep at night, as long as she took some sleeping pills, too, but everything—from rolling up her sleeping bag and zipping her pants to focusing her binoculars and cutting her food—took twice as long as usual. "The trip was turning into a survival experience, but I was there, I felt I could do most of what was left, and we had a chance at some very good birds that I'd come a long, hard way to see. It was now or never for me with these particular species."

She got something of a respite for the next few days, on the islands of Mindanao, Cebu, and Negros. The group stayed in hotels, for once, and their hikes, as she wrote in her memoir, were "non-life-threatening." Her wrist was still swollen and painful and her whole hand still useless, but she was finding her targets, including the "gorgeous" Flame-templed Babbler, a new genus for her. It had an "[extraordinary] orange-yellow bill blending into orange-yellow foreface," "flame-orange" brows, and a "melodic, warbly" song, her notes say. Still, she scrawled periodic expressions of frustration, such as "Drive up awful road," "*Rain all day*," and, after she spent fifteen straight hours in the field, "TOO LONG DAY!"

The final few days of the trip comprised a trek up and down a mountain on the island of Luzon that continually tested Phoebe's strength and will and that she described in her letter to Doris as "a god-awful slog." On the first day, they didn't get going until after lunch, and the terrain wasn't steep, but they were crossing farmland, where there was no shade, on a "hot & sunny" afternoon, according to her notes. There were horses available, and she decided to ride one to save energy for the days ahead. One person who walked instead ended up exhausted and had to quit the trek. The next day, horses were no longer an option, and the hike was "long, arduous, and miserable." They spent nine hours walking uphill on a steep and muddy trail fringed by "arm-slashing" razor grass. "[T]his was simply survival and finding the targets for me—certainly not much fun or other pleasure involved, and of course constant awareness of my hurt wrist," she later wrote to friends.

On the third day of the trek, the group walked along a forested trail on a ridgetop and saw most of the birds they'd been hoping for, including their main target, Whiskered Pitta, a secretive little ground-dweller that nonetheless has a spray of pink whiskers and a burning red belly. They'd heard one calling, followed it down a ravine with "adrenaline surging," and played a tape so it would call again. When it did, someone saw it, fleetingly, as it hopped through the brush; ten minutes later, it reappeared in a tree, giving them "soul-satisfying views" that were "beyond our wildest imaginings," according to Phoebe's memoir. The next day, which she marked in her notebook as "Dave's 69th b-day," they made their way down the mountain, a "long 15 km. hike." As they descended, they saw that over the previous day or two, loggers had arrived and were chopping down and burning the forest. "Immediate, total, heart-rending devastation," Phoebe wrote to a friend.

Whiskered Pitta

By this time, the swelling in her wrist had decreased, and the bone was clearly "distorted," with a "distinct kink," she wrote in her memoir. Her hand was still pretty much useless. Once she got back to St. Louis, she went to a doctor. He "growled" at her for not getting treatment sooner, x-rayed her wrist, and pronounced it broken in three places. The bone had started to heal, but crookedly, and at this point it was too late to reset, he said. She would likely be permanently disabled—lacking full strength, feeling, or mobility in her injured hand.

To protect her wrist from further injury, the doctor put it in a cast, "which is now handicapping me more than I ever was on the trip!" she complained to Doris in an e-mail. She'd be wearing the cast for two weeks, until mid-May, after which she would "have to do some serious, intensive therapy to regain strength and mobility (as for writing—I can now barely scrawl my name). How well I can achieve this at my age, only time will tell. It won't come back fast, I know that. A big frustration now with this cast on is that I can't work on my card file, which requires a lot of handwriting." She didn't plan to skip any upcoming trips, though. "Only an easy 10 days in the Mediterranean (Cyprus and Corsica) coming up in late May, and even the doctor thinks I can manage that all right. (I didn't really tell him all the awful things I did in the Philippines after the injury!) Next big one is a month in Peru in July with Field Guides. Should be much more civilized than the Philippines." However, her future held "NO MORE EXPEDITIONS," she declared. "Next to Irian Jaya, this was certainly the toughest trip I've ever done, and had I known conditions ahead of time, I doubt that I'd have signed on."

Despite having damaged her wrist and dominant hand irrevocably, she claimed, somewhat unconvincingly, to have no regrets, since she'd seen nineteen life birds and two new genera. She wrote to Pete, the guide, "Bad news on the wrist . . . Those may have been some of the most costly birds of my career, but in retrospect I guess I'd make the same decision again. If I'd had it x-rayed and treated in Manila, I'd have had to abort the trip, and as long as I could struggle through and still use binoculars I didn't want to do that. So I guess I DID hear something crack internally when I fell!" She also thanked him "for all your dedicated efforts and masterful bird-finding, and for supporting me in a decision to continue, which I still feel was probably the right one under my circumstance." In her memoir, she wrote, "In the long run, I think I would make the same choice again—though I hope I never have to. In any case, I can live with the present results, and there is that nice, replete feeling of having seen Flame-templed Babbler, Lina's Sunbird, and especially [Whiskered] Pitta."

Just as she'd praised David Bishop to his employers in the wake of the rape, she wrote a letter to Mark Beaman, the Birdquest owner, in which she raved about Pete and his co-leader, Tim Fisher, probably to make sure they didn't get in trouble for not sending her home. "Pete & Tim were both incredibly dedicated, and neither EVER gave up on anything—hence our first-rate results." However, "I do think the elderly/unfit need to be discouraged from this trip. Had I known in advance what many of the 'hikes' were going to be like, I probably wouldn't have undertaken it . . . I don't regret now having done the whole thing—but I *have* at least learned a lesson for the future." Of course, she'd also claimed to have learned a lesson about her physical limitations seven years earlier, after the Irian Jaya trip.

In her memoir, too, she suggested that she'd learned a lesson about what she could and couldn't take on. "My horizons were still broad, but I sensed them gradually narrowing. No more major expeditions, for instance; the peril-to-bird ratio was simply getting too high!"

Her trip to Cyprus and Corsica was indeed easy, with comfortable hotels, fine dining, and leisurely walks. The same can't be said of her next trip, a five-week tour of Peru that included a week of hiking, camping, and horseback riding at high altitudes, although it was nothing compared to the Philippines. Among other feats, she made it, with the help of a horse, to a misty bog at 11,500 feet, where, after a search of several days, she saw the "stunning, glowing" Golden-backed Mountain-Tanager, whose yellow feathers are splattered, Jackson Pollock style, with tiny, confetti-like bits of purple, white, and red. She also saw the Bay-vented Cotinga, which isn't nearly as striking but represented her two-thousandth genus, "leaving me with only nine to go to get down to the final 100 genera," as she wrote in her memoir.

When she returned, in late July, she wrote a long e-mail to Steve Martin, who was fully recovered from his nearly disastrous foot infection and would be joining her in the fall in Madagascar. She implied that she'd struggled in Peru, but she showed some optimism. "My wrist is now something I think I can live with, and I'm no longer conscious of it 24 hours a day. Strength is returning slowly, and I found I could use my scope okay in Peru, though sometimes I have to tighten the screw knobs with my stronger hand. Essentials like holding binoculars or using a computer are no problem, and I can grab someone's hand or a tree to pull myself up a slope." On the other hand, "the thumb motion is not quite normal, and the wrist is definitely kinked, so handwriting continues to be a problem. I have to hold the pen in a slightly different way, but I'm adjusting. Just made over 600 handwritten entries on my file cards from the Peru trip, and the results look better than they did a month or two ago. I've also lost some feeling in the thumb and fingertips, so there's a loss of dexterity there, but not much. I just drop things more frequently!"

She sent in a proud notice to *Winging It* for its "Milestones" column: "Phoebe Snetsinger made a recent trip to Bosque Unchog at 11,500 ft. in the Central Andes of Peru, and tallied *Doliornis*

(Bay-vented Cotinga) for her 2000th genus (out of the slightly over 2100 genera existing worldwide)." Privately, she was still tallying her life list, in accordance with the taxonomy she'd devised and was continually updating. As of late summer, she'd seen 8,659 of the 10,226 species she recognized, which meant that if she rounded up, she'd gotten to 85 percent—the figure she'd predicted she could reach but not surmount.

On September 12, 1999, about a week before Phoebe was to leave for her cleanup of Australia, an elderly Canadian birder disappeared in the Congo forest. The man, Roy Baker, had been on a tour of Gabon that was being led for Field Guides by Phoebe's friend Terry Stevenson, the artist who'd taken her around Zaire and Burundi. Since then, Terry had been Phoebe's guide on four other trips to Africa. When Baker disappeared, his group was looking for the Gray-necked Rockfowl, a close relative of the White-necked Rockfowl that Phoebe had staked out in the Ivory Coast, and just as secretive; at the time, hardly any birders had seen one. Recently, however, an ornithologist in Gabon named Patrice Christy had discovered a nest in a cave deep in the forest. He was getting regular looks at some birds, and he'd agreed to take the Field Guides group to the cave. The rockfowl would be a lifer for all of them, including Terry.

Terry thought a big group of people would spook any rockfowls, causing them to run for cover, so he decided that they'd walk to the cave—which was just a couple of miles from the road, along a narrow, overgrown trail—in two shifts: he'd lead a "fast" group of about six people; thirty minutes or so later, Christy would follow with a "slow" group of six more. Baker, who was seventy, first said he wanted to be in the slow group, Terry recalls, then changed his mind and set out with the fast group. In the middle of the walk, though, Baker changed his mind again—according to one person in the group, he'd taken a fall and was having trouble keeping up—and told Terry he wanted to stop and wait for the slow group. With some reservations, Terry told him that would be okay, but he made him promise to stay put until the others came along.

A short while later, the slow group came upon Baker's backpack—but not Baker—on their way to the cave. They figured he'd left it there on purpose, to make the walk easier, and they didn't think anything of it. Meanwhile, the fast group was returning to the bus, but via a different trail. The two groups didn't meet up again until the slow group got back to the bus, at which point everyone realized, with horror, that Baker was missing. Terry ran back along the trail, but there was no sign of him other than the backpack, and no one answered when he shouted his name. Terry rushed to the village police, who combed the thick, dense forest, to no avail. Field Guides hurriedly hired its own search team, and it looked for Baker nonstop for several weeks, also without success, though a towel that he'd worn around his neck turned up a few miles from where he'd vanished. No one had any idea what had happened. It was possible he'd been kidnapped; it was possible he'd been attacked by an animal; it was possible he'd wandered off the trail and had a heart attack or lost his way. Baker's grief-stricken children, two of whom also joined the search, blamed Terry for the misfortune, saying he shouldn't have left their father alone and had been too focused on seeing the rockfowl himself. They lambasted him to his face and in the press, and prepared to file a wrongful death lawsuit against both him and Field Guides. (A couple of years later, the case went to trial in Austin, Texas, where Field Guides is based, and the jury found that neither the company nor Terry was liable for Baker's death.)

Phoebe didn't know Baker, but she probably heard about his disappearance fairly soon after it happened, and it seems to have gotten her thinking, once again, about the possibility that she'd die on a trip. On September 18, when he'd been missing for six days, she wrote a letter about what she wanted done with her body after she died, as she had twice before, but this time, perhaps in an attempt to make things as easy as possible for her family, she dropped the request that her ashes be returned to them and that they spread them in a special place.

> To my family, friends, traveling companions/guides, tour companies, or whomever it may concern:
>
> In the event of my death while away from home, either in the USA or en route to or within a foreign country, I wish my body to be disposed of by cremation locally, with my ashes also disposed of locally. In the event my death should occur on a cruise, I request an informal burial at sea. Please return my belongings to my family at my home address.
>
> Sincerely,
Phoebe B. Snetsinger

She added at the bottom, "My husband & children all have copies, & concur with my decision."

With that, she left for Australia, where she had an ecstatic time. Her targets were fourteen of the continent's "most difficult and remote birds," as she wrote to a friend, but, through a combination of luck, skill, and perseverance, she and her guide, a Brit named Tony Clarke, were able to find all but two of them. They covered a rain forest near Cairns, on the northeastern coast, where Phoebe had "wonderful close-up experiences" with some birds she'd seen before and some she hadn't; drove south for a few hours and spent a night in some scrub successfully hunting down night birds with the country's reigning owl expert; and drove farther south and birded a sandy national park near Brisbane where she "almost stepped on" her target, a well-camouflaged Ground Parrot.

Toward the end of the trip, they flew to Adelaide, on the southern coast. Equipped with a four-wheel-drive car, a GPS, a satellite phone, and camping gear, they made their way north, toward the vast, red outback. Mainly, they wanted to see the Scarlet-chested Parrot, which was generally—albeit rarely—seen deep in the desert, far from any towns or roadhouses. Within a couple of days, they'd reached the northernmost roadhouse. They got a good night's sleep and filled up on water, food, and diesel, thinking they'd need to drive north for several more days before entering the parrot's range. But the next day, after just a few hours of driving, on a dirt road flanked by scattered trees and sand dunes, they saw a dead tree bedecked with about a half-dozen Scarlet-chested Parrots. "WOW!!" Phoebe exclaimed in her memoir. With patches of blue, red, yellow, and green, the birds were "unbelievably gaudy" and "extraordinary," she wrote in her notebook, adding in the margin, "Lighting up the landscape, the day, & my life!" A few minutes later, a heavy rain began, and they drove back the way they'd come, toward the roadhouse. So much rain ended up falling that had they remained in the desert, as they'd planned to, they likely would have gotten stuck on the gluey road for days. "Lucky day!!" Phoebe wrote in her notebook that night. Later, she added in the margin, "One of the luckiest days of my life!"

"Just back from 'cleaning up' Australia," she wrote to her friend Martin Edwards soon after her return, in late October, as she was getting ready to go to Madagascar for a month. "We connected with ALL of our targets (10 lifers and some probable splits) . . . Best was a dead tree with about 8 male Scarlet-chested Parrots perched in it." Two of her lifers had also been new genera, which left her with 107 unseen, "so want to whittle it down to 100," she told Martin. "Several possible for me in Madagascar, and should be able to get the balance next year." Already, she had trips planned for the year 2000 to Papua New Guinea, New Zealand, Panama,

Brazil, and Peru, all of which she'd visited many times, and to two new places—the Cape Verde Islands, off the Atlantic Coast of Africa, and Bhutan.

On some level, she may have thought that she'd slow down and live a more settled life when she got to this latest goal, but at the same time, she was hoping she wouldn't have to—not then, and maybe not ever. As she wrote to a friend, once she got down to a hundred unseen genera, she could "go after an endless list of high-priority targets for as long as time, health and money hold out!" Toward the end of her memoir, she wrote, tellingly, "As my husband points out, this game never *really* ends. It's simply a matter of perspective; as I see it, one of the wonderful aspects of birding is that it *is* endless. There's always, as long as one lives, some new place to go, some exciting new thing to find. No one knowledgeable will ever say, 'I've done it all— now what?' "

As Phoebe prepared for her trip to Madagascar, she learned from the Field Guides office that Roy Baker was still missing in Gabon and that Terry, who was back home in Kenya and would be her guide in Madagascar, was suffering over the tragedy and over the Baker family's anger. Based on what she had heard, Phoebe felt that Terry had done nothing wrong, and she was intensely concerned about his well-being, as she'd been concerned about the well-being of so many of her birder friends and their loved ones when they'd faced difficulties over the years. In an e-mail to Steve Martin and his wife, Kathy, both of whom would be in Madagascar, Phoebe wrote, "[Terry has] said he won't return to Gabon, and of course he's questioning his decision to leave the guy alone. Hell, in my opinion Terry is the world's most caring, careful and responsible tour leader; he always just does EVERYTHING RIGHT! I'm just sick that this has happened to him and to FG, and with those awful family repercussions . . . Terry normally has an incredibly upbeat and positive personality, and I love him dearly, so I just hope Madagascar will be a positive experience. He's a sensitive guy, he's suffering greatly and he needs some really positive reinforcement, which I sincerely hope we'll all be in a position to give."

Phoebe still "needed" twenty of the endemic birds of Madagascar, some of which she'd have a chance at on the Masoala Peninsula, in the northeast. Masoala was remote and sparsely populated, with an undisturbed tract of rain forest that scientists had been working in for years but that had been closed to all other visitors until recently. Most of all, Phoebe was hoping to see the Helmet Vanga, the only member of its genus, an improbable-looking bird with a small black body, cat-like yellow eyes, and a giant, downwardly curved, electric-blue bill. In addition to Terry, the trip would be led by John Coons, who had been Phoebe's guide a number of times over the years.

The trip got off to a bad start for her. On the second day, November 13, in a small town on the eastern coast near Masoala, she picked up a bad stomach bug, and she spent most of that night in the hotel bathroom throwing up. The next morning around five, the group set out in a small boat for Masoala, a ride that must have been uncomfortable for her, at the very least. When they arrived, in the late morning, they set up camp on the beach and walked into the nearby forest to look for birds. They didn't go far, but they took a steep trail splattered with tree roots, and on the way back to camp, perhaps out of exhaustion, Phoebe tripped on one of the roots and sprained her ankle. (It really was just a sprain this time.) She was in pain and frustrated with herself, as John Coons recalls. "She kept saying, 'Oh, goddamn it, I can't believe I stepped on that.'" Someone cut her a walking stick, and John helped her hobble down the hill. At camp, a man in the group who happened to be a doctor looked at the ankle, decided that there had been no serious damage, and wrapped it in a cloth bandage.

The next day, the group did another short but steep trek in the hills, toward a Helmet Vanga nest that a researcher had recently found. Phoebe could walk, but barely, and John lagged behind to help her along. Twice, they had to pick their way across a creek by hopping from rock to rock, which she somehow managed, with John's help. The suffering paid off, however: When they got to the nest, an adult bird was in it with two little chicks. Phoebe got so close that she could make out all the adult bird's intricacies—not just the "huge arched blue bill" but also the thin line of black on the upper mandible; not just the "staring" yellow irises but also the dark pupils they surrounded. "Fabulous view," she wrote in her notebook, in her labored new handwriting. She limped back to camp and ate lunch.

In the afternoon, Phoebe went with the group on another walk, and, to her delight, they happened upon another lifer and new genus for her, the Short-legged Ground-Roller. It's a chunky, fifteen-inch-tall, mostly green-and-white bird with fine brown markings on its belly that resemble fish scales and "long drooping buff whiskers" that look like an old man's beard. Just three days into the trip, Phoebe was down to 105 unseen genera—only five short of her goal.

Terry was acting as if nothing was wrong, but she was still worried about him. She didn't talk to him about what had happened in Gabon, but at some point early in the trip, in the best handwriting she could muster, she wrote a heartfelt letter to him in her notebook; as usual, she was more inclined to intimacy in writing than face-to-face.

Dear Terry,
Ever since Peggy Watson at the Field Guides office told me about the awful Gabon incident, I've been wanting to

communicate to you my heartfelt sympathy for your trauma &
total support for your decisions & actions. Writing it out is probably the best way for me to express how I feel about the whole
thing, since I know it just wouldn't come out right if I tried to
say it.

There is no doubt in my mind whatsoever that you acted in
a totally responsible manner. For as long as I've known you, I've
had nothing but the utmost admiration for your leadership skills
& talents and your consistently careful, responsible attitude . . .
I personally would trust you with my life. The irony devastates
me that this incident & the subsequent dreadful family repercussions happened to the world's most careful & considerate &
responsible leader, and to the tour company that consistently
runs their trips in the best possible manner.

If my position in the birding world gives me any particular
credibility, & thus if any supportive statement from me would
ever be of benefit to you or Field Guides, I want you to know
you have only to ask & I'd be more than happy to help.

It has been a delight to be on another of your tours—and it
has done me immense good to see you acting so normally, despite recent trauma, with all your usual confidence, competence
& utterly charming sense of humor.

Godspeed Terry—May your troubles be behind you & lots
more happy & successful tours in your future.

She also wrote some miscellaneous reminders to herself in her
notebook: She wanted to get a Long Road Travel Tent, which was
lightweight and could also be used atop a bed as a mosquito net;
she needed new pajamas; she had to fix the patch on her pants; she
needed to pack a long sleeping pad and some peanut butter for
Bhutan; she had to e-mail her friend Bob Braden, who was also
friends with Terry, to tell him about Roy Baker. She noted that

Terry would be leading a tour of Egypt in 2001 that would include snorkeling and visits to archaeological sites in addition to birding. "Possible w. Dave?"

The group spent two more days on the Masoala Peninsula, then made their way via boat, small plane, and van to a forest full of lemurs and birds in the southeast. Phoebe had been there a couple of times before and wasn't expecting to see anything new, but she did: the rare, threatened, and little-known Madagascar Sparrowhawk. According to John, Phoebe was the only one in the group, including himself and Terry, who was certain of the field marks that distinguished the species from a similar-looking one, Frances's Goshawk.

They flew from the southeast to the southwest, a dry landscape of thorny plants and baobab trees that Phoebe had also been to before. She didn't see any lifers for the next couple of days, but she got "amazing close views" of a pair of Long-tailed Ground-Rollers near their nest, according to her notebook. Like the Short-legged Ground-Roller, which she'd seen in Masoala, the Long-tailed Ground-Roller is tall and chunky and has scaly markings, but its most notable feature is its long, peacock-like green tail that sticks up high in the air, making it look like an angry cat.

The group's last day in the southwest was November 23. They got up around four A.M. for a final morning of birding in the desert, and Phoebe snagged her fifth lifer of the trip, a Red-shouldered Vanga. Despite its reddish shoulders, it's a drab bird, much like a sparrow, but it has the same glaring eyes as the Helmet Vanga, and it was a good get because it had just been rediscovered two years earlier. "Exc. close repeated study of male in tape [response]," she wrote in her notebook. Terry remembers that she was "really jazzed."

They were to spend the rest of the day driving north along the western coast, toward a forest where Phoebe had a chance at another lifer, Appert's Greenbul, a little peach-and-green bird that had been found and named only about thirty years earlier. They'd then continue north to a hilly rain forest, much like the one in Masoala, and spend four days there. On the plus side, Phoebe would have a chance at five more lifers in this forest, including another new genus; however, the only hotel in the area was notoriously filthy, with moldy walls and a rat problem.

The group consisted of about twelve people, including the guides, and they split up into two vans for the long drive north, each with a local driver and each with two columns of seats separated by a center aisle, as in a school bus. Neither van had seat belts or air-conditioning. It was hot out, and both vans were stuffy, but one of them—the one Phoebe, her friends the Martins, and Terry happened to be in—turned out to be stuffier than the other because its windows didn't open all the way. When the group stopped for lunch, Phoebe and the Martins ate fast and claimed seats in the other van.

Once they were on the road again, Phoebe took an ornithological paper about Appert's Greenbul out of her bag and asked Steve Martin if he wanted to read it. "You bet," he remembers saying. The van wasn't full, so Phoebe sat with her back to the window and stretched her legs onto the seat across the aisle, to get comfortable and elevate her ankle, which was considerably improved but still stiff. She was in the third row of seats, on the left side of the van, behind the driver. Within a few minutes, she fell asleep. John Coons, who was right in front of her, dozed off too.

A few minutes later, the driver suddenly lost control of the van. It careened from the right side of the road to the left and hurtled, head-on, toward a concrete post on the shoulder. John woke up to screams, realized what was happening, and—assuming the driver had fallen asleep—slapped him on the shoulder to awaken him.

The driver cranked the steering wheel sharply to the right to avoid the post, but it was too late. The left side of the van scraped against it, and, a moment later, the van tumbled over onto its left side. "It felt like slow motion," John says. When the van came to rest, his eyes were caked with dust and he seemed to have sand in his mouth. He saw Phoebe lying to his side and yelled at her to get up, but there was no response. When he looked closer, he saw that she was dead.

No one knows if she even woke up before the crash. Since she was sitting with her back to the window, the back of her head took the impact when the van rolled over, and, in all likelihood, she was killed instantaneously.

No one else was seriously hurt. John got on his radio to tell Terry while Steve, in a state of disbelief, covered Phoebe's body with some curtains.

She was sixty-eight. It had been thirty-four years since she'd started birding, eighteen years since she'd gotten her melanoma "death sentence," nine years since her last recurrence, and four years since she'd gotten to eight thousand species. Following her taxonomy, she died with a life list of 8,674 out of 10,223 species, or 84.8 percent of all living birds. More important, her death was quick, as her friend Joe Wright's had been twenty years earlier in the Himalayas, and, as she'd written admiringly of Joe, she had died "in some godforsaken place with her binoculars on," having lived "so fully and with so much spirit" to the end.

EPILOGUE

WHEN THEY HEARD that their mother had died, the four kids all flew to St. Louis to be with their father and each other and to be in the house, "our closest physical tie to her," as Tom says. It happened to be Thanksgiving week. Tom had recently gotten engaged to his longtime girlfriend, Christina Herrmann, and they'd been planning to spend the holiday with Dave and the Herrmanns at the Herrmanns' home in Rochester, New York. Tom and Christina found out about the accident as soon as they landed in Rochester, and they immediately turned around to go to St. Louis.

Field Guides and the American embassy in Madagascar were arranging for Phoebe to be cremated there. "We knew her intent was to have her ashes spread where she died," Tom says, "but after a few days we decided we wanted the ashes back," to spread them in a place that was meaningful to them and to Phoebe. They decided on the Tetons, one of the places where the family had vacationed together in the 1970s and that Phoebe had once suggested as her final resting place. "It was a fairly quick decision. We recognized that we were going a little against what she said, but it was a sort of compromise." They also decided to have a memorial service for her in Webster Groves around Christmastime.

As he went through her things, Dave made some discoveries that underscored the distance between him and Phoebe. A while back, he'd told her he didn't want her to keep a gun in the house anymore, and she'd said she'd get rid of it, but it was still in her closet. He also found the poetry she'd written in the 1970s, much of which was difficult for him to read. "Her poetry makes clear that she was craving more human connection than she was getting," he says. "We obviously had communication problems. Maybe she talked to her friends about things more than she talked to me." He found her memoir, too, which he knew she'd been writing but hadn't read. He was "surprised"—and surely stung—that there wasn't "more personal stuff" and that one of the only sustained passages about him was about how angry she'd been when he asked for a divorce.

He sent an e-mail to about a dozen of her good friends to announce her death, and they spread the word. On Thanksgiving day, two days after the accident, the *St. Louis Post-Dispatch* ran an obituary under the headline "Phoebe Snetsinger; Renowned Bird-Watcher, Was In Guinness Book of Records." It began: "Phoebe B. Snetsinger, a St. Louisan who was considered by many to be the foremost bird-watcher in the world, died Tuesday from injuries she suffered in a vehicle accident in Madagascar, where she was on a bird-watching tour." A friend from the Webster Groves Nature Study Society described her in the article as "an extremely knowledgeable, brave woman" and as "rather quiet, but always friendly and willing to talk to anybody about birds." The obituary hailed her toughness, too. "The grueling task of touring the birds' habitat meant she had to duckwalk through underbrush, climb mountains and sit for hours in mosquito-infested rain forest, just for a fleeting glimpse of an uncommon bird." *Winging It* also ran a prompt obituary, with the headline "Birding World Loses a Legend." "Phoebe's energy and enthusiasm inspired birders worldwide;

her abilities made her a legend within the [American Birding Association] and one of the few birders to attract the attention of the general public . . . No one can say for sure that Phoebe's life list will never be bettered. But there will never be a more inspiring example of the sheer love of birding. Phoebe Snetsinger will be greatly missed and long remembered by birders around the world."

Over the next couple of weeks, her death was marked in dozens of newspapers in the United States and abroad, much as her father's death had been nearly thirty years earlier. The *New York Times* wrote, "Phoebe Snetsinger, who saw and recorded more birds than anybody else, died on Nov. 23 in a van accident on a birding expedition to Madagascar, shortly after viewing an exceptionally rare Helmet Vanga." In recounting her odyssey from housewife to globetrotter, the obituary noted that she "turned a cancer 'death sentence' into a new life." Bret Whitney described her in the piece as "a celebrity in our bunch," and Stuart Keith said, "She gave so much to the birding world and had so much more left to give." The *Independent* of London said Phoebe was "[t]he world's most famous bird-watcher, a globetrotting American woman who ticked off more species in her notebook than anyone else" and quoted a well-known British birder as saying, "In my several meetings with her at various points around the globe, I was always bowled over by her sheer enthusiasm for birding." Her death was also recorded in, among other papers, the *Guardian* of London, the Toronto *Globe and Mail*, the *St. Paul Pioneer Press*, the *Star Tribune* of Minneapolis, the *Detroit Free Press*, and the *Milwaukee Journal Sentinel*.

Some of her far-flung birder friends grieved together in an Internet chat room that had recently been launched, BirdChat. The day after the accident, Terry Witt, one of the friends of Phoebe's whom Dave had notified, wrote, "I have been waiting to see if someone else would be the bearer of these tidings but since there have been no other postings, I have the unfortunate news to report that one of the finest field birders in the world was killed in a bus accident while on a tour of Madagascar . . . She was one of my best friends, a wonderful person in every respect, and I am sure that she has touched many others in her extensive travels." People started responding right away. "What a terrible tragedy," wrote Aileen Lotz, the author and birder, from her home in Colorado. "So many of us were affected by her incredible courage in beating the cancer, by her incredible knowledge of the birds, by her incredible persistence in pursuing and learning the birds of the world . . . How many of us have lost a wonderful friend, and, in the opinion of many of us, the finest birder in the world." A woman from San Diego with whom Phoebe had taken a trip in the 1980s recalled that while she was "a terrific, knowledgeable birder and a real 'celebrity' . . . there was not one ounce of 'birding snobbery' in her blood, and she always seemed happy to 'associate with those of low position' in the birding world . . . Yes, she will be missed." Said a retired couple from Tennessee, Dollyann Myers and Ron Hoff: "We had just met her in Peru a few months ago, where we told her she was our hero for fighting off cancer and pursuing birds with a passion. We certainly couldn't call her a friend, having only met her briefly, but we will miss her presence in the birding community. We've lost another great one." A couple from Arizona pictured Phoebe in heaven, which they described as "that endless rain forest where the birds are all lifers and where binoculars are unnecessary—and where there are enough field guides to identify every bird seen. Phoebe, we hope to meet you again there someday ourselves."

Some of the birders who grieved in the chat room had never met Phoebe. "I didn't know her, but having cancer myself, she was and is an inspiration to me," wrote a man from California. "I am not on her level, but I try to enjoy every day, to travel in nature, and to see new birds."

The memorial service, held at a restored barn owned by the Webster Groves Historical Society, was crowded with Phoebe's family and friends: Dave, the four kids, and their significant others; Phoebe's brothers and their wives and children; dozens of Webster Groves Nature Study Society members; Doris and one of her daughters; and some of the other birders Phoebe had traveled with over the years. Several people spoke about what she had meant to them. "My mother was not like other mothers," said Marmot, in a loving speech that also hinted at the tensions in their relationship. "When I was a kid, I sometimes longed for some of the things that I envisioned a normal mother would be like. I wished my mother would take more than ten minutes to help me pick out clothing at the mall that was in line with current fashion, instead of clothing that simply worked well and was durable. But there were other ways that my mother outshone all the others. I never knew another mom that woke her kids up in the middle of the night so that they could witness the lunar eclipse. Or let them stay up past bedtime to take them on a late-night prowl to Kirkwood Park to find an elusive Chuck-will's-widow." Sue, in a similar vein, said, "The most important bits she passed on to me were through examples in the way she lived her life. Don't be scared, explore & adventure, live a full life, and enjoy special moments to the fullest— they only come once. There were times when that was difficult to deal with, times when I was a bit scared, or unsure, and I wanted someone to worry about me. I know she did, but what she would say was 'just go for it.'"

Some of Phoebe's traveling companions couldn't make it to the service but remembered her in letters to Dave. "I still can't write to you without feeling a lump in my throat and a void in my heart," wrote John Rowlett, who was bedridden with a heart infection caused by a parasite he'd picked up while guiding a tour. "[My wife] joins me in conveying to you and your family our deepest sympathies for the loss of dear Phoebe, whom I had come to love in a special way over almost 20 years." After apologizing for having to miss the service, he said, "I will be there in spirit all evening and will be celebrating Phoebe's fortitude and zest for life, as well as her love of knowledge, her drive for 'getting it right,' and her passion for birds. She was the sharpest and best-informed world birder I knew."

Marmot took home many of Phoebe's bird books; Tom took her index card files, notebooks, and other papers. To honor her memory, he decided to submit her final life list total to the American Birding Association, even though she hadn't participated in the rankings for several years. It was a tribute that took some time to put together. Since the ABA still recognized just 9,700 species, Tom had to go through Phoebe's notes, species by species, and figure out what her count would have been had she still been using the organization's taxonomy. He came up with 8,398 species, which turned out to be about five hundred ahead of anyone else that year, despite the fact that many people were counting "heard birds." No one else had yet passed eight thousand.

Phoebe left her estate to Dave and the children, and they decided to make a substantial contribution to the Nature Conservancy in her memory. They directed the money to two projects, one in Brazil and one in Missouri. With the Snetsingers' donation and some matching funds, the Conservancy was able to buy a vast tract—22,500 acres— of savanna in central Brazil and turn it into a nature preserve. The land, which had been threatened with development, abuts a national park and is home to hundreds of bird species, many of which migrate to North America each spring, and such glorious mammals as the Giant Anteater, the Giant Armadillo, and the Jaguar. In Missouri, the Snetsingers' donation allowed the Conservancy to buy seven thousand acres of forestland along the Current River in the Ozarks, one of the rivers the family had canoed on the 1970s, when they had their farm. The land is the summer home of dozens of species of warbler and contains some of the last remaining bamboo stands, or canebrakes, in the state.

Upon Phoebe's death, the family had asked that any donations in her memory be sent to the Webster Groves Nature Study Society. Eventually, more than ten thousand dollars was collected, and at Dave's request it was used to help restore a park in Webster Groves that had once been a favorite birding spot of Phoebe's. Over the years, the park's woods had become overgrown with invasive honeysuckle bushes that were preventing the native oak and hickory trees from spreading their seeds. The honeysuckle was removed and replaced with native plants, and a sign was erected to honor Phoebe, "the world's all-time top birdwatcher."

Dave and the kids also decided to edit and publish Phoebe's memoir. It was up to date as of her departure for Madagascar; the last passage she'd written was about her successful cleanup of Australia. In an epilogue, Tom described the Madagascar trip and the van accident. "When the bus crashed, Phoebe, binoculars in hand, was killed instantly. Undoubtedly, she was dreaming of the Red-shouldered Vanga or the hoped-for Appert's Greenbul . . . She went out, as she had always hoped, at the top of her game, in the middle of doing what she most loved to do."

Tom also shared some observations on his childhood memories and his mother's character. "Was she running from a death sentence, as she sometimes stated, or was she embracing an aspect of life that offered her immense fulfillment? Perhaps, it was both . . . If Phoebe had a motto by which she lived her life, it was: *carpe diem.* Her advice to all of us—family, friends, and all of those whose lives she touched—would be the same: Embrace life and live it to the fullest."

The family enlisted Peter Kaestner to write the foreword, even though he hadn't known Phoebe well, as he was one of the birders she had most admired and the one she had hoped would eventually break her record. Clearly, her admiration was requited. Kaestner wrote of their first meeting, in the early 1990s in Malaysia: "Nervous at my first encounter with this modern-day goddess of birding, I gathered up my courage, walked up, and introduced myself. Her trademark smile—warm, sincere, and welcoming, immediately put me at ease." He praised Phoebe's "personal integrity and birding skill," as well as her "wealth of patience for people who may have been lacking in both." She was, he wrote, "my hero."

The memoir was published in 2003 by the American Birding Association, which had never before published a book but was inspired to when the Snetsingers sent in the manuscript. There were color illustrations of some of Phoebe's favorite birds, and there was a map of the world showing all the places she'd been. The title was the one she had given it years earlier, *Birding on Borrowed Time*.

Today, the four Snetsinger kids, now in their late forties and early fifties, are all married. Penny and Harlan still live in Connecticut, in a secluded house where they've built a big ballroom dance studio and which they've surrounded with thousands of daffodils. In 2002, when Penny was forty-four, she and Harlan adopted a little girl from China and named her Robin, as a tribute to Phoebe. They also have a pot-bellied pig, Harry, who lives in their mudroom. Penny still teaches chemistry at Sacred Heart.

After she finished her master's degree, Marmot worked for many years in the biology department of the University of Montana, studying how best to integrate computers and the Internet into the classroom. In 2005, she was the lead plaintiff in a lawsuit brought by the American Civil Liberties Union against the University of Montana for excluding the partners of gay employees from its health plan. The Montana Supreme Court ruled in Marmot's favor, forcing the university to change its policy and to offer insurance to Nancy, a physical therapist. Marmot and Nancy now have a daughter, Zoe, and live in Seattle, where they spend their spare time hiking, canoeing, and camping. Marmot works as a craniosacral therapist and an artist.

In 2002, Sue married her longtime boyfriend, Rich Fredrickson, and settled with him near Arizona State University in Tempe, where he was getting a Ph.D. in biology. They've since had two children, a son, Eli, and a daughter, Ana, and moved to Missoula. Rich is working at the University of Montana; Sue spends most of her time taking care of Eli and Ana, though she does some work from home as a biologist for the Pacific Biodiversity Institute, which aims to save endangered species and forests in the Northwest. The family spends a lot of time outdoors together, and some of little Eli's favorite books are field guides to birds. "No doubt my mom's spirit is around us, alive and well," Sue says.

Tom and Christina also got married shortly after Phoebe's death and now live in a beautiful spot amid farmland and hills not far from the Oregon coast. Tom works for Oregon State University in Corvallis as a researcher for a long-term study of the Northern Spotted Owl, the same species Sue studied in Washington. The bird is now protected under the Endangered Species Act. Tom has learned to hoot just like the owls do, and as he makes his way through the towering fir forests where they live, they come out to greet him as a friend.

In the spring of 2006, he took a sabbatical to join hundreds of other birders in looking for the Ivory-billed Woodpecker, which had been considered extinct from around 1940 until 2005, when some ornithologists published a paper in *Science* saying that they'd seen the bird, repeatedly, in a swampy oak-and-cypress forest in eastern Arkansas. A massive, multimillion-dollar search was launched, led by Cornell University, and Tom was hired to supervise the many volunteers who came to help. "I knew I probably would not see the bird, but I'd be contributing, and there might be a chance of seeing it," he says. The woodpecker, if it still exists, is huge—nearly two feet tall—with striking black-and-white plumage and a pointy crest the color of a fire engine, but it's difficult to distinguish from the slightly smaller and relatively common Pileated Woodpecker, and during the several months Tom spent in Arkansas there were no definitive sightings. The search has continued since then, without success. In Tom's view, it's possible that there are a few Ivory-bills left, but if so, they must be very few, eking out an existence in much-degraded habitat, and he thinks the species is unlikely to be saved.

One day in 2003, four years after Phoebe's death, Dave asked his longtime neighbor in Webster Groves, Barbara Redmond, for a ride to pick up a new car he'd bought. Barb and her husband had been casual friends with Phoebe and Dave when both couples were raising their kids on the block; Barb, her husband, and their six kids had even stayed with the Snetsingers once after a fire in their house. Barb had since divorced, and her kids, like Dave's, were long gone. In return for the ride, Dave took Barb out to dinner, and they found they had a lot to talk about. They started dating, and in December 2004, when Dave was seventy-four years old, they were married. They couldn't decide whose house to live in, so they decided to keep them both and go back and forth.

Barb had worked in a doctor's office for a while, but mainly,

Dave says, she was a "supermom." They have the sort of warm, loving relationship that he'd wanted—and missed—with Phoebe for so long. Barb has joined Dave's magic club, and they're active members of a Unitarian congregation that combines spirituality with progressive causes such as working to combat racism and homophobia. They travel around the country visiting their children and grandchildren and take trips to cities and natural spots all over the world. In our conversations, Dave rarely expressed anger toward Phoebe and said he honored the memory of the "many good years" that they shared early on. But he also said, "The kids, they understand my life with their mother, and they know I'm happy now."

Phoebe thought she was living at the best possible time to see the birds of the world, but in one significant respect, birding has gotten even better since her death. In the same way that online dating sites have introduced couples who, in another era, never would have met, birding sites have made it possible for birders around the world to connect with one another and with birds they'd never fathomed. For example, on birdingpal.org, you use a map of the world to click on the country you want to visit, and a list of local birders, complete with e-mail addresses, appears. The "pals" will give you advice on good birdwatching sites and, in some cases, will take you there themselves, which has made it easier for people without a lot of money to bird abroad. On surfbirds.com, birders post reports on their trips, saying how, when, and where they found certain species. There are photographs of birds with identification tips, links to "birdwatcher-friendly" hotels, and a message board with recent rare bird sightings on each continent. The Cornell Laboratory of Ornithology Web site allows you to listen to thousands of recordings of birdcalls that have been collected over the last several decades but were previously unavailable to the public.

The birds, for the most part, are still holding on, but no one knows how long that will be the case. Since Phoebe's death, three species, including the Hawaiian Crow, which she saw with Tom in the early 1990s, and the Poo-uli, which he rediscovered with his Hawaii Rare Bird Search Team, have almost certainly gone extinct in the wild. According to BirdLife International, a British research and advocacy group, almost two hundred birds are "critically endangered," meaning they're likely to go extinct within the next few decades; some of these have populations of less than fifty. If habitat destruction proceeds apace, 250 more species could be lost by the end of the century. While a few formerly endangered birds have been saved in recent years by conservation work, the outlook for many more threatened species has deteriorated.

In the meantime, birders are racking up bigger numbers than ever, though that's partly because almost everyone counts "heard birds" now. Phoebe's final life list total of nearly 8,400 was recently passed by two birders, both retired British businessmen, and Peter Kaestner, now fifty-five years old and the U.S. consul general in New Delhi, is close behind, with nearly 8,200. He's begun counting heard birds, he says, but "reluctantly." He fully intends to get to number one, and perhaps even to nine thousand species, but he's patient. Over the years, he's been posted in Zaire, Papua New Guinea, the Solomon Islands, Malaysia, Guatemala, Australia, Colombia, Brazil, Namibia, Egypt, and now India, and in each of these countries he's pretty much cleaned up the birds. However, he spends a lot of time at work and with his family—his wife also works for the State Department, as a computer specialist, and they have two teenaged daughters—so he doesn't often travel far from wherever he's posted. For birding purposes, he'd like to be assigned to Peru or China next, but a lot depends on which embassies have openings for both him and his wife and where his daughters can get a good education.

As in Phoebe's day, nearly all the top listers are men. According to *Birding*'s most recent tally, there are only two women in the top thirty: one from Nevada, Marian Cressman, with 7,085 birds, and one from Tennessee, Dollyann Myers, with almost seven thousand. (This is the same Dollyann who posted a message on BirdChat mourning Phoebe's death.) Both women are retired, and both travel and bird with their husbands, either taking organized tours or hiring local guides off the Internet. The top woman lister, however, is actually Pearl Jordan, of Denver, who doesn't participate in the *Birding* tally but has a life list of more than 7,300 species, only about seventy of which are "heard-only." Jordan, now seventy-four, was a single mother of three who worked full-time as a computer specialist for an oil company throughout the 1970s and '80s, sometimes attending night school too. "It was a struggle," she says. In 1985, when she was fifty-one and her youngest child was leaving for college, she read a newspaper article about a lake that was a good place to watch birds. Though she'd never paid attention to birds before, she decided to check it out, and while she was there she met some birders who told her about the Denver Field Ornithologists, a club with free field trips on the weekends. "That was where I learned what birding was, and how to bird." She went abroad for the first time about ten years later, upon her retirement. She can't afford standard bird tours, but she uses birdingpal.org and often travels with Ornifolks, a collective that was founded in 1991 and has blossomed in the age of the Internet. Ornifolks members take turns organizing trips, which are advertised on the group's Web site, and they keep costs down by camping when possible, cramming into cheap hotel rooms, and using local birders as their guides. Sometimes Jordan travels alone, which she can afford only by buying last-minute plane tickets, taking public buses, staying in youth hostels, and sleeping in the airport during overnight lay-overs. She's been running low on money lately and has had to slow her pace; as a result, she didn't meet the goal she'd set of listing 7,500 birds before her seventy-fifth birthday, in August 2008. She hopes, as Phoebe did, never to have to stop traveling.

Though Phoebe wasn't very introspective in her memoir, which she wrote when she was in her late sixties, decades earlier, when she was a housewife in her early forties, she showed a remarkable ability to reflect on her life and, based on her insights, to imagine a radical change in course. There would be many turning points for her—the "death sentence" she got in 1981; the rape a few years later; and, to a lesser extent, the achievement of her world record in 1995—but perhaps none of these was as significant as the trans-formation that she quietly underwent in the early 1970s, when, through her poetry, she took stock of her "comfortable," "pedes-trian" existence and decided it couldn't make her happy. She took little action at the time; her children were still young, her vision for the future inchoate. Still, she sensed, correctly, that the present was just a prelude, "a stodgy, graceless, larval time," as she wrote in 1971, a year before her initial melanoma diagnosis, in the poem she called "Mayfly." "Someday," she wrote, she'd metamorphose, cast-ing aside "the cramping shell . . . that housed me once too well." With uncanny prescience, she declared that, like an insect, she wouldn't live long as a fully realized adult—but having thus far spent her life wingless, she would, at last, get to soar: "I will have at length that day sublime," she wrote, "one final flight as recompense."

ACKNOWLEDGMENTS

A big thank-you to all the people who helped make this book possible:

The remarkable Snetsinger family—David, Penny, Tom, Marmot, and Sue—as well as Barbara Redmond and Christina Herrmann.

Joe, Peter, and Georgia Burnett.

The many other people who shared their memories of Phoebe and their own stories with me, with special thanks to Claudia Spener, Marjorie Richardson, and Bill Rudden of the Webster Groves Nature Study Society and to David Bishop, Doris Brann, C. G. Cederlund, Martin Edwards, Ben King, Steve Martin, Rich Stallcup, and Terry Witt.

The talented folks at Field Guides, especially Rose Ann Rowlett (a great role model for women who like science), John Rowlett, Terry Stevenson, Peggy Watson, Bret Whitney, and John Coons.

Joel Abramson; Peggy Beman; John Wright, son of Elizabeth "Joe" Wright; and the Ela Township Historical Society in Illinois.

Rebecca Layton, for the stylish illustrations.

Tait Johansson and his sister, Ailyn Hoey, with fond memories of our years in Vermont.

The Long Island Bird Club, which pointed me in Phoebe's direction.

Jim, Judy, and Doug Miller, who harbored me in St. Louis and even helped me with research; Alys Fair, my long-lost great-aunt and host in Phoenix; Amanda Rocque and Bryon Farnsworth, my hosts in Denver; Carrie Budoff Brown, my host in Philadelphia; and Andrea Monroe, who put me up in Chicago.

The participants in the two Field Guides tours I took—to Kenya in 2005 and Peru in 2006—for their tolerance.

Stephanie Ross at the Leo Burnett Company and Bryan Patrick at the American Birding Association.

The librarians at the American Museum of Natural History, Missouri Botanical Garden, Swarthmore College Rare Book Room, University of Illinois archives, Brooklyn Public Library, and New York Public Library.

Professors Richard Locke, Patty O'Toole, Lis Harris, and Pruthu Fernando at Columbia, and the members of my writing workshops there from 2001 to 2003.

My early reader-victims, who urged me on: Jean Tom, Charles Stowell, Sabi Ardalan, Cara Solomon, Sarah Taylor, Amanda Rocque, Sam Apple, and Mandy Rice. My reader-victims in the summer of 2008, who helped me with fact-checking and polishing: Tom Snetsinger, Dave Snetsinger, John Rowlett, Rose Ann Rowlett, Caroline Kim, Joe Burnett, Peter Boesman, Martin Edwards, and Magnus Aurivillius.

My proofreader and niece, Kate Borowitz.

The MacDowell Colony, for all the time, space, and support. Also, Aryn Kyle, Sandra Lim, Jen Vanderbes, Jo Solfrian, Rebecca Layton, Julian Rubenstein, Cassie Jones, and my other MacDowell buddies in the winter of 2006.

The Hon. Raymond J. Dearie, whom I now consider a family member, and his staff and clerks from 2003 to 2007, for the encouragement and laughs.

Bobbie Roessner at the *Hartford Courant*, for teaching me how to write a feature story, and my other editors at the *Courant* and the *Rutland Herald*.

My terrific agent, Simon Lipskar.

Kathy Belden at Bloomsbury USA, who saw the potential in a very rough draft, helped me learn how to write a book, and did everything possible to see it through. Thanks also to designers Kimberly Glyder and Amy King, to copy editor Phillip Gaskill, to production editor Jenny Miyasaki, and to Colin Dickerman, Karen Rinaldi, and Alan Kaufman.

My parents, Carmen and Beth-Ann Gentile, and my grandparents, Henry and Dorothy Fischer. My grandfather, whom I called Menu, believed in me and in this book, and I wish he could have lived to see it finished.

And most of all to my husband, Andy Borowitz, who, against all odds, has turned me into a sap. I can't express how much I love you.

NOTES

I conducted my interviews from 2001 through 2008, but mainly in the earlier part of that period. Most were face-to-face or phone interviews; a few were over e-mail. I interviewed the following people:

Joel Abramson, Peter Alden, Manny Alvarez, R. Jay Andree, Magnus Aurivillius, Maurice Barnhill, Paul Bauer, Mark Beaman, Peggy Beman, Anne Selden Berry, David Bishop, Peter Boesman, Hugh Buck, John Burke, Georgia Burnett, Joe Burnett, Peter Burnett, Claes-Göran Cederlund, Dick Coles, John Coons, Paul Coopmans, John Danzenbaker, Harriet Davidson, Raven Davis, Helen Dowling, Martin Edwards, Ela (Ill.) Historical Society (various members), Victor Emanuel, Betsy Fikejs, Dean Fisher, Ted Floyd, Martha Gaddy, Ron Goetz, Theresa Goetz, Joel Greenberg, Bob Groves, Susan Gustafson, Christina Herrmann, Pearl Jordan, Peter Kaestner, Jon Kastendiek, Stuart Keith, Ben King, Vivian Liddell, Steve Martin, Harold Morrin, Pete Morris, Dollyann Myers, C. J. Pollard, Bill Rapp, Nigel Redman, Marjorie Richardson, Robert Ridgely, Phil Roberts, John Rowlett, Rose Ann Rowlett, Norman Ruck, Bill Rudden, Gerry Shemilt, Barbara Spencer, Claudia Spener, David Snetsinger, Marmot Snetsinger, Penny Snetsinger, Susan Snetsinger, Thomas Snetsinger, B. K. Stafford, Peary Stafford, Rich Stallcup, Terry Stevenson, Sarah Swank, Ron Tasker, Richard Webster, Bret Whitney, Pete Winter, Terry Witt, John Wright, and Marion Zimmerman.

The following are some notes on my written sources, my research process, and bird and place names, as well as a few amplifications.

Introduction (Pages 1–7)

The newspaper I worked for in Vermont was the *Rutland Herald*.

The ornithological nomenclature I use follows *The Clements Checklist of Birds of the World*, sixth edition, by James F. Clements. However, in some of the cases where Phoebe called a bird by one name and Clements used another, I followed Phoebe.

The Natural History and Antiquities of Selborne, was published in 1789.

Chapter 1 (Pages 8–36)

Throughout the book, I refer to Phoebe's husband by his nickname, "Dave," instead of "David," to distinguish him from another significant person in her life, David Bishop.

Dave asked me to clarify that he never ended up using radiation in his research.

Among other sources, I relied on The Birds of North America Online for accounts of the species that Phoebe saw near home (http://bna.birds .cornell.edu/bna). I also used the Peterson field guide and *The Sibley Guide to Birds*, by David Allen Sibley.

In addition to the primary sources I mention, I used several secondary sources for my account of the early days of birding, including *The Heyday of Natural History*, by Lynn Barber; *A Passion for Birds: American Ornithology After Audubon*, by Mark Barrow; *Birders: Tales of a Tribe*, by Mark

Cocker; *Dean of the Birdwatchers: A Biography of Ludlow Griscom*, by William E. Davis Jr.; and *A World of Watchers*, by Joseph Kastner.

My information on Peterson came from his many writings, including *Birds Over America* and *Wild America*, and from *The World of Roger Tory Peterson: An Authorized Biography*, by John C. Devlin and Grace Naismith.

Kingbird Highway: The Story of a Natural Obsession that Got a Little Out of Hand, a memoir by Kenn Kaufman, describes the revolution in birding in the 1960s and '70s, as do the early volumes of *Birding*.

Chapter 2 (PAGES 37–67)

The Burnett family history I refer to is *Rare Birds: An American Family*, by Dan Bessie, a cousin of Phoebe's.

The biography of Leo Burnett I mention is *Leo Burnett: Star Reacher*, by Joan Kufrin. I also read the many articles that were written by and about Leo in the press, including several profiles in *Advertising Age*, and a couple of histories of the advertising industry. Leo's quotes are mainly from the Kufrin book (pages 2–5, 7, 16–17, 30, 97, 164, 221, 242) and from three collections of Leo's speeches and memos published by the company: *Communications of an Advertising Man* (page 73), *Leo: A Tribute to Leo Burnett* (page 84), and *100 Leos: The Wit and Wisdom of Leo Burnett* (pages 18, 79). I also quoted from a speech Leo delivered in 1963 at the University of Missouri titled "A Second Look At Yourself." ("I always figured that I was less smart than some people . . .")

The Leo Burnett Company remained privately held until 2002, when it was bought by the public French holding company Publicis Groupe. The agency's headquarters is still the skyscraper that was completed in 1989, at 35 West Wacker Drive in Chicago.

My most important sources on the history of women in the 1940s, '50s, and '60s included *Why Young Mothers Feel Trapped*, a collection of personal essays published by *Redbook*; *The Feminine Mystique*, by Betty Friedan; *The Fifties: A Women's Oral History*, by Brett Harvey; *Educating Our Daughters: A Challenge to the Colleges*, by Lynn White; the inaugural issues of *Ms.*; and various articles from the archives of the *New York Times*, the *Chicago Tribune*, *Time*, *Newsweek*, and *Life*. Some helpful secondary sources were *Marriage, a History*, by Stephanie Coontz; *No Small Courage: A History of Women in the United States*, a collection of essays edited by Nancy F. Cott; and *To Have and to Hold: Marriage, the Baby Boom, and Social Change*, by Jessica Weiss.

I learned about the Snetsinger clan in *A Prairie Farmer and His Family*, an unpublished memoir by Helen Snetsinger, Dave's mother, which is held at the Ela Historical Society in Illinois.

Chapter 3 (PAGES 68–100)

My understanding of melanoma comes from the following papers and texts: *Clinical Oncology*, by Martin D. Abeloff et al.; "Malignant Melanoma in the 21st Century, Part 2: Staging, Prognosis, and Treatment," in *Mayo Clinic Proceedings*; and *Melanoma: Prevention, Detection & Treatment*, a patient's guide by Catherine M. Poole with DuPont Guerry IV. To get a sense of what a cancer diagnosis meant from a social and psychological standpoint in the 1970s, I read *The Dread Disease: Cancer and Modern American Culture*, by James T. Patterson; *Illness As Metaphor*, by Susan Sontag; and "History of Psycho-Oncology: Overcoming Attitudinal and Conceptual Barriers," a paper by Dr. Jimmie C. Holland that was published in the journal *Psychosomatic Medicine*.

I don't know how much money Phoebe inherited from her father (and later from her mother), but the sum must have been in the millions in today's dollars.

The Snetsinger farm was in Steelville, Missouri.

My sources on the birds of the world included dozens of field guides and treatises; *Threatened Birds of the World*, an encyclopedia published by BirdLife International and Lynx Editions; and *The Life of Birds*, both the book and the DVD set, by David Attenborough and the BBC. *Ornithology*, a textbook by Frank B. Gill, was helpful too. In addition, I took two semesters of ornithology while studying writing at Columbia University.

I went to Kenya in the summer of 2005, on a tour led by Phoebe's friend Terry Stevenson.

The Rowletts' mentor in Texas was Edgar Kincaid.

Chapter 4 (PAGES 101–115)

Many doctors would not have given Phoebe as specific and definitive a prognosis—or "death sentence"—as hers did, according to several doctors I spoke with. It's more responsible, these doctors say, to tell the patient what the median one-year or five-year survival rate is for a certain condition, while allowing that some people live far longer or shorter.

I learned about bird extinctions from *The Song of the Dodo: Island Biogeography In an Age of Extinctions*, by David Quammen, and from *Rare Birds Yearbook 2008*, edited by Erik Hirschfeld for BirdLife International.

Chapter 5 (PAGES 116–138)

Unfortunately, I was unable to interview some of Phoebe's peers on the world birding circuit, including Michael Lambarth, Sandra Fisher, Norm Chesterfield, and Harvey Gilston. A few of them had died by the time I began work on the book, while others preferred not to participate.

I learned a lot from *The Birds of Paradise: Paradisaeidae*, a treatise on the family by Clifford B. Frith and Bruce M. Beehler.

Jared Diamond wrote about his boatwreck off Irian Jaya in "The Price of Human Folly," which was published in the magazine *Discover*.

Chapter 6 (PAGES 139–160)

The history of Papua New Guinea and Port Moresby is described in *Law and Order in a Weak State: Crime and Politics in Papua New Guinea*, by Sinclair Dinnen.

Chapter 7 (PAGES 161–187)

A friend of Bob Stjernstedt's, Simon Barnes, wrote about him in an article in the *Times* of London, among other places.

I went to the Manu reserve in the summer of 2006, on a tour led by Rose Ann Rowlett. We stayed in a remote and rustic but very clean lodge, so I was surprised when I got home and came down with dysentery. I was in bad shape for two weeks.

I've changed Bill's name to protect his privacy. (No other names in the book have been changed.)

Chapter 8 (PAGES 188–213)

The "splitting" trend continues, so the total number of bird species continues to grow.

The Rufous-tailed Antthrush is now called the Brazilian Antthrush.

"Irian Jaya" is no longer the name of the western half of New Guinea. In a concession to the native Papuans, the Indonesian government renamed the province "Papua" in 2002. Since then, the territory has been divided into two provinces, "Papua" and "West Papua."

In 2000, following DNA analysis, MacGregor's Bird-of-paradise was reclassified as a honeyeater and renamed the Ochre-winged Honeyeater.

Not long after Phoebe's trip to Irian Jaya, a road was built up the Snow Mountains to the lake where MacGregor's Bird-of-paradise (or the Ochre-winged Honeyeater) lives, making it possible to get there quickly and without suffering. On the other hand, from 2000 until mid-2008, the State Department warned against travel to Indonesia, citing a threat of terrorism.

Chapter 9 (PAGES 214–240)

Mobutu was finally ousted in 1997, whereupon Zaire's name was changed to Democratic Republic of the Congo. A civil war followed, killing millions of people over five years.

The *Washington Post* article about the plane crash that killed Ted Parker was written by Susan Cohen and published in the Sunday magazine. The remembrance of Ted in *Birding* was by Kevin Zimmer, a guide for Victor Emanuel Nature Tours.

Chapter 10 (PAGES 241–249)

The article about Peter Boesman's snake accident, "A Bushmaster Bite During a Birding Expedition in Lowland Southeastern Peru," was by Dr. Norman H. Mellor and John Arvin and was published in the journal *Wilderness and Environmental Medicine*. With help from his wife, Peter resumed birding less than a year after the accident, and since then, in the tradition of Ted Parker, he has recorded thousands of birdcalls in South America and compiled them onto CDs.

Chapter 11 (PAGES 250–277)

The lone Spix's Macaw reappeared not long after Phoebe left Brazil, only to disappear again—for good—in 2000. The species is presumed to be extinct in the wild, though there are about seventy birds in captive breeding programs.

The *Outside* article about the hostages in Colombia was by Wade Graham and was published in September 1998, about four months after the hostages' release.

Chapter 12 (PAGES 278–300)

Citing a threat of terrorism, the State Department now warns against travel to the Philippines and has deemed the island of Mindanao particularly dangerous. Some birders still go to the Philippines, however.

My account of the Roy Baker incident comes from my interviews with Terry Stevenson and from articles in the *Toronto Star*.

ABOUT THE ILLUSTRATIONS

The illustrations were painted for this book by Rebecca Layton, an artist based in Brooklyn, New York. She used watercolor on paper. More of her work can be found at www.rebeccalayton.net.

INDEX

Page numbers in *italics* indicate an illustration. Also, people with whom Phoebe spent the most time are indexed by their first name as well as by their last name.

A NOTE ON THE AUTHOR

OLIVIA GENTILE earned a B.A. from Harvard and an M.F.A. from Columbia. She was an award-winning newspaper reporter in Vermont and Connecticut and now lives in New York City.